This book is dedicated to my first patient

Lyn Miller

Taking Medicine

AUSTIN MACAULEY PUBLISHERS™

LONDON · CAMBRIDGE · NEW YORK · SHARJAH

A CIP catalogue record for this title is available from the British Library.
ISBN 9781786935199 (Paperback)
ISBN 9781786935205 (E-Book)
www.austinmacauley.com

First Published (2017)
Austin Macauley Publishers Ltd.
25 Canada Square
Canary Wharf
London
E14 5Lq

Acknowledgements

I'd like to acknowledge the Arvon Foundation as I found the course that I attended at Totleigh Barton so valuable. It was an amazing experience in wonderful surroundings, although the prospect of being snowed in was daunting. I particularly appreciated the encouragement of Naomi Alderman and Helen Oyeyemi, the two writers in residence.

I owe so much thanks to my husband Dave. He's always believed in me and supported me. He helpfully agreed to lend me back three years' worth of letters that I'd written to him which I then used to jog my memory for some of those student details. And he miraculously thought up a title for my book. Thank you for everything, Dave.

I'd also like to thank Austin Macaulay who have enabled the publication of this book. Each individual who's been involved in the project has been approachable, helpful and enthusiastic and I'm grateful for their input and support.

One

Tears streamed down Alison's face as she leaned over the cadaver. The formaldehyde fumes rising from the newly opened thoracic cavity nipped her eyes fiercely, stung her nostrils and caught at the back of her throat making her cough and splutter. She was unable to wipe her face as her hands were encased in surgical gloves greasy with fat and with pieces of pickled tissue attached. She knew from her dissection of the upper limb, earlier that term, that the first few days were the worst for this discomfort which would settle once most of the vapours had been released.

To gain some relief Alison straightened up and looked around the room. It could be considered a macabre sight, but she'd become accustomed to it. On her first day at medical school she, and most of the other students, had been nervous about what awaited them in the dissection room. All of them had studied biology at school so had wielded their scalpels over the bodies of frogs, fish and perhaps rabbits but that seemed very different from a human dissection. The room was painted white giving a clean, clinical feel. The multiple tall, arched windows which reached almost to the ceiling on the north and south facing long walls made it light and airy. Under the windows on each side of the room stood two rows of fifteen tables and on every table, was a body with its feet pointing towards the central aisle. To preserve them, the cadavers had been embalmed and were shrouded in sheets when the students weren't working. Among the students there was an uneasy balance between respect for the people who had left their remains to allow aspiring doctors to learn their anatomy and a more flippant, jokey attitude, which probably enabled the students to actually carry out their work. The students had been allocated in groups of six to a table and most groups gave their body a name and made up stories about how they imagined its past life. Alison's group called their body Maggie. She had a full set of false teeth and still wore pale pink nail varnish on her toenails.

Alison caught the eye of her friend Linda who was one table down and across the aisle and who was also spluttering and snuffling. "I'd worried that I might feel sick or faint doing this," Alison thought, "but I never imagined that my nose and eyes would turn into taps."

"Alison, some of us are doing some work here," said Robert, drawing her attention back to their task. Alison frowned and tried to concentrate. She felt a bit intimidated by Robert who was ultra-keen on anatomy and, they all felt sure already, was destined to be a surgeon. However, he did actually carry her and their group along with his enthusiasm and seemed to have a talent for finding and

10

demonstrating the features they were looking for, so he was popular with the students on his table.

"It's just that the fumes are getting to me, Robert. I think I'll have to take a break," she replied.

"I really think you should keep going until we've found the left coronary artery," he muttered.

Feeling guilty, Alison began to pack away her instruments and could see that Linda was stripping her gloves off at her table. White coats flapping, they bustled up the aisle between tables and tried to avoid the glances of the anatomy demonstrators. Alison shrugged her lab coat off and stuffed it into her grey metal locker. The girls clattered down the stone stairway, hurried through the vaulted hall and pushed through the heavy metal-studded wooden doors to emerge into the sunshine and delicious fresh air of the medical quad. It was a crisp November day and there was a perfect square of cloudless blue sky above the Italianesque courtyard.

'The union for a coffee?' asked Linda. Alison nodded and they headed through the passageway by the McEwan Hall to the turreted building which housed the Students' Union.

When they were settled in a quiet corner of the refectory with their coffees, Linda asked Alison about her plans for the weekend. "Isn't this the weekend that Gordon's coming down?"

"Yes," said Alison, "he's got the weekend off for once. His train gets in about teatime, so he'll be here in time for the ceilidh on Friday night."

Alison's boyfriend, Gordon, was currently working in the Caledonian Hotel in their home town of Oban. It was difficult for him to get time off at a weekend and this would be his first visit since her arrival in Edinburgh. Having completed a college course in hospitality management in June he was pleased to find a job as a trainee hotel manager back in Oban. He could stay with his parents and save some money. He was also close to the yacht club, so was able to sail in his free time, his favourite pursuit. Alison had so much that she wanted to show him in Edinburgh, she was sure the weekend would just fly past. It also fitted in well with the Sports Soc. ceilidh on Friday evening. It was the kind of occasion that was fine to attend on your own, as everyone mixed in together for the dances and some, like the 'Dashing White Sergeant', were danced in groups of three, but it would be great to have her own partner. And it was a chance for Gordon to meet some of her new friends. She was aware that quite a few of the first year students thought that she was quaint in keeping up with a boyfriend from home. There had been a lot of pairing off into couples since term began. However, Alison and Gordon had been an item for two years now. They'd met in the summer holidays just after Gordon had finished school for good.

"Isn't it hard being so far away from each other?" Linda wondered.

"Oh, we're used to that. Gordon was away in Glasgow at college during term for the past two years, which was probably just as well, as I needed to study hard to get the grades to come here. And now I still need to keep working

– I don't know about you but I'm finding everything's really tough. I've had to get my head round a whole new language before I could even begin to learn anatomy, which has just so much to remember."

"And don't get me started on all those formulas in biochemistry."

"So, it's probably a good thing that he's not here to distract me."

"Did you always want to be a doctor?" Linda asked.

"Well I always liked biology at school and the idea of being a doctor grew from that. I suppose it was a way of applying an interest. I don't think I ever had a great calling to relieve suffering like some of the others describe."

"Especially the religious ones," Linda commented.

"And then there are the ones whose whole families seem to have been doctors since the time of the ark. I don't suppose they had much of a chance to think of a different career." Alison then went on to describe to Linda her dream that Gordon would eventually open an outdoor centre with sailing and climbing and other activities and she'd be the local GP. She imagined herself driving along the shore road towards Gallanach on a house visit and seeing a flotilla of yachts on the Sound, their white sails bright against the green of Kerrera. She'd smile to herself, knowing it was Gordon with his sailing students.

"Gosh, you seem awfully sure of things already," said Linda, who was beginning to have serious doubts that medicine was the right course for her.

"Well, first I have to get through the anatomy oral on Friday, never mind the rest of the five years of medical school. So, I'd better get back to the left coronary artery. Hopefully Robert will have dissected it out beautifully by now."

Alison headed back up to the anatomy department to the work in progress. The diagrams in her anatomy textbook showed the important features in contrasting colours, blue for veins and red for arteries. The reality of cadaveric dissection was that everything was a pinkish grey colour so the features were much more difficult to demonstrate. She couldn't help wondering why people had left their bodies for dissection. Did they feel a debt of gratitude to the medical profession for helping them or a close relative? Or were they really interested in science? She didn't believe in an afterlife but she did wonder what they would make of the students' activities in the dissection room if they were able to watch what was happening to their bodies now. She could see Robert hunched over Maggie's chest cavity as she approached their table.

"Oh, you're back," he commented. "Come and hold this. I need another pair of hands," gesturing with his forceps which were attached to a piece of greyish red tissue that she tried hard to identify.

***

The oral on Friday morning was nerve-racking. Alison felt shaky and her mouth was dry as she waited in the corridor for her turn to be grilled. Robert exited looking slightly flushed. Then the demonstrator asked her to go in and guided her to the professor who was standing by one of the cadavers. She felt disorientated looking at a different dissection. And this was a man. She'd become accustomed to 'Maggie's' features and was distracted by the male body's white moustache with yellowing at the hair tips, he'd obviously been a smoker. He also had a colourful array of tattoos on the areas of skin which were still intact. She could make out an anchor and wondered if he'd been a sailor. She managed to concentrate and give coherent answers to the professor's questions about the chambers of the heart and so began to feel a bit more confident. But her answers on the route of the right phrenic nerve were more hesitant and uncertain. She escaped feeling relieved that it was over, but unsure that she'd passed.

She didn't really want to look at the noticeboard when the results were posted at noon and, because she was small, had a struggle to see over the other heads to find her name. Fifty-four percent. Well that was a pass but it was galling to just be scraping through after all the work she'd put in. She used to get eighty percent at school without too much effort at all. However, she quickly saw that she wasn't the only one to just have made it; most of the marks were under sixty percent. And she noticed that Linda had failed. "Poor Linda, she'll be very upset," Alison thought. Robert's mark was ninety-one percent.

Later on Friday afternoon, Alison was wobbling on a small ladder, stretching out to attach a swathe of tartan material to one of the pillars in the ceilidh hall. Her friend Karen was holding the bale of red and yellow Buchanan tartan and giving instructions,

"Try to attach it a bit higher up so that it drapes evenly like the other side," she suggested.

Maybe you should be up the ladder, you're taller after all," said Alison.

"Well I maybe have an inch on you, but you're doing a grand job. How did the anatomy oral go then?"

"Oh, it was scary. You know I get so flustered when they're asking me things. Even if I know them my mind just goes blank. Anyway, I scraped a pass so I can put it behind me."

She landed back on the floor safely and they inspected the effect.

"I think it looks quite festive. Once the band's set up and a few folks are dancing it'll be fine. It's a good sized hall. Have we sold many tickets?" Alison asked.

"Yes, I think we've sold the lot. I had a rush on them at orchestra practice last night. I'd been worrying before that we wouldn't get enough people." Karen replied.

Karen was Alison's badminton partner. A keen badminton player at school, Alison had signed up with the sports society in Fresher's week hoping to get onto one of the teams. After a few casual games, she'd been approached by Karen who needed a new doubles partner as her previous teammate had graduated. They started practising together and seemed to be a good pairing, making it onto the 2nd team. The club members were a sociable bunch and Alison enjoyed meeting students from different faculties there. Medical students were renowned for their cliquishness. Karen was in her second year of a French language degree but she was also very musical, playing flute in the orchestra. When fund-raising ideas for the badminton team's proposed visit to Italy were being raised, one of the ideas was a dance. Karen managed to get some of her musical friends to make up a ceilidh band, so was quickly welcomed onto the organising committee. Alison had been roped in to help with decorating the hall but she would need to leave soon to meet Gordon at the station.

"I think we're done for now anyway. I'll chum you down the hill," Karen offered.

The girls left the hall which belonged to St Columba's by the Castle church and turned right, following the curving street up towards the Lawnmarket. They were of a similar height, but Alison's shoulder-length, almost black curls were a contrast to Karen's straight, silky, blonde hair. It was already dark and the orange streetlights had misty haloes round them as the day had been damp. The towering bulk of the Highland Tollbooth St John's church marked the entrance to the Royal Mile. They passed an antique emporium, a kilt shop and a cafe advertising scones and shortbread, all closed for the night now. At the corner of George IV Bridge Karen was heading right, back towards her Marchmont flat.

"See you later," they promised and waved.

Alison waited for the green pedestrian crossing light, and then cut diagonally across the junction. She hurried past the front of the Sheriff Court building. St Giles Cathedral was a dark shadow ahead on her right, but her route took her left into St Giles Street where a short walk brought her to a gap in the railings and the top of 'the New Steps'. She pattered steeply down in angled tiers to Market Street. At the bottom, her view was straight across the railway lines and Princes Street gardens to the floodlit Scott Monument, its shape always reminded her of Thunderbird three on its launch pad.

She glanced at her watch, ten to six, she'd be in plenty of time as she only had to turn onto Waverly Bridge and then down the ramp into the station. She was feeling excited, but also nervous about meeting Gordon and the coming weekend. She'd found that time snatched together in a long distance relationship can go wrong. Somehow it becomes almost too precious and important so that small arguments or imperfections that you'd take in your stride if you have plenty of time to sort things out can be blown out of proportion. However, she felt it might be more relaxed here, just the two of them, without all the other family ties and expectations that Gordon's weekend visits home to Oban had contained.

Waverly station on a Friday evening was bustling with activity under the high glass roof. Taxi brakes squealed and the tannoy announcements echoed off the walls. Alison gazed up at the arrivals board. Gordon would have had to change trains in Glasgow. She found the correct notice and went to wait by platform twelve. As she stood her mind wandered back, remembering how it was that she and Gordon had first started going out together, more than two years before.

Suddenly she was enveloped in a huge hug and being swung round in a circle with her feet off the ground. She squealed partly with fright, partly with glee. Gordon had arrived and crept up behind her while she was daydreaming. At six foot tall to her mere five three he could easily sweep her off her feet, and she enjoyed being enclosed in his arms, strong from sailing and climbing.

"Hey, I've missed you," he said after replacing her on the ground and kissing her. "What have you got planned for us?"

"Well tonight's the ceilidh, you did remember to bring your kilt, didn't you?"

"Yes, I've got it, but I was hoping the dance would be tomorrow. I'd really rather it was just the two of us tonight."

"I can guarantee it's going to be good fun," she coaxed him as they made their way arm in arm up the slope and out of the station.

Two

The ceilidh was in full swing but Alison was having a break from dancing, enjoying a cool drink while Gordon was leading Linda through the steps of 'Strip the Willow'. As she was from south of the border, country dancing was a new experience for Linda. The band was very lively; Karen's orchestra friends were doing a great job. Above the fiddles, accordion, clapping and stamping of feet there were shouts of "Heee-uch."

'Woops, sorry,' someone apologised as they were spun out of the dance by a fierce burl and collided with Alison nearly spilling her drink. All the Scots had been brought up on these dances, learning them at school and dancing at weddings and parties. Their youthful versions could be a bit over-enthusiastic, boys often sending their partners careering across the room with their twirls and then laughing.

"Oh, that was fun," panted Linda as she came up after the dance. Alison was pleased to see her smiling and obviously enjoying herself as she'd been tearful and upset by failing her anatomy oral earlier in the day. "I think I'm beginning to know some of the steps and I can see why Country dancing took off so well in Scotland, it certainly gets you warm. I can also see why you're hanging onto Gordon all the way from Oban; you didn't mention that he looks like a Viking God."

"In a kilt?" asked Alison, laughing, but secretly pleased that her friend approved. The band was striking up for an 'Eightsome Reel' and Gordon appeared at her shoulder and slipped his arm around her waist.

"Want to give this one a go, Alison?" he asked and led her to a group of three couples waving to them to join in and make the set complete. The men all had their sleeves rolled up and a few, like Gordon, wore kilts. The couples bowed and the dance began. When they came to the middle section and Gordon was in the centre of the circling dancers lifting his feet high, making his blue and green kilt swing, Alison felt her breath catch at the sight of him. She was strongly aware of how physically attractive she found him, and remembering their lovemaking snatched in the short time they'd had in her room just a few hours earlier, she felt a deep contentment. "If I was a cat, I'd be purring," she thought.

Next morning on the top of Arthur's Seat Alison's jacket was ballooning and flapping in the wind and her hair was whipping round her head. Climbing the hill to show Gordon the lie of the city underneath seemed a good way to start their sightseeing especially since it was almost on Alison's doorstep. She thought the hill would appeal to Gordon; although she knew the climb wouldn't be much of a challenge to someone who regularly climbed

'Munros'. To have a big hill in the middle of a city was definitely different and the last rocky scramble to the top took her breath away. Being a relative newcomer to the city Alison could only name a few landmarks. The castle was an obvious one, moulded to its rock, and Pollock halls where they'd started out from crouched by the gates to the park with the swimming pool built for the commonwealth games behind.

"I think that dome over there is the old college of the university and that flatter one is the McEwan hall, right next to the medical school," she told Gordon. In the other direction, they could see across the Forth to Fife and follow the coastline to the east where the water began to open out to the North Sea.

"I love that there are open spaces around Edinburgh. When I came here I thought it might feel claustrophobic after Oban, but there are still hills, and the sea close by. And actually, it's been quite nice being unknown, not bumping into a neighbour or someone's mum around every corner." Alison remembered experiencing the tantalising sense that she could re-invent herself here because no one had any preconceived ideas about her. "In fact, you know how at school I was considered to be very serious and studious? Here in medical school people think I'm quite flighty – there are some seriously academic types and I'm not one of them," she remarked.

"You seem brainy enough for me," Gordon replied. "I enjoyed the climb and I think it's great that your room is so close to the park. Now let's go down and you can take me to your favourite pub for lunch."

"We should check what's on at the cinema tonight on the way past."

"Do you know where there's a good record shop?" They planned the rest of their day as they began the clamber back down from the volcanic summit.

On Sunday, it was wet with soft rain blowing in drifts across the sky. The grey outside made it pleasant to stay cocooned in Alison's room. It was very basic in its design and furnishings, a single bed, a small wardrobe with drawers and hanging space, desk and chair with bookshelf above and a sink unit with cupboard space below and a mirror above. She had two functional reading lamps, one on the bedside cabinet and one on her desk. Alison had added some softening touches. She'd brought a downie cover from home which was a melding of pinks from palest to deep rose and happily toned in with the window curtain provided which was of pink and white stripes. She'd pinned two art posters to the wall alongside her bed, Monet's 'Poppy field' and Van Gogh's 'Café terrace at night'. On her desk stood a pair of framed photographs, one of Gordon, wind tousled from sailing and one of her border collie, Jess, chasing bubbles in the back garden at home. There were some hefty medical tomes on the bookshelf but also some paperback novels. Propped in the corner was a heavy duty blue plastic bag containing the half skeleton that she had on loan for the year to help her learn anatomy. The bones were loose apart from the hand and foot which were correctly articulated. She'd tidied it all away for Gordon's visit as Karen had been very squeamish when she arrived one time and found the hand lying out on Alison's bed. She'd borrowed an airbed and sleeping bag from Karen for the weekend. Being squashed two to a single bed might sound romantic, but didn't turn out to be at all practical for sleeping. It very quickly felt cramped and very hot, especially with a restless sleeper like Gordon who seemed to be re-enacting rugby games in his dreams. Getting up late, they'd brewed some coffee and spooned up cereal. Then they spent the day playing her guitar, chatting and listening to The Police *Outlandos d'Amour*, which Gordon had bought the day before. Gordon was especially pleased that the disc he'd bought was blue.

"I'm sure there'll be a limited number of blue ones. It might be valuable one day."

"I think that's the highlight of your visit," said Alison.

"Oh, I wouldn't say that." As he replied, he raised his eyebrows and looked towards her. Her stomach lurched and she felt melting deep in her abdomen as they began to kiss again.

That evening, they ventured out enveloped in waterproofs as they'd agreed to meet Karen and her boyfriend Chris at Potterrow. They huddled together against the wind and rain, rushing up Buccluech Street to gain the warm atmosphere of the bar. Gordon had met Chris briefly at the ceilidh on Friday and the two had quickly bonded over boat talk, as Chris had done some sailing on the Forth out of Port Edgar with sea scouts. They set up a game of pool, each couple a team, and seemed to be evenly matched with the men playing steadily and the girls laughing in amazement if they managed to sink a ball.

"So, you actually live in the real world of work?" Chris asked Gordon.

"Yes, but I'm still a trainee manager at the hotel and I'm a trainee instructor at the sailing club, so nothing very grand there," said Gordon. "The hotel's always busy so it's good experience for me. Oban's popular with tourists in the summer and because of the ferry terminal for the islands custom stays quite steady through the winter too."

"Wow, good shot," Alison encouraged Karen as she potted a ball neatly in the side pocket. "Your shot again. I think you're going to beat us." They played best out of five, with Karen and Chris winning three to two games. Chris, an excellent mimic, kept them amused with a running commentary on the play in the style of various TV stars and politicians. They were particularly amused by his rendition of D.J. Tony Blackburn and comedian Eric Morcambe.

"If you don't make it to fame as a musician, you can always become an impressionist," Alison joked.

"Well, I still hope to at least be a successful musician, not many get to be famous. I hope you're going to come along next week to our orchestra concert. Did Karen tell you I'm the leader?"

"Only about a dozen times, she's so proud of you. I've got my ticket and am looking forward to it, although I'm not that familiar with classical music. It'll be funny to see you two all serious and dressed up. Anyway, I think we'd better call it a night now. Gordon has to catch an early train back tomorrow so that he can work the evening shift."

"Yeah, I need to get the seven fifteen from Waverly to make my connection in Glasgow. It's not very civilised. I think next time I come down I'll try to drive, if I can borrow my Mum's car, it would be more direct. Good to meet you both and I hope the concert next week goes well, Alison will tell me all about it."

The rain had stopped, making their walk back to Pollock halls much more pleasant.

"So, what am I to tell your Mum when I come across her fixing the flower arrangements in the hotel lobby later in the week?" Gordon asked. Alison's Mum owned a florist business in the town and had the contract to supply the hotel flowers.

"Oh, you can just tell her I'm fine and about the things we did at the weekend. I don't think I'm going to make it back to Oban before the Christmas break, not that she'd be expecting me any sooner. I do phone her once a week."

"I know, but she's bound to want to talk about you." Last summer Alison's Mum had grown possessive of her as the departure date for university had drawn nearer. Her older sister, Helen, had already left home working as an air stewardess out of Glasgow airport. It seemed like a case of imminent 'empty nest syndrome'.

"I think she's got things back into perspective again. We're getting on fine when I phone her and she's not been quizzing me so much. She didn't even ask me about the sleeping arrangements for your visit."

"Well I hope she won't ask me about that in the middle of reception." Gordon protested.

"I'm sure she won't, she doesn't really want to know." Alison replied." I think Helen has eased the way there. It's just that Mum and Dad's generation were brought up firmly with 'no sex before marriage'. So, she likes to think that Helen and I are going to be the same. And as long as we're discreet she can continue to pretend it's not happening. I've no idea what Dad thinks, he'd never dream of mentioning such things. I suppose he's left it for Mum to deal with."

"My Dad once gave me a talk about 'being responsible.' That was the sum total of the father to son advice."

"Well, I'm sure it's always been a tricky subject to raise between parents and children. Nothing new there."

Alison's alarm clock startled them awake at six o'clock the next morning. It was still very dark as they waited on Dalkeith Road at the bus stop. It was also chilly with a penetrating damp left over from all of yesterday's rain. They were glad of their thick jackets, scarves and gloves.

"You could have let me go on my own and stayed on longer in bed. Your lecture isn't until nine," Gordon said.

"I know, but I wouldn't have gone back to sleep. I'd rather come with you and hopefully I can find an open café for some breakfast."

They caught the number thirty-three bus when it arrived and took it down to Princes Street alighting just past the Scott Monument. The city was still very quiet as they approached Waverly, although a few taxis zoomed past them down the hill into the station.

"It might be fun to have a car next time you come," Alison said, "It would let us explore a bit farther afield, maybe to the Pentlands or down the coast."

"We can talk about it, but it might not be the weather for it next term, maybe summer term would be better for the car. I was considering whether I could get a group together from the rugby club to come down for one of the Scotland international games next term."

"That's a great idea. I've never been to Murrayfield."

They were at the platform now and the train was already waiting.

"Hey, I've really enjoyed my visit. It's been good to see where you are and put faces to the names you tell me about. You're good at writing to me. I probably get two or three letters for every one I send you. I love reading them, but seeing you this weekend has brought everything to life."

"It's going to feel a bit lonely now, once you've gone. I'll phone you tomorrow night, you should be home if you're working the early shift." Alison gave Gordon a huge hug which he returned. Her eyes were filled with tears, blurring her vision, making him seem hazy as he set off down the platform, turning to wave before stepping up into a carriage.

After seeing Gordon off Alison felt deflated but went in search of breakfast to cheer herself up. She thought there might be a café open on Market Street, so climbed the stairs to the back exit of the station. However, it all looked deserted there so she carried on across the road and up Fleshmarket Close. The clocks had turned back an hour three weeks ago, so at seven thirty the day was just beginning to lighten, but the close with its towering stone walls was still very gloomy. Luckily it was a straight climb, allowing her to see that there was no one lurking farther up. Also a few of the street lights mounted on the wall to her left were still lit. Never the less she had a sense of relief as she emerged breathless at the top of the steps onto Cockburn Street. She wouldn't have liked to venture in there at night two hundred and fifty years ago when there would have been no street lighting. There was nothing stirring in any of the nearby buildings so she walked on up to the High Street. She passed the Tron Church and crossed Hunter Square, where some pigeons scuttled away from her, and then came onto South Bridge. The traffic was beginning to thicken as she headed south towards the university. As she crossed the entrance to old college, she remembered picking out its dome from the top of Arthur's seat two days ago. Its fat columns towered above her, her head didn't even come up to the top of their plinths. Just beyond the Empire Theatre she noticed the shape of a man through the glass doors of a café with the

29

lights on inside. She looked in and the man opened one half-door for her.

"Do you want to come in? We've just opened," he said with a strong Italian accent. "What can I bring you?" Alison ordered a coffee and toast and jam and sat thawing out in the warmth listening to the hiss of the coffee machine. Gordon's visit had been a great success but also unsettling. "I'll need to make a big effort to concentrate on work again," she resolved as she sipped her drink which was rich, dark-roasted and delicious.

She waved to the Italian proprietor as she left, hurrying towards Nicholson Square. "So, it won't do to be late for my anatomy lecture," she thought, as she passed the elegant lampposts twined with diving dolphins at the entrance to the medical quad. There was still a steady stream of students clattering up the stone stairs while unwinding maroon, red and yellow faculty scarves and unfastening coats. At the entrance to the steeply raked lecture theatre she could see Robert sitting in their usual area across the room and four rows up. She climbed up the aisle, slid in next to him and flipped the seat down.

"Hi," he greeted her. "Have a good weekend? Get lots of work done?" Of course she had had a great weekend, but she hadn't done any work. Why did he always manage to make her feel guilty?

Three

Alison turned her face up to the sun and breathed in deeply, enjoying the late spring warmth. It was the beginning of May and the blossom on the trees above her was at its peak, hanging in thick clumps. The bright pink colour reminded her of the cotton-wool balls that her mum used to keep in a jar on the bathroom windowsill. She strolled down the long pink tunnel which stretched the whole width of The Meadows. It was Wednesday and classes finished at lunchtime to allow for those students who participated in sport. There was no badminton scheduled mid-week as there was a competition taking place on Saturday, so Alison was going to Karen's flat for lunch. She passed under the arch made by actual whale jawbones at the end of Jawbone Walk and waited to cross Melville Drive.

Next year she was planning to take over Karen's room in the Spottiswoode Street flat, as Karen was due to spend her year abroad in France. She crossed at the green man signal and followed Learmonth Walk as it climbed the slope of Bruntsfield Links until she branched off at the spur for Spottiswoode Street. The flat was a lot closer to the medical school than Pollock halls and this would be her daily walk. She'd miss being so close to the Queen's Park but from the bay window in the flat's sitting room you could see Bruntsfield Links at the end of the road so she would still be very close to a green space.

Alison had visited the flat a few times before but was noticing things today with the keen eyes of a soon-to-be tenant. Once through the main door the stairway was lit by long windows to the rear of the building. The lower walls were tiled in cream, slightly crazed, with rich bottle green trim. Most of the flat doors were painted a similar green colour to match. When she'd climbed to Karen's door on the third floor, she pulled on the old-fashioned brass doorbell and heard the jangle inside. When the door opened, there was a waft of spice and onion released into the stairwell.

"Hi," Karen welcomed her. "I've made us some spicy parsnip soup. Hope you're hungry." Alison followed Karen down the hall and into the large, bright kitchen at the end. There was a table set for lunch in what would originally have been a bed recess when the flats were built at the end of the nineteenth century. Alison sat down as Karen ladled the thick fragrant soup into earthenware bowls and they buttered hefty slices of bread to accompany it. Both attacked their food with healthy appetites, which Alison was pleased to notice in her friend. She'd thought that Karen looked rather thin and tired after the Easter break.

"So how are the plans for France going? Is anything more settled yet for your attachment?" Alison asked.

"Yes, I know I'm going to be studying in Bordeaux and I'll have a part-time attachment in a secondary school in Pessac, a nearby town. There are a few others from my year who'll be at the same Uni, so it should be good."

"Where'll you stay?"

"I haven't got that sorted out yet, but the department will help us. They have a list of approved landlords which I need to get a hold of."

"I know your French is brilliant compared with mine, but I'd be terrified I wouldn't be able to understand anyone at all," Alison commented.

"Well, I've been on a French exchange with school and it wasn't too bad. Even after a week I felt much more confidant. I've done a lot more French since then, so I should be fine. D'you want some more soup? I've also got some chocolate cake." Alison elected for the cake and a mug of coffee which they took with them through to the sitting room. The furniture was an eclectic mix of things that were slightly worn and unfashionable. The sofa was covered with a brown tweedy material, while the armchairs were flamboyant pink and blue floral chintz. There was an old standard lamp with a heavily tasselled olive green shade and a more modern coffee table, perhaps sixties style, with a tiled top which gave it a vaguely Mexican look. The fireplace was an original feature, also tiled in red and black and the cornices had been carefully picked out in maroon and gold. There were original wooden shutters at the large bay window. Alison went to stand in the bay and looked to the end of the street where she could see a haze of bright green appearing on the trees and behind them the unmistakable shape of the castle.

"I didn't realise you could see the castle from here." she commented.

"You've probably always been here at night when the shutters are closed. You can see it easily in winter but once the trees are in full leaf for the summer it's blocked out. But my room doesn't have this view, it's to the back and looks over all the internal gardens. I'll show you later when you've finished your coffee. And I hope that you'll be able to meet the others, I think they'll be back soon. You've already met Liz, she's studying business management and Elaine is a lawyer. They're both really easy to get on with and neither is too untidy, which I know will matter to you."

"Yes, there's no way I could live with some of the medics I know. Either I'd be a resentful skivvy, tidying up all the time because I wouldn't be able to help myself, or I'd nag them constantly. Anyway, I think it's quite good to share with non-medics, we can be a bit clannish."

"Talking of non-medics, have you heard from your friend Linda at all?" Karen asked. Alison had been shocked when Linda announced at the end of their first term that she had made a mistake and was giving up medicine. Everyone knew she'd been struggling a bit but so were quite a few others in the year group. She'd explained to Alison that the anatomy in particular was really getting to her. She had found the dissection distasteful from the outset and had always had to steel herself to attend the dissecting room. She began to be so distressed by it that she avoided going if at all possible, which of course meant that she'd fallen behind in her grades. She'd thought carefully about what it was that really interested her and decided that it was a curiosity about people and what made them tick. She'd already been considering specialising in psychiatry after her degree, so was going to try to transfer to psychology.

"We've been writing to each other. She's got a job back home in Chester in Marks and Spencer but she'll be back here in October. She's been accepted to start a psychology degree. I miss her a lot, especially for coffee break chats. She said she might come up to Oban to visit in the summer, which would be great."

"That's good that she got a place for next year, I hope psychology will suit her better. Do you want to look at the room now?" They crossed the hallway. "The bathroom's there and this will be your room," Karen said, opening the door onto a spacious room, apple-green coloured walls, high-ceilinged with fresh white woodwork and an old fireplace also painted white.

"I love it," Alison said, stepping inside. "I should work well here," she mused, sitting herself in front of the window at the sunny desk currently strewn with French texts.

"I've been meaning to ask your advice," Karen said, leaning against the mantelpiece. "You know I've not been feeling great since that virus I got at home during the holidays? My glands are still up and I'm tired, sometimes I think I've got a temperature. It's similar to how I felt after I'd had glandular fever, but that's three years ago now. Do you think it can come back? Would it be daft to go to the doctor? It's not as if I'm really ill."

"Well, if you're worried you should go for a check-up. After all you've got big exams coming up soon and you want to be at your best. Maybe you just need some antibiotics or a course of iron to perk you up. Not that I'm an expert. First year medics are still learning about what's normal, we don't know any more than anyone else about illness."

"I think I'll make an appointment, thanks. Oh, that sounds like Elaine coming in. Come and meet her."

***

Come Saturday Alison and Karen were on court playing a pair from the Glasgow university badminton team. Their opposition was a sharp two-some and the girls were trailing behind. Alison felt desperately tired; it seemed that she'd had to cover more of the court than usual today. Were the other players far superior, or was Karen having an off day? She couldn't be sure, maybe a bit of both. Alison ran to the side of the court and stretched, lunging her arm and racquet as far as she could

36

reach but the shuttle flew past and landed beyond her, just inside the line. "Game and match," the umpire called. The four players ran up to the net to shake hands. It was a disappointment for Alison and Karen as their loss meant that they were out of the competition and Glasgow would go through to the next round. They went for showers and met up in the dressing room.

"Sorry, I think I let us down today, just felt a bit sluggish around the court," Karen apologised.

"Oh, don't worry; everyone has their off days," Alison replied. However, she thought that Karen still seemed a bit out of breath. "Are you sure you're OK? Did you make that doctor's appointment?"

"Yeah, it's on Tuesday. Come on, we'd better get up to the bar and be sociable." They collected their kit together and headed out of the changing rooms.

The following weekend on Sunday afternoon Alison and Karen were in very different surroundings, sitting in the lounge of The North British Hotel at the east end of Princes Street. Chris had a job leading a string quartet to entertain the guests who had gathered for afternoon tea. The girls had decided to come and listen this weekend. Their table was smothered in snowy white linen, with matching napkins. The food was presented on silver cake stands and the tea-set was pretty willow-patterned china. There were flowers on each table and larger floral displays on stands scattered around the room which made Alison think of her Mum. They nibbled on their delicate cucumber sandwiches and listened to Mozart rise above the clink of teaspoons and murmur of conversation.

"What would Gordon think of this in his professional capacity?" Karen asked.

"I think he'd be impressed. Afternoon tea in Oban is a lot less refined," Alison replied. "I'm going to try one of these tiny butterfly cakes. Everything's so dainty you don't feel guilty at all."

"Mmm, it's all delicious. By the way, I've been to the doctor," Karen reported. "He thinks I'm just a bit run down after that virus, but he took a blood test and I've to go back to see him in two weeks. I'm glad I went. I feel a bit better."

"Good. Well tuck into some more of this food to keep your strength up, after all we've paid for it up front."

"Don't worry; Chris will eat up anything left-over when he has his break."

***

By the first week in June the weather was really warm and sunny. "Why is the weather always good when I've got exams coming up?" Alison asked herself. She had brought a picnic rug to George Square Gardens along with her physiology notes, trying to make the best of the sunshine. An approaching figure threw her into shadow, and then Karen landed on the rug.

"What a relief that's me finished!" she announced.

"Did it go OK?" Alison asked, secretly jealous of arts students who seemed to finish their exams a whole month earlier than she would.

"I think so. I don't suppose you'll want to come for a drink?"

"No, I'd better not, I can't start celebrating yet – I've got masses still to do."

"We'll be in the pub at Greyfriars, Bobby, if you change your mind. Actually, I might not stay very long I'm not feeling all that celebratory either."

"Why not? I thought you felt all the exams had gone fine?" Alison asked.

"It's not that. I went back to the GP and you were right, I am a bit anaemic and he gave me a course of iron tablets to start. But I've still got this lump in my neck and he wants me to go and see a specialist about it. He thinks I might need to have it removed."

Alison felt a niggle of apprehension.

"How long will that take?"

"Probably a couple of weeks. It'll be at the Western General. I was going to go home this weekend; my parents are coming up with the car to help me empty my room and I'm starting my holiday job the week after next." Karen's family lived in Peebles, a small Borders town about an hour's drive away.

"Well, I suppose it's not too far to come back for an appointment and anyway your mum might want to go with you. I didn't know you had a lump. Is it sore?"

Karen turned her head to the left and Alison could see a rounded oval shape appear, about an inch long, in the hollow in front of her sternocleidomastoid muscle on the right. "No, it's not sore and I think you can only see it because I've lost a bit of weight. But I suppose I'll have to see the specialist, they might decide I don't need anything else done. I hadn't mentioned any of this to my parents, now they'll make a big fuss over it all."

Alison's apprehension was growing, but she didn't want to alarm her friend.

"Yes, well they're bound to be a bit anxious about you. Hopefully it'll all turn out to be a fuss about nothing. You know, I think I've changed my mind. Maybe I will come to the pub with you; it's nearly teatime after all." Saying that she began to gather up her books. They folded the picnic rug between them and picked their way between other sunning students to the gate out of the garden.

That evening she phoned Gordon from the pay phone along the corridor from her room at Pollock. Alison was able to voice her concern.

"I'm really worried about Karen. You know I told you how she's always tired and she's lost weight? Now I've found out she has a lump in her neck and it sounds as if her GP thinks she needs a biopsy because he's referred her to hospital."

"What does that mean?" Gordon asked.

Alison was sitting on the floor with her back against the wall. She had her body huddled around the telephone receiver to keep their conversation private, trying to stop her voice from echoing all along the hall. She began to cry.

"Well, it might mean nothing, but from what I've read since I got back here it might be a type of cancer."

"Hey, aren't medical students' famous for thinking they have every serious illness in the text books at some point in their career? Maybe you're spilling some of that over onto Karen and it's not as bad as all that." It felt hard to comfort someone from so far away but Gordon tried.

"Yes, you're probably right. I'm probably overreacting. Karen didn't seem all that worried herself, more put out about the fuss and having to come back up from Peebles for the appointment once she's started her job."

"Well then, try not to imagine the worst. I know she's a good friend, but you need to concentrate for your exams."

"Yes, I'll have to get back to my physiology I suppose. I'll try to phone you again tomorrow."

"Bye for now then."

"Bye," she said and searched for a tissue to wipe her tears as she hung up the receiver.

Four

"Well, hello there, Alison, it's nice to see you home. How are the studies going? It's medicine you're taking, isn't it?"

"Hello Mrs Robertson," Alison greeted the elderly woman who had been her class teacher in primary three, but was now retired. "Yes, I'm a medic and I've managed to get through first year, although it was hard work."

"That's excellent. I'd like some of those apricot coloured roses please. Could you give me eight with a bit of greenery?" Alison was working in her mum's shop again this summer. She began to make up a small bouquet with the roses. "And have you made lots of friends down in Edinburgh? Your Mum told me you're still dating young Gordon McRae."

"Yes, Gordon and I are still dating. I've got a friend from university coming up to visit next week. She's from Chester originally and has never been this far north."

Alison found being back in the small town a bit exasperating after the anonymity of Edinburgh. It was nice that people were friendly, but sometimes they seemed to know too much about her and still be curious to learn even more.

"Oh, that'll be good company for you and you'll be able to show her all the sights. I'm sure your Mum will give you some time off. Now what do I owe you for the flowers?" Alison watched through the display window as she stopped to chat to another woman on the pavement outside. "That will be that piece of information relayed," she thought. "Or maybe I'm getting self-absorbed. I'm sure they have lots of other more interesting conversational topics than me."

Moving back home for the summer was a mixed experience. She had a great sense of relief at having passed her first year exams and was tired after the summer term. Those last few weeks had been a mixture of boredom when studying and panic if she took some time off. She had tried not to compare herself with Robert who seemed to be able to stay in the library for hours on end. Whenever she was giving up for a break she'd see his red head still bent over his notes, or worse he would glance up, shake his head at her and wave as she left. It had been relaxing to settle into the well-known routine of home and the shop and she appreciated their comfortable, spacious house and large helpings of delicious home cooking. Her relationship with her Mum was much more relaxed again, which pleased her. Most days she could see Gordon, work allowing, and she'd enjoyed catching up with old friends from school. So why did she often feel grumpy and discontented? The scrutiny of the community, real or imagined, was part of it. Also, there was no way that she and Gordon could be as intimate as they'd been on his Edinburgh visits, and of course she was worrying about Karen. They'd been keeping in touch mainly by writing but also with an occasional phone call. There were still no answers. Every stage seemed to take two or three weeks. First there was a wait for an appointment to see the consultant, who had recommended going ahead with the biopsy. Now she was waiting for a date for the surgery and then, no doubt, there would be another wait for the result. "If I'm finding it bad, how much more frustrating must it be for Karen?" she thought.

Her musing was interrupted by her Mum arriving back in the shop.

"Been busy?" she asked.

"Steady. There are a few orders for later in the week and I've had some customers in the shop. A woman wants to speak to you about wedding flowers. I took down the details and said you'd phone back."

"Very efficient, thank you. Why don't you head off home now and I'll close up in another half an hour? I was wondering if you'd like to ask Gordon over to eat with us on Monday when your friend Linda arrives."

"Thanks Mum, I'll see if he's free and let you know."

When she left the shop, Alison turned left and then left again into William Street, a short, narrow road leading to the Corran Esplanade. As she gained the open sea front, the breeze played around her, bringing with it a strong scent of seaweed. It was a sunny day and there were lots of visitors milling about, mainly heading towards the town centre. She weaved through the groups, walking in the opposite direction. Oban Bay was on her left and she was almost keeping pace with a Caledonian MacBrayne car ferry. It was setting off for the Isle of Mull and had an accompanying cloud of squalling seagulls. She continued on past St Columba's Cathedral to her parents' house on Ganavan Road.

On opening the front door, she was immediately greeted by Jess who circled around her, wagging her tail so energetically that it made her whole body squirm.

"Hi, girl. Do you want to go out in the garden?" Alison went through the house to the back door and let the excited dog out into the back garden which was fully enclosed by a stone wall. She left the back door open allowing warm air to enter the house; fragrance from the sweet peas that her Mum grew close to the kitchen door drifted in too. She went to the fridge to find a cold drink and noticed that her Mum had left a pile of mail on the kitchen counter. She flicked through the letters and among them found a postcard addressed to her. It was written in purple felt-tip pen and had a view of Neidpath Castle on the river Tweed near Peebles on the front.

"Dear Alison,

Back home after my operation, it wasn't too bad. Have to wait for 2 weeks to get the result, so will try to phone you then. I hope Oban is sunny and that you enjoy Linda's visit.

Love from Karen."

"Just as I thought, more waiting," Alison looked to find the date of the postmark as Karen hadn't written a date on the card. It would probably be another ten days or more until she could expect to hear any more news. She was pleased that Linda's visit was coming up soon as it would distract her from her worries over Karen. She poured juice into a glass and took it out into the garden where she sat down on the wooden bench under the rose trellis in dappled sunshine. Jess immediately came up and presented her ball on the grass at Alison's feet, then crouched down and waited expectantly for Alison to throw it for her.

***

Late on Monday afternoon Alison was waiting at the railway station for Linda's train to arrive from Glasgow. She was pleased that it was sunny as she wanted her friend to see Oban at its best and form a good first impression. After a journey of six and a half hours from Chester she would be tired. The train pulled in and doors began to open. She spotted Linda struggling with a large rucksack farther down the platform and rushed over to help her. They hugged then Alison assisted Linda to heave the bag onto her shoulders.

"Wow, I'm glad to be here. That was a mammoth journey and changing stations in Glasgow was crazy."

"Well you're here safely and, if your bag's not too heavy, I thought you'd enjoy walking home. It's not far and after sitting for so long it might be nice to stretch your legs, but we can get a taxi if you'd rather."

"No, walking's good. And you can show me some of the local landmarks." The friends set out chatting.

As they came out of the station, Alison pointed across the road to the Caledonian Hotel.

"That's where Gordon works. You'll see him later, Mum asked him round for dinner tonight. He'll probably be busy just now, so we'll not go in."

"What's that round castle thing up on the hill? Is it a ruin?"

"It's called McCaig's folly cos it was a grandiose idea, but it was never completed. The views are good from up there; we can go later in the week."

"The views are amazing down here, too. What's that island?"

"That's Kerrera. It's mainly just sheep over there. The hills farther away with the clouds on top are on Mull. We just follow the bay all the way along here to our house."

"Wow." Linda exclaimed when they arrived at the gate to Alison's front garden. "I never imagined that you had all of this on your doorstep." She gestured at the seascape, dotted with islands. "No wonder you were always going on about space and light when we were in Edinburgh."

"Mmm, just one of my quaint Highland eccentricities. So, you'll appreciate the sea view from your room. It used to be Helen's, now the guest room. Come on," Alison grabbed Linda's arm and guided her up the front path. "You've got all week to gaze at the view."

Gordon joined Alison's family for dinner that evening and they all vied to suggest various activities to entertain Linda during her stay.

"You can borrow my car for a day or two as long as I have some notice," Alison's Mum offered.

"I can take you out on the water on Thursday, that's my day off this week," said Gordon.

"Alison said you like to golf. I can give you a round at Glencruitin on Friday afternoon or at the weekend," said Alison's dad, not to be outdone.

"It's true what they say about Highland hospitality being so good," said Linda. "I'd like to do everything!" They all laughed as they dug their spoons into the raspberry cranachan that Alison had whipped up for dessert. She had picked the rasps from the garden earlier that afternoon.

The week with Linda flew past. They climbed up to McCaig's folly for the view and walked the beach at Ganavan. The area bristled with ruined castles and standing stones. So, they had a 'history' day in the car. First, they visited Carnasserie Castle and enjoyed exploring the nooks and crannies, watching swallows swoop around the battlements. Then they carried on through Kilmartin Glen, stopping to examine some of the stone burial chambers and finishing at Dunadd Fort, an important Royal centre of the ancient Gaelic kingdom of Dalriada.

"I'll need to show you the history around Chester," Linda commented on their way home. "Let you walk round the walls and see the Roman remains."

"Yeah, I'd like that. Let's do it sometime," Alison replied.

One of the highlights of the visit for Linda was getting up close to seals when they went sailing with Gordon. She was amused when some of them slid off the rocks and into the water and then appeared very close to the yacht, keeping pace with the boat, seemingly inquisitive about the humans. When it rained, they played cards and board games and throughout the week they chatted non-stop, reminiscing and catching up with each other.

"I'll never forget your face that day in the dissecting room when Alastair and Ian decided to remove the false teeth," said Linda.

"I wasn't even paying any attention. I think they had to use a fair bit of force to pry them out and the upper plate came flying through the air and landed in my lap. It was a bit of a shock, no wonder I screamed."

"And do you remember the biochemistry lecture when the professor was writing that reaction path on the blackboard?" Linda asked.

"Yes, the board must have been about thirty feet long and he kept writing until he'd filled a whole line, then he drew a big arrow and went back to the other end of the board again. He didn't seem to understand why we all started laughing."

"I think he'd lost most of us before the half-way mark on the first line. It was weird going back to Chester after the first term, knowing that I was giving up. I felt relieved because I didn't think I could keep up with the course, but also at a terrible loose end. I kept thinking I should be doing more. I suppose I'd got so used to being busy. The Marks and Spencer job filled in some of the time but the best thing I did was to join the FP hockey club from my old school. It gave me a bit of a social life, too, most of my friends went back to their own studies in January."

"Do you think you'll keep the hockey up when you're back in Edinburgh this time?" Alison asked.

"Yes, I'll try for the Uni team. I think I stand a good chance of getting in after all the training I've been doing recently and hopefully I'll have enough time to play as I don't think my course will be so jam-packed this year."

"Have you arranged a place to stay yet?"

"Yeah, I've got a room in a flat at Newington on Rankeillor Street. There are three other girls and I know one of them, Sally, from Pollock. She was my contact. You were lucky to get a room in the Spottiswoode Street flat."

"Yes, it's really nice and it's just across the Meadows to lectures so I'll be able to sleep for another fifteen minutes in the mornings."

"Mmm, you're not really a morning person, are you? Have you had any more recent news about your friend Karen? It's her old room that you have in the flat, isn't it?"

"I got a post card last week. She's waiting for the result of her biopsy. I think I might try phoning her at the end of this week if I haven't heard any more from her by then."

On Friday afternoon Linda went off to play golf with Alison's dad. "I'll guarantee you won't have played a course anything like this one," he said as they set off. "It's a wee bit hilly."

"Oh I'm sure I'll enjoy it, Mr Scott. I had a round at the Braids course in Edinburgh in Fresher's week. It's pretty hilly. I spent a lot of time looking for balls in the gorse bushes."

After the golfers had gone the house seemed very quiet and Alison decided to try phoning Karen. She sat at the telephone table in the hall gazing at the jewel coloured pattern of light shining on the carpet from the stained glass panel on the front door as she listened to the ringing at the other end of the line. Karen's Mum answered the phone.

"Hello, Mrs Douglas it's Alison Scott. Can I speak to Karen please?"

There was a pause.

"Alison, I'm afraid you can't speak to Karen at the moment. I don't know when you last heard from her, but she got bad news yesterday. We were at the clinic for her biopsy result and it's something called Hodgkin's disease, a kind of cancer. They kept her in to do what they call staging tests so they know how best to treat her, but it will almost certainly mean chemotherapy."

"Oh. I was afraid of that. How did she react to the news?" The coloured light patterns started to blur and leach into each other as tears filled Alison's eyes.

"Like you, I think we'd all thought it might come to this. We'd tried to be positive and hope it was all OK but although none of the doctors mentioned any definite diagnosis, somehow their manner all along made me feel that they thought it was going to be bad. I think Karen picked up on that, too, so she wasn't too surprised but she is very upset. It'll mean she can't go to France. I think that's the main thing that's upsetting her."

"How long will she be in hospital?"

"I don't know exactly, but they may keep her in for her first chemo dose, so probably well into next week."

"I might see if I can come down. I could stay at the flat. Is Chris around just now?"

"No, he's on a tour with the orchestra. I'm sure Karen would appreciate your company, but she'll be coming home to Peebles when she's discharged." Alison felt that Mrs Douglas was staking her claim to look after her daughter.

"I'll need to check with my mum. I know she'd like me to be in the shop when she and Dad go on holiday the week after next but until then she should be fine without me. Can you tell Karen I'll try to come down for a few days?"

"We'll be up to visit her this evening and I'll be sure to pass your message on. Thank you for phoning, Alison."

Alison replaced the receiver and her tears began to flow more freely. She felt very frightened for her friend and in a strange way for herself. People their age didn't expect to get seriously ill. A boy from her year at school had been badly injured in a car crash. But cancer was something that happened to old people, and the treatment was awful and you could die. Jess, sensing her distress, came and put her front paws on Alison's knee and nuzzled up to her face, licking her tears. Alison hugged the dog close and was comforted by her warmth and the familiar musky smell of dog.

"Come on, Jess, we'll take a walk down to the shop so I can talk to Mum. Where's your lead?"

Five

On Tuesday afternoon Alison walked up the driveway of the Western General Hospital on her way to visit Karen. She had travelled from Oban to Glasgow with Linda the day before. There the friends parted, Linda making her way south to Chester for the remainder of the summer and Alison catching the train to Edinburgh. They would meet up again at the beginning of the next university term. "I had a great visit and it was so good to see you. I hope Karen will be OK," Linda had said, hugging Alison. "I'll phone you next week once I know you'll be back in Oban, and see you in October."

Once in Edinburgh Alison made her way to the flat in Spottiswoode Street. She knew that Elaine was away for the summer but Liz had a summer job with the Royal Bank, so would be back at some point. Thinking that Karen's parents were most likely to visit her in the evenings she had decided to make her first visit on the next afternoon.

She climbed the stairs following signs for 'C' corridor. She had little experience of hospitals and, as her course had two pre-clinical years, it would be another year before she was on the wards as a student. The soles of her sandals squeaked on the shiny linoleum corridor as she walked along, peeping into wards as she looked for the number of Karen's ward. She found number ten and entered a bright south-facing six-bedded room. Immediately she spotted Karen in the closest bed, wearing blue pyjamas with a white snoopy-dog motif, her long blonde hair tied back in a ponytail, flipping through a magazine without seeming to concentrate on it.

"Karen, how are you doing?" she asked as she hugged her friend closely, aware immediately of a large white bandage protruding from the neck of Karen's pyjama top and not wanting to squeeze too tight.

"Well I've had better days, but seeing you should cheer me up."

"What's the big bandage for? It's nowhere near where your lump was," Alison couldn't help being curious.

"I had a bone-marrow test. They took it from my breast-bone, although I'm sure you'll know a better name for it. It wasn't pleasant."

"It's your sternum," Alison clarified. "Will you have to have any more tests?"

"I don't think so. I had a CAT scan yesterday and they want to put in something called a central line to prepare for my chemotherapy."

"What's that exactly?"

"It goes into a deeper vein. It's because the drugs can wreck your veins. If you need a lot of treatment, it can get hard for them to find new ones for a drip, so they put in this more permanent one. I should get home after that and just come in as a day patient for the treatment. I hope they might let me out tomorrow or Thursday. Could I come and stay at the flat for a few days? Mum is expecting me to come home to Peebles, but it's so suffocating there. I've had to give up my summer job so I've got nothing to do and I feel Mum and Dad are watching me all the time. I know they love me and they're concerned, but I need to be able to breathe. Also, Chris will be back this weekend and it'll be easier to see him if I stay in Edinburgh."

"Karen, there's no problem with staying in the flat. Elaine is away and I'm only here for a few days. I have to go back next week 'cause my parents are going on holiday and Mum's relying on me to help keep the shop going. So, there will be rooms free that you can use."

"Great. I'll need to arrange to see my director of studies soon while I've got the energy. They think my treatment will take six months but that I might not feel back to normal for another six months after that, so it's probably best if I try to arrange to take a year out."

"I'm sure that Uni will do everything they can to be helpful," Alison reassured her.

"Yeah, I hope so anyway. It's strange to think that I'm going to let people put what amounts to poison into my system. I don't know how I'll feel, but I know it's not likely to be good. Since I've been in there have been a few people in the ward with bad side effects of their chemo. I have to admit that while I'm trying to be positive and take the longer view, I'm really scared." Karen seemed to laugh but Alison thought it sounded close to a sob.

"I think you need to be able to tell someone things just as they are, exactly how you're feeling when you feel like it. I'm happy to be the person you can do that with if you like. Why don't we have an agreement that there are no rules, anything goes any time, serious or silly?"

"Thank you, Alison, I would like that and I can't do it with my parents. I feel I have to be brave for them. And I'm not sure about Chris, but he might not want to be lumbered with a bald, puking girlfriend." There was no doubt now that the sobs were winning through.

"I don't know, but I don't think he'd desert you. He doesn't seem like a light-weight emotionally and he's always been devoted to you."

"But I don't want him sticking around out of duty or pity. I couldn't stand that."

"Why don't you give him a chance, keep an open mind. Things may not be as bad as you're imagining. Here have some tissues." Alison produced some from her handbag.

"Thanks. Will you come with me to the wig place? The thought of that is freaking me out."

"Sure. Do you think we can go this week or can it wait till after my folks get back from holiday?"

"It's probably going to be best to go as soon as possible. Apparently, some people start to lose their hair as early as two weeks into the treatment and they might need time to custom make something."

"OK, maybe we could go on Friday if you're likely to be out by then. D'you have their address or phone number so you could make an appointment?"

They began to make some practical plans and then to talk more generally about the summer and mutual friends. Alison was very glad that she'd come down to see Karen as she'd obviously been feeling frightened and lonely. She hoped that Chris would be able to reassure Karen about his feelings once he was home. They'd always appeared to be a very close couple, maybe because they were particularly tactile, invariably linked to each other somehow if they were within touching distance. But Alison had always thought that there was also genuine emotional commitment on both sides.

***

On Saturday evening, there was a big pot of chili con carne simmering on the stove top in the kitchen of the Spottiswoode Street flat. Alison was setting the table for four and sipping from a glass of Chianti. Karen and Chris were in the sitting room and Liz was due home within the next half hour. Alison decided not to start cooking the rice until Liz appeared but began to put together a salad. Karen had been discharged on Thursday after having her central line inserted on Wednesday. Mrs Douglas had not been pleased at her decision to stay on in Edinburgh but Karen was able to explain that it was easier to see about a wig and to make arrangements for her course if she was here. Her treatment was likely to start in about ten days and she'd promised to go home for a few days prior to that.

"Mum seems to have totally forgotten that I've lived away from home for the past two years and that I've got a life here. I'm pleased that we can get together with Chris and Liz before you have to leave," Karen had confided after the tussle with her Mum. Alison was planning to return to Oban on Sunday afternoon.

"Hi, I'm home. That smells great but it's very hot and steamy in here," said Liz coming into the kitchen and crossing to push up the large sash window over the sink making it screech.

"Thanks, you don't notice it so much when you're cooking but it is warm. Buy anything for your holiday?" Liz was spending some of the money she'd earned over the summer on a month long inter-rail ticket allowing her to tour round Europe. Today she'd been shopping for some gear to take with her.

"I got a few T-shirts and this cool bush-hat," she said, modelling the hat. The green camouflage pattern toned down her fiery red hair but curls still escaped all around the brim.

"A hat's a good idea with your colouring. You're going to have to be really careful not to burn," said Alison. "Do you want to take this bottle of wine and some glasses through to the others? We'll be ready to eat in about fifteen minutes."

Half an hour later the friends were sitting round the table in the dining alcove attacking steaming plates of chili and rice, their glasses topped up with red wine. Alison had found a blue checked tablecloth in a kitchen drawer and had lit some candles and put a small posy of flowers into a cream jug.

"This is really good Alison and not too hot, I've heard from Karen that sometimes your chili comes with a health warning," teased Chris.

"I freely confess that in my first attempt I did overdo the spices," Alison admitted. "I hadn't come across chili at home. We had jars of cinnamon and ginger for baking when I was growing up. Then we stretched to dried mixed herbs for savoury dishes after I learned how to make spaghetti Bolognaise in Home Ec. Anyway, tell us about your tour. I haven't seen you since the SNO Proms concert we all went to in June."

"That was a good night, wasn't it? The Mahler was very atmospheric and I like it when it's less formal, even the picnic style seating."

"I was glad you'd warned us to take a cushion to sit on. The floor was beginning to numb my gluteal region even with the extra padding," Alison commented.

"She means her bottom," Karen translated.

"My love, the music should have transported you beyond such trivialities," joked Chris in his best Bruce Forsyth voice. The others laughed.

"I'm afraid our orchestra tour wasn't up to quite such a high standard, but I thought we did very well. It's a great experience to be away on tour and we had plenty of free time to explore. It's a bit of a coincidence that I was in the south west of France where Karen was due to go next term. We started at Biarritz and finished at La Rochelle with five venues in between. I'd love to go back and see more of the area on a more leisurely trip some time. Will you be going in that direction on your inter-rail trip?" he asked Liz.

"At the moment, the plan is to start off in Paris for a few days then move south to the Riviera and after that go east into Italy. The girls I'm travelling with are keen to see a lot of the famous art and architecture in Florence and Venice. However, a month is a long time so I hope we'll do some beach days too," said Liz. "How was the French food? Did you sample any local delicacies?"

"They were very big on oysters. Every menu had 'Huitres' as a starter. I tried them but I think they're definitely over-rated. They either taste of lemon or garlic, depending on which they're served with and the main substance is a bit of slimy, slightly chewy, salty stuff," said Chris. "If we're all finished, shall I clear all these plates? I'm very hopeful that there will be something sweet to follow."

"You're in luck. Karen went along to Victor Hugo's Deli this morning and bought us a cake selection. Does everyone want some coffee to go with the cake?" Alison checked. She was pleased to notice that after piling the dirty crockery by the sink Chris sat back at the table with his arm along the back of Karen's chair, his hand on her shoulder. They looked relaxed together.

"It was so lovely to be out walking along the Meadows this morning" said Karen. "Even after just a few days in hospital I was gasping for some fresh air."

Over coffee with gateau and pastries Karen began to tell the others about her visit to the wig suppliers the day before.

"Well I don't think they get too many young people in. There were definitely a lot more mature styles on offer and grey was a popular colour. I decided to stick with blonde but I thought it would be easier to have it shorter, so it'll be more like Alison's length."

Alison admired Karen's attempt to make the experience seem light-hearted when the reality had been very strained. The specialist hairdresser had shown them into a small room within her salon where they could talk in confidence. She was very pleasant but some of her suggestions, although practical, had seemed almost too down to earth for a first meeting. She had recommended that it would be simplest to cut Karen's hair short and perhaps even to shave her scalp before her hair actually began to fall out. She explained that although this might be upsetting it was probably easier to cope with, both emotionally and physically than waiting for handfuls of very long hair to clog up the shower and fall all over the house. She offered to arrange a cut for Karen when she came to collect her wig and also told her that as her hair was so long she could either sell it or donate it for future wig-making. These details had caused Karen to break down in floods of tears and she'd been curt with the wig specialist who seemed to take it all in her stride, she was probably very used to all sorts of emotional reactions.

Poor Karen, Alison knew that she was still reeling and distressed from the news she'd received the day before. She'd been visiting Karen on Thursday afternoon when her consultant, Dr Wood, had come to talk to her prior to discharge. Alison had offered to leave but Karen wanted her to stay. Dr Wood looked friendly and approachable. He was small and rotund, and wore a bright blue shirt fronted by a jazzy blue and yellow tie decorated with a gold and lapis lazuli tiepin under his spotless white coat. His eyes looked lively behind gold-rimmed glasses. He pulled the curtains around Karen's bed to make a roofless tent, it felt almost cosy but the hint of privacy was an illusion. Any conversation could easily pass through the flimsy walls of curtain and over the rail into the ward. Dr Wood explained the results of all the staging tests. Karen's bone marrow had been affected which her anaemia had already led him to expect. Her CAT scan showed widespread involvement of other lymph nodes not just the one that had appeared in her neck. These results combined with the symptoms, like the sweats, she had been experiencing all unfortunately indicated that Karen had what seemed to be an aggressive form of

Hodgkin's disease. This meant that the outlook was less positive and that her treatment was likely to be prolonged. The plan was for six cycles of chemotherapy, four drugs to be given through her central line every second week for twenty-four weeks as long as Karen's system was able to tolerate that frequency. She was due to have the first round at the day unit a week on Monday. It was a lot to take in and Alison could feel Karen's hand trembling and icy in hers as she struggled for control. He also gave Karen written information, because Dr Wood acknowledged that she was likely to forget some of what he was telling her. The literature would also answer the questions that patients commonly had about their treatment, including a list of the potential side effects. He reassured Karen that he would see her before her first treatment was given to answer any particular questions she might have thought of. And he suggested she wrote down anything that was worrying her so that she wouldn't forget to mention it when she saw him next. Alison was comforted by his caring manner and hoped that Karen was too. On their way home Karen was quiet and subdued. Alison kept quiet, too, respecting her friend's need to absorb the severity of her situation. She hoped that Karen would be able to talk to her later.

"Alison what are you dreaming about? Probably Gordon. You haven't heard a word we've been saying, have you?" Chris's voice broke into her thoughts.

"Sorry I was miles away." She returned her attention to the present. "This Black Forrest gateau is delicious. I think they've soaked the cherries in something very boozy." She proceeded to fork up the remains of her cake.

Six

"Dear Gordon,

It' hard to believe I've completed the first week of second year already. Everyone seems very keen after the summer break, especially Robert. My subjects are quite similar to last year except that anatomy is all neuroanatomy. This means that we're dissecting a brain which is quite challenging because it all looks much the same to me – even harder to make out any features than in anatomy last year. We have a lot more pharmacology this term including practical sessions. On Thursday, we had our first physiology practical of term which involved measuring how much we sweat, very pleasant. Eight of us spent an hour in a room at one hundred and ten degrees Fahrenheit. We had to do some exercises to begin with and then we sat wearing huge green plastic gloves that came up to our armpits to collect our sweat. The boys had a particularly dramatic reaction, especially Ian who's a keen athlete. He had sweat dripping off his chin. I managed to collect fifteen millilitres of sweat from both of my arms, which was the highest volume amongst the girls doing the experiment, but less than half of the boys' volumes. The shower afterwards was very welcome! Next week we have to take a twenty-four hour urine collection. We were all supplied with three plastic containers for 'morning', 'afternoon' and 'overnight' and girls also got a funnel. Robert is mortified as he is going to a cheese and wine party for the chess club in the evening of the collection and now thinks everyone will remember him as 'that guy with the plastic bucket' for the rest of the year.

The flat is working out very well. I love having more space, not just my room, but also a lounge and kitchen to spread out into. I think that catering for myself is going to be more flexible than last year and also, I can eat healthier food. The Hall canteen had a very stodgy menu. Liz and Elaine are both quite keen to share some cooking and eat together when it's convenient. Last week we ate together on half of the nights, I expect once term gets into full swing this might get less. My shorter walk to the medical school is such an improvement. I've even come home at lunchtimes some days which saves some money on sandwiches. The main down side is having to go out to a telephone box to call you and my parents. Although the box in the corridor at Halls wasn't very private it was at least in the same building. Now I have to go round the corner and along Warrender Park Road. However, not everything can be perfect.

Liz had a lot of stories to tell after her inter-railing trip. Apparently the Italian and Greek men are very predatory on the beach. She said that they got fed up being pestered to go out for drinks all the time. At one point, they met a couple of guys from Cambridge also on euro-rail and joined up with them for a few days. Liz said that was much better as the locals left them in peace. Elaine spent the summer at home in Stirling. Her holiday job sounds exotic, it was at Blair Drummond Safari Park, but it had nothing to do with animals, she was working in the canteen.

She managed a couple of weeks away in September and went to Skye. She said it rained every day – but not all day.

I met up with Linda yesterday and she seems to be settling into her psychology course and enjoying it so far. I don't think her flat is as nice as mine, the rooms are all large but it doesn't have the big bay windows and definitely seems darker. She's joined the hockey club and hopes to get a place in the second team. We went to a pizza place on Lothian Road which had good food and wasn't too expensive, maybe we could go there next time you come down.

I saw Karen on Thursday. She's mainly been staying in Peebles but was in town for a hospital appointment. She's had five doses of the treatment now and looked pretty rough. The most obvious difference of course is her hair. Her wig is quite a good colour match, but the texture is much coarser, so it doesn't really look like Karen with a haircut. Her face is a bit puffy and she's had a terrible crop of mouth ulcers which spread onto her lips, so they're all flaking. She says the sickness has been bad after the treatment, so between that and her sore mouth she hasn't felt much like eating. So far, she's not been venturing out much but she's beginning to recognise a pattern. By the second week after the treatment she's feeling a bit better so is now beginning to feel more confident and her plan is to come to stay here or with Chris for a night or two on a more regular basis every second week. One of the worst things she's finding is just being bored. She's been trying to keep up her flute practice and do some French reading but feels very isolated down in Peebles.

I saw Chris on the Music Soc. stall at the Societies Fair. I decided to join up for badminton again this year. I'd miss the exercise if I didn't go. After all Karen would have been away in France if she hadn't been ill and I do know a few other people

68

quite well, so I hope I'll find someone else to team up with regularly as a partner. I've got used to playing doubles; it would be strange to go back to singles. It sounds as if Chris is finding it hard to cope with Karen. He said she keeps telling him that he doesn't need to stick around if he doesn't want to, almost as if she's pushing him away. I suggested that he can come round to the flat sometime to talk as the staff wasn't the best place to have a serious conversation. I don't know if he'll come. I always think his jokes and mimicking are amusing but it makes it hard to know the person in behind. I suspect he's out of his depth emotionally but maybe his music will help him to express his feelings.

I'm missing you a lot Gordon. Do you have an idea which weekend you'll be able to come down yet? It would help me to have a definite date to look forward to. Let me know so that I can check against any away badminton matches. I'll try to phone later in the week,

Love from Alison xxx"

Dear Alison,

It sounds as if you're settling back into life at Uni. I'm not so sure about all the measuring of bodily fluids – a bit unpleasant and I hate to think what they'll ask you to collect next.

I had a good day out on the water yesterday. I sailed down level with Jura to Loch Tarbert and then back. My next day off is on Friday and the boss has set me up with some American guests who'll pay me to take them out sailing. That suits me OK as I'd probably have been going out anyway.

The first weekend I'm due to be off is the second one in November, so I can come down to see you then. I'm even hoping to have bought a car as Roddy McLeod's Mum is selling her Ford Escort for a reasonable price. It's quite old but in good condition with a low mileage, as she really only used it to visit Roddy's Granny down in Ardrishaig once or twice a week. Since I know you'll ask — it's pale blue. Anyway, if I've done the deal I'll drive it down to Edinburgh. You can have a think where you'd like us to visit.

I'm sorry to hear that Karen is having a tough time. I suppose it's what you'd expect with that type of treatment, but hopefully it will all be worth it in the end. I'm not surprised that Chris is stressed; I don't think that I'd cope very well if you were the one that was ill.

I'll post this on my way to work, as I'm due on reception at two o'clock. Hopefully you'll brave the phone-box and call me soon,

Love from

Gordon. X

Seven

Juggling with her keys and book bag Alison managed to unlock the front door. She'd spent the last two hours in the Medical Reading Room trying to find information for her pharmacology essay on anticoagulants. As she stepped onto the doormat, she noticed a scrap of paper. It was a hand delivered note; she unfolded it and read,

'Karen ill with pneumonia. Back in Western C10.

Chris.'

Checking her watch, she saw it was five thirty. She decided that there was enough time to have something to eat before catching a bus, as she knew that visiting time at the Western General started at seven o' clock. She heated up a portion of the lentil soup she'd made at the weekend and cut some bread to make a cheese sandwich. She tried to remember where Karen was on her chemo cycle and thought that she'd just had her eighth treatment earlier that week. Presumably her white cell count had fallen making her susceptible to this infection. Alison left a note on the kitchen table for Liz and Elaine and set off for the bus stop.

When she arrived at the hospital, now familiar with the route, she quickly found her way to the ward. But on looking in at the door to C10 she couldn't see Karen. One of the beds had the curtains pulled around, so she thought maybe the nurses were attending to Karen and waited outside in the corridor hoping to find a member of staff. After a minute, the door from C10 opened and Mrs Douglas came into the corridor. She was a tall, slim woman with untidy grey hair dressed in 'slacks' and a crisply ironed blouse.

"Oh, Alison I didn't know you were here. I really think that Karen is too unwell for visitors tonight."

"That's OK. I don't need to stay long, but could I just see her for a minute so that she knows I was here?" Alison had met Karen's Mum a few times and while acknowledging that the older woman was under a huge strain, she still always got the impression that Mrs Douglas didn't like her very much and wanted to keep Karen all to herself. "If you're having a break, maybe I could just slip in now until you get back," she suggested.

"Her Dad is with her. She's got no energy for chatting, but maybe she'd like to see you," Karen's Mum conceded grudgingly. "I'm just going to the toilet." Taking this as permission to enter the ward Karen sidled in the door and across to the enclosed bed. Mr Douglas looked up as the curtain parted to allow her in. He was sitting holding Karen's left hand in his. Alison was shocked by Karen's appearance. The first thing she took in was Karen's totally bald head which seemed very smooth and white. Alison had never seen her without her wig before. Without any hair concealing her head, she looked small and vulnerable. Karen's eyes were closed, she was wearing an oxygen mask and was hooked up to an IV line. Her breathing seemed very rapid and shallow and although her face was pale her cheeks burned hot and she looked sweaty.

"Karen, here's your friend Alison to visit you," Mr Douglas said giving Karen's hand a pat. Karen's eyelids fluttered but her eyes didn't open. She raised her right hand slightly. Alison went round to that side of the bed and took her hand in both of hers. It felt clammy.

"Hi Karen, I've just popped in because Chris let me know you were ill. I can see you're very tired so don't try to speak." There was no obvious response from Karen and Alison was unsure what to do or say next. "Just you rest and get better and I'll come back to see you another day." She perched on the edge of the bed still holding Karen's hand until Mrs Douglas returned a few minutes later. Mr Douglas accompanied Alison back out into the corridor. He was a portly man with a very thick head of straight blond but greying hair, cut close, and a very impressive handlebar moustache reminiscent of Lord Kitchener's.

"Sorry, my lass is just too ill to speak to us tonight, but she knows we're there for her," he said. "So, thank you for coming." He seemed a gentler character than Mrs Douglas.

"I can see she's very sick. When did that happen?" Alison asked.

"Just this morning," he replied. "She had her treatment on Monday and was queasy and sick yesterday, as we've come to expect. This morning she complained of a sore throat and seemed to have a cough, so we took her temperature and it was raised. We'd been told to look out for this kind of thing and to phone if we were worried, so we did that and they asked us to come straight in. By the time we got here her breathing was getting bad. They've put her on IV antibiotics and the oxygen, so she should begin to pick up now."

"Has Chris been in?"

"Yes, he happened to phone this morning so he knew we were coming up and he met us here. He's a good solid lad."

"And he's very fond of Karen," added Alison. "Do you think I could phone you tomorrow to see how Karen is? I'll probably leave visiting again until she's a bit better."

"Give us a ring. Probably around lunchtime is best. Bye lass," he said. He kissed Alison's cheek and returned into the ward.

Alison retraced her steps, making her way out of the building. When she reached the exit door, she realised that her own breathing seemed laboured and she felt slightly dizzy. She staggered down a small flight of steps and passed between the two lions which guarded the doorway. She spotted a bench just beyond the lion on her left and sat, head in her hands, trying to take deep, steadying breaths of the cool night air. There seemed to be a weight behind her sternum inhibiting the airflow and she was overwhelmed by a feeling of helplessness. Gradually her breathing began to steady.

"Excuse me, are you alright?" a concerned male voice asked. She raised her head to see a tall white-coated junior doctor with a head of thick dark hair by her side looking at her closely.

"I'll be fine. I've been visiting my friend and I think I just got a bit hot inside," she said.

"You look a bit pale," he commented.

"I think I got a bit of a shock at how unwell she was," Alison admitted.

"I hope she'll be OK, she's in the right place," he replied.

"I'm sure she'll get better. Thank you for stopping," Alison whispered.

Seemingly reassured that she wasn't in need of medical attention he patted her on the shoulder and continued on his way into the building. After a few more minutes Alison felt steady enough to walk down the hospital driveway to the bus stop.

***

On Saturday evening Alison was in Greyfriar's Church to attend the Music Soc's performance of Verdi's 'Requiem'. Chris had sold her a ticket. She'd arrived early and the performers were taking the chance to grab something to eat and drink between their rehearsal and the performance. She spotted Chris munching on a not very healthy snack of a Mars bar and drinking a can of Coke.

"Keeping your sugar levels up I see," she commented. "Has it been going well?"

"The basses were a bit behind on one section, but I'm sure it'll be better tonight," he replied. Alison didn't like to mention that she was unlikely to notice anything wrong unless it was someone falling off the stage or something similar.

"How are you? Have you seen Karen since Wednesday?" she asked.

"I went in briefly last night," he said. "She was still a bit breathless but definitely picking up."

"I phoned her folks on Thursday and the message was that she was much the same, so I thought I'd wait until tomorrow to check if it was OK for me to visit. Her Mum wasn't very pleased to see me on Wednesday."

"I don't think she minded you at all, Alison, aren't you a bit paranoid where Mrs D's concerned? I think she was just very worried and knew Karen wouldn't be up to talking to anyone. She probably thought you'd get a shock, too."

"I did. I hadn't expected her to be so bad."

Chris put his arm round her shoulder and gave her a squeeze.

"Well you should see a big improvement next time you're in," he said. "I'd better go and tune up. Enjoy."

She began to hear the cacophony of the orchestra tuning up. Then the Chorus had to file into their seats in order. The conductor and soloists entered and the audience quietened. To her surprise Alison thoroughly enjoyed the concert. The church acoustics allowed the sound to soar and it was emotionally uplifting to hear. She even got the impression at times that she could feel the music resonating within her body. She was glad that she'd come, having considered bailing out since Karen had originally been meant to accompany her.

***

Monday afternoon saw Alison approaching the Western General again. She'd phoned Karen's house on Sunday morning and spoken to Karen's aunt as her parents were out at church. She'd learned that Karen was a lot better, but would be in the ward for at least another day as she was due to have a blood transfusion. Mr Douglas was planning to return to work the next day, so her parents wouldn't be able to see her until the evening. Karen's aunt was sure it would be fine for Alison to visit in the afternoon, so she decided to skip her pharmacology practical and headed off to visit her friend.

This time when she came to the door of C10 she could see Karen sitting on the top of her bed, swathed in a fluffy pink dressing gown and with a navy blue and white cotton scarf wrapped round her head like an African woman's doek. She had her eyes closed but the oxygen mask had gone and her breathing seemed to be normal. There was still an IV line, today a bag of blood hung up from the metal pole.

"Hi, Karen," Alison greeted her, drawing up a chair to sit by the bedside. Karen's eyes opened immediately and she gave Alison a smile.

"How are you feeling? You look a lot better."

"I'm getting there. I still have an occasional coughing fit. Apparently, I'll feel full of beans once I've had this blood transfusion. Mum told me you were here on Wednesday but I don't remember much from then. Do you like my headgear? Wearing a wig with a fever is unbearably hot and prickly but one of the nurses showed me a few ways to wear a scarf, today it's the African style."

"It's very fetching. Any idea when you'll get out?"

"Dr Wood thinks probably tomorrow. I'm going to have to take a break from the chemo until all my counts build up again and maybe have bigger gaps between the drugs. He's keen that I still try to complete the full six cycles though. Hey, I had one of your colleagues practicing on me today. She said she was in third year and she was learning how to take a medical history. Anyway, she was extremely thorough, so I'm sure she's got the hang of it. That'll be you next year."

"Mmm, I suppose it will."

"Excuse me Karen, can I just check your temperature and blood pressure please?" one of the nurses had arrived. She completed her tasks and wrote the results onto a chart hanging at the foot of the bed. She also examined the rate of the drip flow and slowed it down slightly. "All fine," she commented as she moved on to the next bed.

"Did you enjoy the concert on Saturday?" Karen asked.

"It was good, you'd have loved it. Chris looked so competent and professional as the leader," Alison replied.

"I'm not sure what to do about Chris," Karen blurted out. "I don't feel I'm being fair to him. He's been great, looking after me and very supportive, but I can't cope with him touching me, I just freeze. I think it's because since I've been so ill I don't really trust my body anymore. I certainly don't feel in the least bit attractive or sexy. Sometimes I might want to have a cuddle or just be held close, but I'm frightened that will give off the wrong signals and lead Chris to start getting romantic, so I feel I can't risk him touching me at all. I've tried to explain to him and I've told him he doesn't need to keep seeing me, but I'd really miss him if he went." Karen sounded distressed and Alison sat up on the bed beside her and gave her a long hug.

"I think the main thing is to be honest," said Alison. "If you tell Chris how you feel about the physical side of things, but that you still love him I'm sure he can cope with that. After all it's only a part of your relationship and I know he really cares for you. From what he's said to me he's been more worried that you just don't want to be with him anymore and he does still want to be with you."

"He's mentioned it then?"

"Not in detail, just that he was worried you didn't want to keep going out with him."

"I do. I really love him, but I feel I'm being awful to him."

"Well just tell him how it is, he'll understand and I'm sure you won't feel this way for ever." Alison tried to be reassuring.

"Hello ladies, sorry to interrupt, can I just listen in to Karen's lungs?" It was the tall doctor from Wednesday night. "Oh, we've met before." he said, recognising Alison. "I'm sure you can see that your friend is making a good recovery."

"Yes," said Alison shyly. She felt embarrassed, remembering his concern for her on Wednesday. "I'll wait outside while you examine Karen." She escaped out into the corridor and immediately bumped into another tall man with dark hair, but with curls this time.

"Oh, Chris, sorry I wasn't looking where I was going," Alison was flustered. "I just came out to let the doctor examine Karen. I don't think he'll be long."

"How is she today?" Chris asked.

"She's much better and hoping to be discharged tomorrow. When the doctor's finished, I'll just pop in with you and say goodbye, then leave the two of you in peace."

Eight

The run-up to Christmas was always a very busy time for the Scott family. Mrs Scott had three peak times in her business during the year, Mother's Day, Valentine's Day and Christmas. Usually the whole family got involved to help her and their own arrangements were either neglected or had to be completed before the rush. This year was no exception and on Christmas Eve Alison was working with her Mum and her assistant Fiona in the shop. Alison's Dad had taken a few days holiday from his job at the Bank and had donned a Santa hat to make the deliveries.

"I can't imagine what he wears for Valentine's Day," joked Alison. "Cupid wings perhaps?" She enjoyed the atmosphere in the shop at Christmas, everyone seemed to be cheerful and the young children who came in were all bright eyed, excited about Santa's imminent visit. Her mum kept a basket of mandarin oranges in the shop to give to the children. She didn't begin to feel tired until the number of customers was thinning out and glancing at the clock she noticed that it was almost three o'clock. "Mum, are we likely to have many more people in now? It might be better for one of us to start helping Dad."

"Yes, you're probably right. Do you want to take my car and give him a hand?"

Alison enjoyed her drive around the town. As it was almost dark, decorative lights began to shine out and she admired Christmas trees in house windows. She caught glimpses into festively decorated hallways as she dropped off the floral deliveries. Sometimes there was also a waft of cooking aromas, perhaps mince pies baking or from one house gammon roasting. By the time she and her dad were finished the shop was all closed up and she headed for home feeling very hungry.

One of her mum's holly wreaths was attached to the front door and fairy lights twinkled inside the stained glass panel. When she came into the house, Alison was greeted as usual by Jess sniffing around her legs, tail wagging. She quickly shed her outer clothes and went through to the kitchen. Alison's sister, Helen, had a few days of extra holiday over the festive season this year and so was allocated the job of food shopping and cooking. This meant that there would be some treats in store for the rest of the family once all their work had been completed.

"Hi, Helen, something smells great." She inhaled the warm air which had a rich and beefy scent.

"It's steak and kidney pie and there's lots of it so I hope you're hungry," said Helen as she mashed butter into potatoes. "Could you put these through on the table and then give Mum and Dad a shout please?" Alison put the dish of potatoes on a mat in the centre of the dining room table. The table was beautifully decorated with specially embroidered poinsettia placemats, red candles and red napkins. Crystal candle-holders and glasses shone bright against a snowy white cloth. She slipped quickly into the cloakroom to wash her hands before going to find her parents who were sitting by the fire in the lounge sipping from glasses of red wine.

"Helen is serving up," she said and they followed her through to eat.

"Well I don't think I'll be venturing out again tonight," Mr Scott said after attacking a huge helping of pie, potatoes and carrots. "I'm whacked. What about you girls?"

"I'm going carol singing at nine with a group from the Rotary Club. Gordon's Dad asked me to help out. There'll be mulled wine and mince pies for us afterwards at the Royal Hotel. Gordon should be coming along there after his shift finishes at eleven and we're planning to go to the midnight service. Do you want to come, Helen?" Alison asked.

"I said I'd meet Maggie for a drink, but I could see if she's up for carol singing. We both used to be in the choir at school, so we should be able to manage some Christmas carols. I'll give her a ring after dinner. Who'd like some trifle now?" Helen began to clear dishes from the table.

"What about you, Mum? Do you want to come carol singing?" Alison asked.

"You know I think I will. I think some fresh air and singing would do me good. It would be relaxing after the buzz of these last days. George why don't you come, too? It would be fun." In the end, the whole Scott family and Helen's friend Maggie took part in a rousing carolling session round the streets. It was a crisp, dry night which added to their enjoyment and they were feeling very festive when Gordon caught up with them at the mulled wine reception.

"My, you all have very rosy cheeks. Is it the frosty weather or the mulled wine?" he greeted them.

"Probably both" said Alison's dad. "Let me find you a glass and a mince pie, after all you've been working hard while we've been enjoying ourselves." Gordon slid onto the bench seat next to Alison, put his arm round her shoulder and gave her a hug. Alison smiled and as she relaxed into his embrace felt happiness bubbling up inside. What a great evening spent having fun with her family and now even better with Gordon close.

"You working tomorrow, Gordon?" Helen asked.

"Yes, I'm on the early shift, so Mum is planning that we eat around six in the evening. I'll be looking forward to that all day. Then I'm off for two days, so it's not too bad."

"And you're joining us on Boxing Day," Alison's Mum confirmed. "Helen's boyfriend Neil will be driving up, so come around five. That should be fine."

"We'd better move or we'll be late for the service," said Alison. "Anyone coming with us?"

The others elected to go straight home, so she and Gordon set off for the candle-lit traditional service of nine lessons and carols.

Christmas morning got off to a slow start. Gone were the days of eager children waking at five o'clock to see if Santa had been and left their stockings stuffed with goodies. Instead the family gathered slowly in the kitchen where warm croissants and bacon were waiting with orange juice and coffee. They took their second cups of coffee through to the lounge where presents were heaped under the Christmas tree. After an appreciative present-opening session Alison and her Dad went out with Jess for a walk while Mrs Scott and Helen began preparations in the kitchen.

"How's your friend Karen getting on now?" her Dad asked as they wandered along Ganavan Road towards the beach.

"She's a lot better but still pretty washed out. She had a month's break from her chemotherapy after the pneumonia. So now she's had one treatment since then and I think they're planning to only give one every four weeks instead of every fortnight. There should be another three to complete the course and then I suppose she has to wait and see what happens."

"It's tough for a youngster to cope with. Her family must be very worried."

"She's amazingly positive most of the time. I'm not sure I'd be so brave," said Alison.

"Well none of us know how we'd react and thankfully our family seems to be healthy and hearty. What's the dog got in her mouth?" They went over to investigate. Jess was pawing and sniffing at the edge of the water, dancing back and forward with the small waves, and then stopping to shake her head vigorously. As they got closer, they could see a dead seagull protruding from her jaws. It took a lot of coaxing for Jess to give up her prize.

"Your Mum won't want her bringing that back to the house."

The rest of the day was spent eating and relaxing in front of the fire with some television thrown in. Alison spoke to Gordon on the phone to wish him a Happy Christmas. They'd agreed to exchange presents when they saw each other on Boxing Day.

The clear frosty spell of weather came to an end on Boxing Day; which brought grey skies and a strong wind, sweeping rain and sleet ahead of it. Today it was Alison's turn to help in the kitchen, which was a pleasant cosy place to be on such a wild day.

"It's not good weather for Neil driving up from Glasgow," her Mum worried. "I hope he's sensible and drives carefully. At least he should make it all in daylight."

Alison didn't know Neil well. She had only met him once last term when Helen brought him through Edinburgh for a day to visit. They had been together since the spring, meeting via Helen's work, as Neil had been a frequent traveller on the Glasgow to London flight. He worked as an architect for a Glasgow firm, but they currently had a large contract in the financial centre of London requiring his attention, hence all the flying. He had asked Helen on a date after smiling at her for a few weeks.

"At least there won't be a lot of heavy traffic and lorries on the road today so the spray won't be so bad," Alison pointed out. "What do you want me to do next? The soup is made. Will I start on the pastry?" Mrs Scott had always encouraged both girls to help in the kitchen and they'd often had evening sessions of baking together to fill the freezer or to donate to a 'bring and buy' stall at school, so they worked together companionably in the kitchen.

Mid-afternoon Alison was curled up on the sofa by the fire engrossed in the latest John le Carre novel 'Smiley's People' that she'd been given for Christmas. The doorbell rang and she uncurled and padded to answer. On the doorstep was Neil surrounded by a swirl of sleet, laden with presents.

"Neil, come in quickly out of the cold. Can I help you carry anything? Helen, it's Neil," she called.

Once Neil's luggage had been retrieved from his car and he'd shed his parcels and coat the family gathered in the lounge to greet him properly. His glasses had misted up in the sudden heat of the house and he took them off to wipe them clean. He was fair-haired with a blonde moustache and grey-blue eyes.

"How was your trip Neil?" Mrs Scott enquired. "I didn't envy you driving in this weather."

"Oh it wasn't too bad. The roads were quiet so I made good time?" he replied.

"Will we all have a cup of tea? We'll not be eating until later, Neil, after Gordon Alison's boyfriend joins us, so you'd better take a cup to warm you up." Alison's Mum turned to go and organise afternoon tea.

"I've brought a contribution I hope you'll find useful," said Neil handing over a wrapped parcel to Mrs Scott.

"Thank you very much, Neil," she said as she headed towards the kitchen.

"And these are for you two," said Neil offering gifts to Alison and her Dad. "Helen told me which brands to buy," he confided as Alison unwrapped a bottle of Nina Ricci L'air Du Temps perfume and Mr Scott a bottle of Glenlivet single malt whisky. As they were thanking Neil, Mrs Scott returned with a loaded tea trolley.

"Thank you for all the goodies, Neil. That will save me baking for a few weeks. Now how do you take your tea?"

After chatting over cups of tea Alison and her parents drifted out of the room, subtly, in order to leave Helen and Neil on their own for a spell. Alison took her new book up to her bedroom and was soon caught up in the story again. She was surprised by her Mum shouting up to her that Gordon had arrived, as she hadn't heard the doorbell ringing. She raced downstairs to greet him and handed him a large parcel wrapped with snowman paper. He in turn gave her a dainty package. She opened it to find a jewellery box and in it nestled a delicate brooch with clusters of small fresh-water pearls gathered at the tips of five golden fronds.

"Oh, thank you Gordon. You saw me looking at that in the jeweller's, didn't you?" she asked, pinning the brooch onto her dark red dress.

"Yes, I thought you were admiring it, so I went back another time to buy it for you." Gordon was opening his parcel which contained a thick Icelandic style jumper in shades of blue and green. "This is super and will be very warm. I'll try it on." He took off the red V-necked sweater that he'd been wearing and modelled his gift.

"Come and meet Neil," said Alison. "He arrived a couple of hours ago." She took him into the lounge and introduced the men. Gordon was still wearing his new jumper.

"It suits you," Helen said. "It's a good fit and Alison definitely chose the right colours, but I think you might get a bit warm wearing it in here with the fire on." She looked at Neil and got up from the sofa. "Now that Gordon is here I'll go and fetch Mum and Dad." She returned to the room a minute later with her parents in tow.

"Now that we're all together, Neil and I would like to tell you that we're going to get married and are now officially engaged." Helen announced. Alison squealed and leapt up to hug her sister and then Neil.

"Congratulations. When did you decide?" she asked.

Alison's Mum and Dad seemed rather dazed at first but then joined in the hugging and congratulations and Mr Scott went out to the garage to find a bottle of Champagne he had put away there.

It should be nicely chilled," he said. Alison and her Mum admired Helen's diamond solitaire which was substantial without being too showy.

"Neil proposed over drinks after we'd been to see *The Nutcracker* ballet about ten days ago. I accepted, of course, and then we chose a ring at the weekend. It had to be made smaller so Neil collected it and brought it up with him today, which fitted in brilliantly with telling you all." Helen explained once the fizz had been poured and toasts made to the couple.

"And when do you plan to be married?" Mrs Scott asked.

"We thought in the summer, probably early in July so that Alison is finished with her exams and can be my bridesmaid," said Helen.

"Places will be very busy then, the most popular are probably already booked," warned Mrs Scott.

"They will be for Saturdays, but I thought we might go for a Thursday or a Friday so we could still be lucky. I can start making enquiries in the next few days before I have to go back to work and I can take Neil around and show him the possible venues." Helen and her Mum quickly got into the details of wedding planning. Alison listened with half an ear but was also aware of the conversation between Neil and Gordon.

"I just got my RYA instructor's certificate a couple of months back. The hotel job has been handy because it was next to the sailing club so in my time off I completed all the sailing and assessments. But I feel I've probably got as much out of hotel work as I want now and I've applied to The Outward Bound Trust to become an assistant instructor. The sailing certificate will hopefully help, but I'd need to train in other areas," Gordon explained.

"That sounds interesting. Where would you be based?"

"I'm hoping near Fort William, but they have other centres in Wales and the Lake District. I've got an interview in January." Alison knew about Gordon's plans and was pleased for him that he'd been offered an interview, but it seemed that if he got this job he'd be moving even farther away from her. She had once tentatively suggested that he might move to work in one of the Edinburgh hotels to be nearer her.

"Alison, you know I don't want to spend my life being a hotel manager. The training was just to give me experience in the hospitality line if I ever get my own centre, or help to run or manage a centre," he'd said. She knew that it was the outdoor life that really interested him and was very proud for him when he attained instructor level in his sailing. She just sometimes wondered if they would ever really be together as a couple. She was beginning to recognise that she actually liked living in the city and might want to continue to do so. She definitely wasn't so sure now about returning to a small town to work and settle down. How would that fit in with Gordon's intended lifestyle? But on the other hand, she did love Gordon and part of what she loved about him was his outdoor ruggedness and that he had a strong vision for his own future. Sometimes it all just seemed too confusing to try and work things out, so she tended towards just drifting along for the moment, taking each thing as it happened. She supposed all the wedding talk was making her feel unsettled about the course of her own relationship, but she felt that she was definitely much too young to be thinking about marriage yet.

Nine

As she walked home across the Meadows, Alison felt low and discouraged. This afternoon's physiology practical had been embarrassing because she'd fainted whilst taking a blood sample from Robert. She could remember putting the tourniquet on above his elbow and easily finding a good vein. He was skinny and had a fair complexion, which helped. Her hands had been trembling when she attached the needle to the syringe, making it tricky. Then she'd sat on a stool next to him poised to put the needle into his arm. By then her hands were also sweaty, so she didn't feel in control. She did get the needle into the vein but was worried that it would slip out when she put pressure on the plunger to draw the blood back. She could see some blood coming into the syringe – there was a high-pitched ringing in her ears. Then she heard Robert calling to Ian at the next bench along, his voice sounding as if it were emerging from a deep well.

"Ian, can you catch Alison? I think she's going to faint."

Apparently, Robert had noticed her face turning a greenish grey colour and Ian did a great job of catching her just as she began to topple from the stool and lowering her gently to the floor. This is where she came to a minute later. Luckily, she had let go of the syringe still half-full in Robert's arm, so he wasn't hurt. But it was so disheartening. She knew that she wasn't normally worried about the sight of blood or needles. She hadn't been one of those girls who'd fainted in the queues for immunisations at school, and she'd had blood taken from her own arm in earlier experiments with no problems. So, was it about inflicting pain on someone? And how was she going to cope with being a doctor if she couldn't take a blood sample? She knew that she'd also have to put up with several days of teasing from Robert and Ian until a fresh drama cropped up. She decided that she'd had enough of medicine for one day, so planned to do something mindless, like going to the laundry. And she wouldn't take any work with her.

Later Alison was sitting in the steamy atmosphere of the Marchmont laundry waiting for her washing to finish in the drier. She'd brought along a magazine to read, however because lots of students lived nearby and frequented the same laundry she had spent more time chatting than reading. Morag from her year had just left after a prolonged description of the dress that she had bought to wear at the Medical Faculty Ball next week. Apparently, she'd found a bargain in the Oxfam shop in Morningside. Morag's theory was that you got a better quality of clothes in the charity shops in the posher areas of town. Alison was luckily able to borrow a dress from her sister Helen. She was due to meet up with her Mum and sister this Saturday in Glasgow to shop for wedding clothes. She could also collect the dress for the ball from Helen's flat while she was through. It used to annoy Alison when she was younger and growing up in Helen's shadow that she and Helen were so alike. Everyone used to comment that they were like 'peas in a pod'. So, in her teens, when Alison was struggling for recognition as an individual with her own character, she'd found their similarity galling. Once Helen left home there was less direct comparison and now it was quite handy to be able to swap clothes, not that Alison owned anything that Helen was likely to want to borrow. The arrangement was fairly much one way.

A loud buzzing caught Alison's attention, letting her know that the drier was ready to be emptied. She folded the warm fragrant laundry and stacked it into two bags so that she wouldn't be lop-sided for the walk back to the flat.

When she arrived back, Elaine was in the lounge tackling a pile of ironing. Elaine was often described as 'bouncy' or 'bubbly'. A small, curvaceous, blonde bundle of energy, she was famous for tanking up that energy with chocolate bars, and also for the contents of her wardrobe. For a student, her clothes were very formal, perhaps she was dressing up as the lawyer she hoped to become.

"Hi Alison," she said, "seems like tonight is laundry night." She shook out a white ruffled Laura Ashley cotton blouse which would be a challenge to iron.

"I won't get around to ironing tonight. I'm due to meet Karen and Chris for a drink in half an hour. Want to join us?"

"No, I've got masses of work to do after this, so I'd better stay home. Give Karen my love, though. She must be nearly through with the chemo."

"Yes, just one more dose to go. She can't wait for it to be done with. I'd better get ready, maybe see you later then."

Alison dumped her laundry on the floor in her room, leaving it in the bags. Then she applied some mascara and blue eye shadow, brushed her hair and sprayed on some of her Christmas perfume. She considered changing but decided just to wind a mauve chiffon scarf round her neck before grabbing her jacket and setting out for Deacon Brodie's Tavern on the High Street. Karen was staying at Chris's house in Stockbridge for a few days, so they'd agreed to meet at a pub which was about halfway between there and Marchmont. Alison followed her familiar route along Jawbone walk to cross the Meadows then continued onto Middle Meadow Walk which ran between the Royal Infirmary on her left and the Medical school on her right, the crown of St Giles Cathedral seemed to be suspended on the horizon. She continued along Forrest Road and passed the Greyfiars Bobby statue at the beginning of George IV Bridge. As usual there were a few tourists gathered around it and she saw one lady pat Bobby's head. Recently there seemed to be a fashion for rubbing his nose which looked bronze and shiny compared with the matt black finish on the rest of the statue.

The pub was on the crossroad at the far side of the Lawn market. She spotted Karen and Chris sitting at a table with drinks in front of them and waved to them. She stopped at the bar to order a half pint of draught cider and, as her drink was being poured, admired the beautiful wooden ceiling which had carvings of thistles and roses, the details painted in rich purple, red and green. She put her drink and two packets of crisps on the table and leaned in to hug Karen hello. Her friend felt very frail in her embrace, her shoulders bony and the skin on her cheeks rough against Alison's face. She still had sores at the corners of her mouth from chronic thrush infections. Alison hoped that once the treatment was finished Karen would soon be able to start gaining weight and would look less fragile.

"Things OK?" she asked.

"I was just telling Chris that my mum and dad have got me some tutoring jobs," Karen sounded animated. "After prelim exams, there are always a few kids who've not done as well as expected whose parents decide to get them some extra help. The French teacher at Dad's school remembers me from my days there and knew I might be free. So, he asked Dad if I'd be interested and has since recommended my services for tutoring."

"How many kids will it be?" Alison asked.

"So far I have four signed up. I'm going to see each of them for an hour every week, after school or in the evening. But Mum has also found me a flautist who needs some extra help. I think it's one of her piano students who

98

wants to brush up on flute." Karen's Mum was a piano teacher who gave lessons in her own home and her dad was head of the Maths Department at the local secondary school.

"You'll have to spend most of your time in Peebles then," said Alison.

"During the week I'll have to, but I can come up to Edinburgh at weekends. I'll aim to keep them free of students. The tutoring will only last up until the school exams in May and maybe after that I'll feel well enough to take on something more full-time. We'll see."

"Maybe we'll all come down to visit you on the bus one day." Chris suggested.

"Yes, a Wednesday afternoon trip could work." Alison agreed.

"That would be nice. So, how did Gordon get on with his interview?" Karen asked.

"Great," said Alison. "He got the job. He'll be based at the Outward Bound centre near Fort William most of the time, but he'll have to visit other centres as part of his training. He's told the manager at the hotel that he's leaving, so now he's working a month's notice. Then he'll have a couple of weeks of holiday before he starts."

"It sounds brilliant experience, just what he wants to do." Chris commented.

"Yes, but it will be harder for us to meet up as he'll be farther away and I don't think he gets many weekends off," Alison sounded wistful.

She had a similar conversation on Saturday with her mum and Helen as they caught up on news over coffee before their shopping began.

"Maybe it won't be so bad," her mum said. "But in future it might be easier for you to come to Oban and meet up there rather than expecting Gordon to travel to Edinburgh every time."

"Or meet in Glasgow," Helen suggested. "Neil and I might even have a spare room for guests once we've bought a flat."

"Thanks," Alison said. "How's the flat-hunting going? Anything you like yet?"

"It's taken us a wee while to build up our enthusiasm again after losing the one we liked in Shawlands. We were so psyched up, it was a real let-down to be beaten at the auction. We'll probably go and see a few that are new on the market for viewing tomorrow, and just hope there's one that will suit us."

"And what about dresses Helen?" her mum asked, getting down to that day's agenda. "Do you have a style in mind or a colour that you'd like Alison to wear?"

"I did browse through the bridal section in Frasers last weekend, just to see what they had. I didn't try anything on. There was one dress I really liked the look of for me and a bridesmaid's one which I liked, but Alison would need to approve. It was a deep turquoise, sort of a kingfisher colour."

"Well why don't we look there first?" said Mrs Scott.

Six hours later, footsore, but happy that they'd achieved their aim, the three women were drinking restorative cups of tea in Helen's flat.

"I can't believe that it was Mum who caused all the problems," teased Alison.

The sisters had chosen the dresses already picked out by Helen, after trying a few others in addition for comparison. However, Mrs Scott had a real problem finding something that she considered to be 'suitable' but not 'fuddy-duddy'.

"Well a lot of those outfits were more the kind of thing your Gran would have worn," she complained. Eventually she had discovered a smart dress and jacket in a shade of antique gold which suited her when they visited a boutique hidden away on Ingram Street. Next, they had the challenge of locating matching hat, bag and shoes.

"You know I think we did extremely well to find outfits we all like in one day," said Alison.

"Hear! Hear!" agreed Helen, and in celebration I'm now going to open a bottle of wine.

With her glass in hand, thoughtfully refilled by Helen, Alison went through to her sister's room for another session of trying on dresses, this time for the ball.

"Does everyone still wear long?" Helen asked. "I think it's getting less fashionable. The last two dresses I've bought are mid-calf length. Anyway, take whatever you want." Alison felt very elegant wearing a grey-silver silk with spaghetti straps which swirled around her calves as she tried a few dance steps around the room.

"Would this one be OK?" she asked.

"Yes, you look great in it," said Helen.

"It's a pity that Gordon isn't coming to the ball. He won't see me looking shimmery and sexy."

"Are things OK with you guys?"

"On the surface they are. We've not had an argument or anything. But I'm frightened that we're drifting apart. After nearly four years together we're seeing less of each other than ever before. Sometimes I really miss him, but I'm aware that I'm getting used to it," Alison replied.

"Is there someone else?"

"I don't think so for Gordon – he wouldn't have time. I used to get asked out by other students, but most of them know I have a boyfriend now."

"Who are you going to the ball with?"

"A guy in my year; Robert. But really, we're all just going together in a group, he's just a friend."

"I don't know what to advise you, Alison. Probably best just to give things more time."

"Yes, that's what I think too."

***

The Medical Faculty Ball was an annual event held in the Assembly Rooms in George Street. Alison's group arrived enthusiastic and determined to sample all that was on offer. The venue was entered via a spacious hall where there was a bar and a list of the music programmed for the next six hours. A photographer encouraged people to pose for him. Thickly carpeted stairs led from right and left to the first floor. On this level were two large rooms – the Ballroom and the Music Hall. Each had huge glittering chandeliers and each hosted a different type of music for dancing, on arrival a jazz band in one and a Scottish Country dance band in the other. In the basement was another dancing venue where disco music played. Alison had a very lively evening, dancing with all the men in her group when asked. Robert surprised her by his ability to dance a quickstep, and he owned up to having been sent to ballroom dancing lessons as a child. There were other dancing partners there from her year that she met up with during the course of the night. She attempted a waltz with one of her anatomy demonstrators from last year and jived with Dr Armstrong her physiology tutor. She thought she caught a glance of Dr Wood from Karen's ward across the Ballroom but didn't come close enough for conversation. Her group was still there to join in with singing 'Auld Lang Syne' at two a.m.

Alison had enjoyed the occasion thoroughly. A few weeks later she received a copy of the official photograph taken of her group posing on the red-carpeted stairway.

She found a frame for it and put it on the mantelpiece in her bedroom along with Gordon and Jess.

Ten

As she gazed out of the bus window at the passing Borders countryside, Alison could see that green was now well established on the grassy hillsides and budding trees. There were lots of lambs playing around their munching mothers. Today she was on her way to Peebles to visit Karen and as she travelled she was thinking about her trip at the weekend. She'd been summoned up to Oban by Helen to take part in some wedding planning. It had worked out well as she'd also been able to see Gordon, who had a free weekend and had come down from Fort William.

"He was so enthusiastic about his new job," she thought. She had to admit that he seemed really happy, and he looked very fit too as he was spending most of his time out of doors. "We got on fine, just as we usually do – but is it enough?"

The bus slowed down as it came into the thirty mile an hour zone of the town and Alison began to pay attention. Looking out for the Park Hotel on the left. According to Karen's instructions the bus stop was a few yards farther on. Karen was coming to meet her at the bus stop, as Alison didn't know her way around.

"Alison," Karen was calling and waving, and seemed to be bouncing up and down on the pavement as Alison alighted from the bus. "You got here. What do you want to do? Are you hungry?"

"I bought a sandwich and some juice and had them on the bus, so I'm OK for now. It's a really nice day, so it would be good to be out in the fresh air. Do you feel up for a walk?"

"We could go along the river a bit. I manage that OK 'cause it's flat. Hills still do me in. Do you want to call by the house first and collect the dogs? That would earn us some Brownie points from Mum."

"Fine," Alison agreed and they set off towards Karen's house. Their route took them down to the riverside and across a pedestrian bridge over the racing Tweed.

"You're looking good," Alison told her friend. "You've definitely put on some weight and your colour's better."

"Thanks. I'm feeling much better, but not back to normal yet. My mouth has finally healed up, so I'm able to eat more. But I'm still not as hungry as I used to be."

"How about your hair?" Alison asked. It was obvious that Karen was still wearing her wig.

"There is some fuzz coming in, but not enough to go without headgear yet."

Karen stopped at a wrought iron gate and immediately there was a fury of barking from two West Highland Terriers in the garden.

"They're a bit territorial," said Karen. "You've got a dog at home, so you'll not be scared of them." She opened the gate and led the way in to the garden, allowing the dogs, Kirsty and Heather, to investigate Alison. "I'll go in and get their leads and let Mum know we're taking them out."

Alison squatted down and patted the two dogs, which, after sniffing her, had rolled onto their backs, presenting their tummies for tickling. Mrs Douglas appeared at the door with Karen when she returned with the leads.

"Hello, Alison, it's a good day for a walk. I hope you'll come back and have tea with us," she issued an invitation.

"Thanks, Mrs Douglas, that would be lovely," Alison replied politely. The friends headed back to the riverside path and began to walk on the footpath along the south bank of the Tweed.

"How's your tutoring going?" Alison asked.

"I like it. It's making me think more about French again and the kids are quite refreshing. You know how teenagers are? They're very wrapped up in their own lives so they're not too bothered about mine. They just treat me like a teacher, no kid gloves or worried glances."

"Do you think they'll pass their exams? They must be coming up soon."

"They should do OK if they keep their heads and don't panic. Now where's Kirsty got to? She must have fallen behind, we'll wait for her. Kirsty come," Karen called.

"Is she getting old? She seems slow."

"No, she's expecting her puppies in about ten days. Didn't you think she was a bit plump? Mum breeds Westies. Heather is one from Kirsty's last litter that she decided to keep. Here she comes. Good girl. Between Kirsty and me we'll just have to dawdle."

"Well we're not in any rush," Alison reassured her.

"No and we don't want to get back too early and have to suffer listening to lots of piano lessons before tea," said Karen. "Why don't we sit on this bench for a bit and enjoy the sun?"

They settled on a wooden bench facing the river and began to discuss Karen's visit the previous week to see Dr Wood at the outpatient clinic. That had been her first review since finishing her chemotherapy and so far, all her results were fine.

"He wants to see me back in another three months, and he said that if I'm OK then he'd be happy for me to go to France in September. However, he wants me to be close to a major medical centre with a haematology facility, and preferably to come back to see him every three months for my check-ups. But it sounds as if I can start to think about another placement."

"That's great. Do you still feel up to going away?"

"I know at first I'll be nervous, there's no doubt this illness has knocked my confidence. But I feel I've got to get back on track with my life. In the end that's what will help most." By now the girls had resumed their stroll and reached a second pedestrian bridge to the west of the town. They crossed the river, pausing to look down at the swirling current, and set off back towards Peebles along the north riverbank. Alison told Karen about her visit home last weekend and the plans for Helen's wedding so far.

"And Gordon was there?" Karen asked.

"Yes, he's so happy in his new job, he can't stop talking about it. He obviously enjoys it so much more than the hotel work. He's already mentioned that he's hoping for promotion to full instructor before the end of the year."

"And how about his feelings for you?"

"I think he's still quite happy with our part-time relationship. He's busy at his work and now he also has lots of like-minded company. It's me that gets lonely," Alison admitted.

"Does he know that?"

"I don't know. I tell him I miss him and that I'm lonely, but he thinks I'm very busy studying and have lots of friends – which is true. I think he feels that I'm exaggerating when I complain about having to go to parties on my own, because it's not as if I don't know other people there, but it's not the same as going as part of a couple. He's not unsympathetic, but neither of us can see any obvious solution. How about things between you and Chris?"

"We're much better. I'm less prickly than I was, beginning to relax more about things. I'm hoping to get a summer job in Edinburgh and stay in Chris's flat. I haven't told Mum that yet though."

"Don't worry I won't mention it," Alison reassured her.

"And how's badminton going? You're obviously not playing today."

"It's good. I've mainly been paired with Maria."

"She's a good player, sharp around the net."

"Yes, I like her, but there's also a girl called Caitlin, who's new this year. She's been getting some games with Maria, too. Anyway, it suited me for her to play last weekend and today so that I could do my visiting."

When they returned to the house, Mrs Douglas provided a traditional High Tea of bacon, eggs and tomato, sliced bread and butter, scones and jam and several types of home-made cakes. She obviously had a talent for baking in common with Alison's Mum. Over tea Mrs Douglas chatted about her piano pupils and the expected new puppies, and Alison felt much more at ease in her company than she'd ever done before. Maybe Chris had been right and she'd misjudged Karen's Mum. Mr Douglas asked her lots of questions about her course and she kept them amused by describing her latest physiology practical which had involved having her blood pressure taken in various positions, lying, sitting, and standing, at timed intervals after exercising (which involved running up and down the department stairs ten times) and also while she had her head fully immersed under water.

"So, this week I ended up looking like a drowned rat, but I didn't faint," she concluded. She'd already told them about her previous experiences at physiology practicals.

When it was time for Alison to leave to catch the bus back to Edinburgh, Karen was looking rather pale and tired. Alison was confident she could find her way to the bus stop, but Mr Douglas wouldn't hear of her going on her own and he accompanied her with Heather, the younger Westie. As they walked along, Mr Douglas was greeted by several teenagers, he was obviously a popular teacher.

"It was good of you to come down to visit Karen," he said. "Now that she has a bit more energy she's beginning to get bored. I expect she'll want to move back up to Edinburgh once her pupils have taken their exams. Margaret and I will miss her, but it's a step in the right direction for her recovery."

"She is definitely looking so much better, it's great. I won't be around in Edinburgh to see much of her over the summer, though. My sister's wedding is almost immediately after term breaks up. Then my Mum wants to go on holiday and make the most of having me around to help in the shop. This will be my last long summer break. After third year we move to clinical rotations and that only gives us two weeks off in the summer and two weeks off at Christmas."

"They keep you very busy on your course, don't they? I expect there's a lot to cram in." They saw the bus approaching the stop. "Well good luck for the rest of term and your exams, lass." He waved to her as the bus drew away.

Alison dozed on the return bus journey. She'd been reassured by her time with Karen. The treatment seemed to have worked and Karen looked to be gradually recovering from the effects of the chemotherapy.

On her arrival back in Edinburgh, she decided that a bath and then an early night were what she wanted most. Back in the flat she could hear Fleetwood Mac playing softly behind Elaine's door. She called, "Hello," but got no reply. Maybe Elaine had fallen asleep with her music on. When she went into the bathroom to run her bath water, she noticed an unpleasant, slightly sour odour which she realised was becoming characteristic. She wondered if there was a problem with their drains, maybe she should ask the others. Adding some Fenjal bath oil to the water soon substituted a pleasant herbal fragrance and she relaxed back to a drowsy state in the warm water and was dead to the world almost as soon as her head hit the pillow. From the depths of her sleep she was vaguely aware of noise from the bathroom next door, but it wasn't loud enough to rouse her fully and in the morning, there was only a suggestion of a memory.

***

Alison had arranged to meet Linda for lunch on Friday. The morning passed quickly, a nine o'clock pharmacology lecture, then some time studying in the library. Linda was waiting, as they'd agreed, outside Teviot Union, but since it was another sunny day they decided to buy sandwiches and have a picnic. They found a south-facing bench in Greyfriar's Churchyard and settled there to enjoy a chat and their lunch. It was amazingly peaceful, shielded from traffic noise because it lay tucked away behind the tall tenement buildings. They brought each other up to date with their courses. Linda was enjoying her work, even the statistics.

"And I think I've met someone special," Linda confided. "We've been getting friendly over this term and he's asked me out tonight on a proper date."

"I thought you had a glow about you today," said Alison. "Even your freckles look brighter than usual." Linda was self-conscious about her skin, as many freckled people are, and so was a good target for teasing. "Tell me more."

"Well I met him in the queue for the photo-copier in the library a few weeks ago. Then we seemed to bump into each other quite a lot there. He's studying engineering. We went for a coffee together on Monday and we're going to the cinema tonight."

As far as Alison was aware, this was the first relationship that Linda had ventured into since coming to university and she seemed very excited, so Alison hoped that the romance would grow. However, she was aware of feeling rather envious as Linda told her about Colin. Apart from seeing Gordon last weekend her own relationship currently consisted of sporadic phone calls in a draughty public phone box and letters which were becoming less frequent.

"But I've got nothing to wear. Say you'll come with me to help me get a suitable outfit." Alison allowed herself to be persuaded.

On their way out of the Kirkyard they stopped to look at auld Jock's grave on the eastern pathway. There, so legend tells, his faithful dog Bobby had famously kept vigil for fourteen years until his own death. Then the little dog was also buried in the cemetery alongside his master and in the company of a lot of notable Edinburgh dignitaries.

"And now Bobby's probably more famous than any of them," Linda commented.

Down on Princes Street they headed for Etam where they usually could find affordable clothes. After browsing the display racks, they went, giggling, into the changing room with a bundle of clothes each to try on. Alison wasn't intending to spend any money, but chose a few outfits to keep Linda company.

"What d'you think of these dungarees?" she asked, modelling a pair with blue and white stripes.

"You look like Andy Pandy, all you need's the hat," was Linda's verdict.

It was just as well that Linda had an assistant as she had Alison running back and forward between the shop floor and the dressing room with alternative sizes and colours; but she eventually settled for a figure hugging corduroy skirt in a deep pink and a long sleeved T-shirt in a dusky lilac shade which toned in well. By the time they left the shop Linda was happy that she'd be adequately dressed for her date. Alison thought wryly that her date tonight would be with her physiology notes again.

Eleven

On the morning of Helen's wedding Alison woke up early at six o'clock. Unusually for her she felt instantly awake and knew that there was no point in trying to doze off again. She knelt on her bed and parted the curtains to peep through the gap. Oh dear, drizzle. Well, it might clear up. She decided to go out for a walk with Jess who would probably be a bit neglected today. Although she knew that her mum had arranged with Andrew, a teenager from along the street, to come by to feed and walk the dog later this afternoon. Andrew quite often provided dog-walking services for Jess. This suited him well as his family didn't have a dog, despite his pleading, and it earned him some pocket money. Alison left a note on the kitchen table to say she'd gone out, and then collected her waterproof jacket and Jess's lead.

She decided to go into the grounds around Dunollie, a ruined castle just along the road from the house. Outside the rain was very fine, just hanging, a smirr in the air. It was warm with very little wind and the tiny droplets gathered on every surface. They nestled in Alison's hair and tickled her face like a gentle fizz. Once off the road Alison threw a ball for Jess who went charging after it, leaping into the air to try for a catch. When it was retrieved she brought it straight back and dropped it at Alison's feet, ready for another chase. Alison scanned the terrain carefully, looking out for any sheep. Jess liked to go after anything that ran away from her, so she loved sheep. She knew she could begin a woolly stampede, with an accompaniment of frenzied baaing, with just a glare and a couple of intent steps even from the other side of a fence. Alison didn't like to think of the disruption should she come across the creatures on a hillside while off the lead. And she was also sure that the farmer who sometimes had his flock grazing here would take a stern view if the dog was bothering them. The low cloud came well down the hills, cutting off the summits and making the valley seem more enclosed and smaller than usual. They walked on until Jess had had a good workout, luckily with no sheep encountered. The dog was panting heavily by the time Alison arrived back at the house so she filled a water bowl from the garden tap at the back door and Jess lapped noisily. Then she rubbed her coat down with an old towel, trying to dislodge most of the grass seeds and loose vegetation from under her legs and tail.

"Is that you back Alison?" Mrs Scott called from the kitchen.

"Yes, I woke early so I thought I'd tire Jess out. Now I'm starving." She collected a bowl, spoon and a cereal box and joined her Mum who was sitting at the kitchen table with a cup of tea and a newspaper.

"It's a good job we're going to the hairdresser this morning, your hair has really frizzed up with all the damp," her Mum commented. It was true. Alison's hair which was naturally curly and tended towards loose ringlets was currently huge with corkscrew curls.

"Is there a weather forecast in the paper? Is it meant to dry up?" Alison asked.

"Yes, I think so, but it will probably stay quite dull."

"Well that won't matter as long as it's dry. In fact, strong sunshine could be bad for the photos 'cause it makes everyone screw their faces up."

By the time the three Scott women left for the hairdresser at ten o'clock the day was definitely beginning to dry up and brighten slightly.

"Make sure you wear a blouse or a cardigan so you don't need to take clothes off over your head later," Helen advised. Alison was impressed by how calm and organised her sister seemed. No point, however small, escaped her. She was sure that her unruffled poise and attention to detail must make her very good at her job. At the hairdresser's they were treated like VIPs, with cups of coffee, biscuits and a manicure while they waited their turn to have their hair styled.

"And where will you be going for your honeymoon? Or is it a secret?" Michelle, the hairdresser, asked Helen.

"No, it's not a secret. I get a good deal on flights with my work so we decided to fly to San Francisco. We're staying there for five days, and then we've hired a car and are going to Yosemite National Park."

"That sounds a bit different," said Michelle.

"Yes, I'm really excited about it, and about today."

When they returned to the house they tried to eat a snack lunch, but Helen's excitement seemed to have spread to the whole family and no one was very hungry. Helen had a last phone conversation with Neil, who was staying with his family at a nearby guesthouse. Alison overheard her sister give him instructions about having his luggage delivered to the reception venue. Soon it was time to get dressed and help Helen with her dress and makeup. Alison and her Mum set out for the church in the first limo, leaving Helen and Mr Scott to follow shortly in a beribboned Bentley.

The church was beautifully decorated with the same creamy, yellow roses that Helen and Alison were carrying augmented by trailing greenery. Mrs Scott had worked hard with Alison's help the day before, and she had a spray with a matching rose pinned to her jacket. She entered the church and was ushered to sit in the front pew. The groom and his brother, who was best man, were dressed in kilts with white heather sprays in the buttonholes of their tweed Argyll jackets. They waited by the altar for the bridal procession to begin. Alison stayed behind in the church porch and soon caught a glimpse of the bridal car approaching. She went down the steps to help Helen out of the car and make sure that her dress was properly draped.

Then time appeared to speed up, ceremony, photographs, meal and speeches all passed in a blur. Alison hardly seemed to draw a breath until the first duty dance with the best man was over and, most of her responsibilities completed, she could go and sit next to Gordon and relax.

"You've done a great job and you're looking lovely," Gordon complimented her.

"Thanks, I think it's all gone well, don't you?"

"Definitely. Now you can have a rest. Can I get you a drink?"

"A coke would be great, thanks." Gordon got up and made his way to the bar leaving Alison to watch the dancers, including her parents, execute the steps of 'The Duke of Perth'. Helen's friend Maggie came to sit beside her.

"I think Helen has carried the day off beautifully," she said. "I'm so jealous, she looks perfect and she has that brilliant trip coming up and her new flat in Glasgow. Here am I still living with my folks in Oban."

"But you had some time away at college. You could have stayed in Glasgow."

"You're right, but I like the variety of animals that I see up here. In Glasgow, it was all pets." Maggie worked as a vet's nurse.

"You'll just need to save up for your own place," Alison suggested. Then the next dance was announced, a

'Military Two-step', and Gordon came to claim Alison as his partner.

The dancing was interrupted at ten o'clock for the departure of the bride and groom. The wedding guests lined the hallway and the couple ran out between them through a blizzard of confetti to a waiting taxi. At the taxi door Helen stopped to throw her bouquet back towards the crowd and Maggie was the one to catch it. The dancing resumed until midnight when the band played 'Auld Lang Syne' and the reception was over. Gordon came in the taxi with the Scotts back to their house, helping to carry presents, left-over cake and Helen's discarded wedding dress. Although she'd had an early start to the day Alison was still wide awake, high on the buzz of the occasion.

"Let's go and sit out in the garden," she suggested. "I'd like a hot chocolate; do you want one?" She made the drinks and they went out to sit on the bench under the rose trellis.

"Don't you think we'll get eaten by midges?" Gordon asked.

"There's a bit of a breeze now. That should keep them away, but we can always go in again if they bother us."

"Helen and Neil had a grand send-off. It made me think that you and I should get engaged," Gordon said.

"Don't be daft; it's the occasion and the alcohol that are talking. How much have you had to drink?"

"Not so much that I don't know that I'm proposing that we make a commitment to each other to get married.

It's hardly a new thought for me, after all we've been going out for four years now."

"But Gordon we're seeing less and less of each other. I couldn't begin to think about a commitment to marry you if you can't even give me the commitment of living in the same place as me for a while. I have to be in Edinburgh for at least another three years of Uni and then a year for my house jobs. If you can't live with me there, then I don't see much future for us."

"You know I can't do the work I want to in the city."

"I know, but you could compromise and do different work for a while until I'm through with my course. I don't see the point in getting engaged and then living apart for another four years."

"It has to be me that makes the compromise?" he clarified.

"Well I can't move the university and I don't think you'd want me to pack in my course."

"No, I wouldn't want that. Look we're tired. Maybe we should sleep on this and talk again tomorrow."

But Alison doubted that she'd sleep at all as he kissed her goodnight and they agreed to meet for coffee in the morning before he set out for Fort William. How could he be happy to continue on in this way for all that time? That night she was very restless, tossing and turning, her mind refusing to switch off and let her rest.

"It's because I love you, so I'm happy to wait until we can be together. I suggested getting engaged because it would bind us closer to each other, and also to let you know that I'm serious about us," Gordon explained the next morning.

He was holding her hand across the kitchen table at his parents' house where they were having coffee. Gordon's parents were both at work. Alison had to acknowledge that this statement emphasised the patience, loyalty and fortitude that were major parts of Gordon's character. She hoped that she was loyal, too, but she knew that she couldn't carry on much longer with living apart. She tried to explain this,

"I just miss you too much, and I find it hard supposedly being part of a couple but really being on my own most of the time. It seems to me that if you're really serious about us you'd want us to be together. If you came to Edinburgh to live and through time things worked out, then I could imagine getting engaged and married. But if you have no intention of moving closer then I wonder if we should break things off."

"I don't believe this. I want to get engaged and you want us to break up?" Gordon was upset.

"I don't really want us to break up, but it seems that we can't be together any time soon. So maybe it would be best." Alison was beginning to get tearful.

"It's not the best for me, but if that's how you're thinking, then we'd better take a break. As from now, you're free of me."

Gordon got up from the table and left the kitchen, slamming the door behind him. She could hear him stamping up the stairs and his bedroom door close, not quite so loudly. When it was obvious that he wasn't going to return, she emptied her half-finished coffee into the sink, rinsed out the cup and left it on the draining board, then let herself out of the house. She felt numb, her mind sluggish. What had she done? Should she go back and try to mend things between them? She walked slowly home as if in a daze, went up to her room and lay down under her duvet. She felt chilled and extremely tired. She fell asleep.

***

The next two weeks were a lonely, miserable time for Alison. Her parents had left immediately after the wedding to have a holiday and of course Helen was on her honeymoon. She was running the florist shop during the day along with Fiona, her mum's assistant, and returning to an empty house apart from Jess in the evenings. She'd heard nothing from Gordon, who'd returned to Fort William, and didn't want to bump into either of his parents, which was quite likely as his dad's pharmacy business was close to the shop. The time of year and the shop routine also reminded her strongly of the beginning of their relationship four years earlier. She tortured herself with reminiscing.

It had been during the summer holidays after her fourth year of school and Alison was in the shop, helping out. She'd put the finishing touches to a creation in blue and white for a new baby, cornflowers, agapanthus, white roses and spider chrysanthemums, softened with baby's breath and maidenhair fern. She'd tied the azure ribbon and attached the small, bobbing blue-teddy helium balloon, then misted generously to keep the flowers fresh. "There, all ready for the proud dad to collect," she'd thought.

Her tasks completed, she'd decided to go to the coffee shop around the corner, where they also sold snacks to take away, and buy a filled roll for her lunch. Her mum was at the Oban Bay Hotel arranging wedding flowers so she'd put up the "Back in five minutes" sign on the door and locked up. The lunchtime street had seemed warm after the cool of the flower store and she remembered crossing over George Street to walk on the sunny side. When she'd arrived at the café, there was a small queue. She'd recognised one of the people serving behind the counter, a popular boy from school. He was tall, darkish blond and tanned. She knew that he'd played rugby and sailed and she'd noticed he had well developed muscles showing under his green apron and short-sleeved polo shirt.

"Not off on an exotic holiday abroad then?" He'd asked as he made up her sandwich.

"No, I'm helping my Mum in the shop, but we'll be going to France once Fiona, her assistant, gets back from her holidays."

"I'm working here for the summer to save up for college. I expect I'll see you around then," he'd said.

When Alison arrived back at the florists, the cool air had helped her to recover her composure. She was annoyed by how she had flushed after a little attention from Gordon, who would probably not remember her existence after five minutes had passed. She was sure he'd just been making polite conversation with a customer.

Two days later as she'd emerged from the shop at closing time she'd noticed a long lanky figure leaning against the wall just down from the display window. Gordon had straightened up and smiled and Alison tried to remember to keep breathing and instructed herself not to gabble.

"Hi, Alison, I thought you'd be finishing about now so I waited for you."

"Oh," she said

"I was wondering, if you're not busy, whether you'd like to come to the sailing club disco with me on Saturday night? I could pick you up from your house."

And of course, she'd said yes.

Emerging from her memories she sighed heavily, earning a glance from Fiona who was concerned about her.

"Do you want to call it a day and finish early?" Fiona asked. "It seems quiet, I'm sure we don't both need to be here."

"Well, OK," Alison replied. "And I'll let you away tomorrow if it's quiet then."

When she got to the house there was no greeting from Jess, she must still be out on a walk with Andrew. She slumped down on the sofa and stared into space. After a few minutes, the phone began to ring. She considered ignoring it, but roused herself to go and answer. It was Karen, who'd been phoning regularly since Alison had told her what had happened with Gordon.

"I think you should come down to Edinburgh a bit earlier than you'd planned," she suggested. "Then we can keep you busy. The festival will be on and I'm planning my 'Bon Voyage' party."

"Well I might," Alison said, not wanting to commit herself. She heard the back door open and Jess came bounding through the kitchen, she could hear her claws clicking and skidding trying to get a grip on the shiny linoleum floor. "Hi Andrew," she called. "Thanks for walking Jess, but I can feed her. I got home early."

"OK," he called. "I'll be back tomorrow," and he let himself out.

"That was Andrew," Alison explained to Karen who was still on the line. "I think I talk more to him than to anyone else at the moment."

"That's a bit quick, you don't want to start something on the rebound," Karen warned.

"He's about twelve years old, Karen, and walks the dog for pocket money." Alison initially sounded affronted, but then saw the funny side of Karen's misconception and began to laugh. Karen on the other end of the phone was pleased that she'd managed to amuse her friend.

Twelve

Alison arrived back in Edinburgh in the middle of August. She had never felt the need to escape Oban before and it made her feel sad. She realised that this summer marked the end of long holidays as she was about to enter her clinical years. She wouldn't be able to visit Oban again for more than a few days at a time, maybe it was just as well.

This was the first time that Alison had been in Edinburgh during the Festival and she couldn't believe how different the atmosphere was. The streets teemed with life, particularly around the High Street and the university area. There were masses of tourists and she heard snatches of conversation in American accents and foreign languages as people passed by. Sometimes she caught the lingering scent of a French cigarette or a cigar. Adding to the crowd there were performers out on the streets advertising their shows. Some of them were in costume, handing out fliers with details of their act and others put on excerpts from their plays on street corners. There were bursts of impromptu music and sounds of applause and all of this activity lasted on well into the night. The price for tickets at the official Festival was, in the main, prohibitive for students but the Fringe tickets were much more affordable and there were also some free shows on the Fringe. Alison had arranged to meet Karen outside the entrance to Old Assembly Close on the High Street just down the hill from St Giles Cathedral. As she was waiting, she was entertained by a juggler who was keeping an orange, a feather duster and a chain saw circling around his head. She dropped a coin in his hat on the pavement and spotted Karen approaching from the direction of the Cathedral. She hadn't seen Karen for nearly two months and her spirits lifted as she saw how well her friend looked. She was wearing jeans and a close-fitting T-shirt which showed that she had regained some curves. Her blond hair was cropped close, but it was obviously her own hair and the boyish style looked dramatic.

"Karen, you look great," Alison exclaimed as she hugged her friend. "Seeing you has really cheered me up. I love your hair."

"Thanks. I like it, too, and it feels so light and airy after wearing wigs or hats for so long. I think I might keep the shorter style, what do you think?"

"I think it's really glamorous, you look a bit like that pop singer Annie Lennox."

"And, how are you?"

"Oh, I'm OK," said Alison. "I must say I love Edinburgh in the Festival. It seems so lively and cosmopolitan."

"Yeah, it's like being abroad without the bother of travelling. Do you want to go to the show that's coming on down the close here? There's a square that opens out on the left where they put on free performances. Chris caught this one yesterday and thought it was good, it's by a group called Pookiesnackenburger. He described it as lively music with some funny antics thrown in."

As the girls wandered down the narrow close, they could hear frantic drumming and a voice over a loudspeaker funnelling up towards them, encouraging people who were passing by to gather. They joined a thickening crowd to watch the show.

After watching a lively performance, the friends emerged back out onto the High Street and decided to go to one of their favourite cafes for a late lunch. It was situated on Victoria Street a steep curving street in two tiers which wound from George IV Bridge down to the Grassmarket. Since they were after the main rush for lunch they were able to find a table by the window at the 'Laird's Larder'. They watched crowds of tourists wend their way up and down the hill and enjoyed bowls of thick Scotch broth accompanied by rustic style oatcakes and butter.

"So, tomorrow night we're going to the Cambridge footlights, then on Friday it's your party and you set out for France next Monday?" Alison checked their arrangements.

"That's right. Can you help me with shopping for the party tomorrow? Then we'll have all day Friday to get things ready."

"Sure, I don't have a lot planned over the next few weeks apart from some sewing. We're expected to wear smart clothes once we're on the wards and I don't own any skirts or blouses having lived in jeans and rugby shirts for the past two years. Elaine said I could borrow her sewing machine, so I'm hoping to save some money by running up a couple of skirts."

"There's a good material shop over near Pollock Halls."

"Yes, 'Remnant Kings'. I thought I might make a detour past there on my way home."

"OK, so will you come down to Stockbridge tomorrow afternoon?" Karen asked. "We can get the shopping and then have tea at the flat with Chris before we go out to the show."

Later, as she was browsing through dressmaking patterns in 'Remnant Kings' not really feeling very inspired, Alison reflected that currently Karen was the one who radiated life and energy and was carrying her along in her enthusiasm. It was strange how their roles had flipped; she felt that everything was an effort meanwhile Karen was bursting with health and vitality. Eventually she found a 'Style' pattern with a simple pencil skirt that she felt she could attempt to make. She then wafted between the stacks of cloth bolts fingering lining silks, gaberdines and tweed mixes and eventually choosing a mid-blue tweed material and a grey heavy cotton. The assistant cut the required lengths and then helped her to gather matching lining materials, threads and zippers. As she walked along Grange Road heading back towards the flat with her package, she realised that she was going to miss Karen dreadfully when she left for France.

On opening the front door, she was greeted by Joan Armatrading being played at full volume in Liz's room. Liz had been working at the bank again earlier this summer, but unfortunately, she had to re-sit one of her exams and so she was now engaged in studying for it. Alison was glad not to be alone in the flat in her current wobbly emotional state. When she'd first arrived back, she had immediately removed Gordon's photograph from the mantelpiece in her bedroom and shoved it, still in its frame, into the bottom drawer of her dresser underneath her woolly jumpers. Alison stuck her head round Liz's bedroom door and offered to make coffee.

"That would be great. I'll come through for a break," Liz said. "What's in the package?" she asked as she came into the kitchen, stretching. Alison had filled the kettle and now showed Liz the material explaining about having a dress code from now on. "You'll be vying with Elaine now. I'm going to be the odd one out on the fashion scene."

"I don't think my clothes will ever be anywhere as elegant as Elaine's. I'm only hoping to pass muster not to suddenly become a fashion icon." Alison reassured her.

"Talking about Elaine, I wondered if we should be saying anything to her when she gets back, or should we just wait to see how things are?"

"What do you mean?" Alison was puzzled.

"Well I thought you'd have noticed the vomiting. She's done it sporadically since I've shared with her but it definitely got worse at the end of last term."

"Oh." It all suddenly added up. The sour smell that she'd thought was the drains. But, now that she thought back, it hadn't been noticeable since she'd arrived back in the flat. And then the vague impression of noises in the night returned to her, retching noises?

"She's been making herself sick? Has she ever talked about it?" Alison asked.

"Not to me, but I think generally it tends to be a secretive type of thing." Liz replied.

"I feel that I must be really unobservant, but then Elaine always seems so together. I'd never have imagined it."

"Maybe it's worse when she's stressed, could be why it was bad at the end of term with exams," Liz suggested.

"I think we should probably see how she seems when she gets back and only speak to her about it if we think she's getting bad again. I'm glad you mentioned it, though, at least now we're both looking out for her."

"OK," Liz drained her coffee mug and got to her feet. "I suppose I'd better get back to economics."

***

On Friday evening the Bon Voyage party for Karen was in full swing in Chris's flat in St Bernard's Row. Karen had suggested that guests wear French costumes so there was a plethora of navy and white hooped T-shirts and berets. A few girls were dressed to look like Can-can dancers and, seeming strangely out of place, there was one Nun. Alison had helped Karen to buy French cheeses and pates, olives, gherkins and grapes and a dozen baguettes. Karen had thought that numbers might be low as it was still holiday time, but there seemed to be plenty of people squashed into the available space.

Alison had arrived with Liz and she recognised a few people from the badminton club. She tried to be enthusiastic for Karen's sake but wasn't really in the mood for a party, finding the noise level excessive and the jostling annoying. She burrowed herself into a relatively sheltered corner in the kitchen and nursed her glass of Beaujolais. From there she could overhear Karen telling people about her plans for the year abroad. Her placement had been switched to Paris on the advice of Dr Wood so that she was close to medical facilities should the need for them arise. However, she hoped that this would prove cautionary but unnecessary and to get by with reviews at three monthly intervals at his clinic back in Edinburgh.

"It's going to be hard for us to let her go, isn't it?" Chris asked, appearing by Alison's side.

"She'll be fine, but I'll miss her," she replied.

"I was sorry to hear about you breaking up with Gordon, he seemed a nice chap."

"Danger of a long-distance relationship," said Alison. Then when she realised that Chris was just entering into that role she quickly added, "If it goes on for too long."

"Do you think you'll get across to visit Karen?" Chris asked her.

"I'm not sure that I can afford it, although I thought I might look for a Saturday job to try and earn some extra cash. What about you?"

"Her folks are planning to go for the September holiday weekend, so I'll try to make it over for a weekend in October sometime. It'll depend a bit on concert schedules and I won't know those definitely until the beginning of term."

"Keep in touch with me, won't you?" Alison asked.

"Sure, I'll pop in for a coffee. Woops, I think the music has run out – I'd better go and do my DJ duties."

Chris proceeded to squeeze his way across the crowded kitchen making for the music centre in the dining alcove. Alison decided to call it a night and, giving Karen a hug on the way past, she also negotiated a path across the kitchen and then let herself out of the flat. Once out on the front path she took deep breaths of fresh air and then strolled home through the still bustling festival streets.

***

On Monday of the next week Alison received a post-card with a picture of the Kelvingrove Museum on the front. It was from Helen, informing her that the wedding photographs had been developed and suggesting that Alison phone to arrange a meeting. As she went out that evening to phone, she reflected that she was certainly spending a lot less of her time enclosed in the local phone box. She didn't miss its draughty interior with the dim light and faint whiff of urine. She and Helen agreed that Alison would come through to Glasgow on Thursday and spend the night at Helen and Neil's flat as Helen had two days off then. The anticipation of a trip to see her sister definitely made Alison feel more cheerful and on the next day there was another event to lift her spirits. She'd decided to take a break from sewing and went for a walk along the Meadows. As she passed Victor Hugo's delicatessen, she felt a sudden craving for some salami and crusty bread for lunch, so decided to call in. She noticed a hand-written sign in the window 'Help wanted, Saturdays' and asked the woman behind the counter about it. The woman went to find the owner, who after a short chat with Alison offered her the job beginning this weekend. That fitted in perfectly with her return from Glasgow, and earning some money made the prospect of visiting Karen in Paris much more likely. Mrs Scott was pleased to hear more animation in Alison's voice when she took another walk to the phone box that evening to call home.

"I know it's early days," she said to her husband, "But I think Alison is beginning to pick up."

"That's good to hear," he said. "I was worried about her. But you know, I think that the best distraction for her will be starting her new term and beginning to deal with patients. It will give her studies a whole new focus."

Thirteen

Everyone looked so different on the first morning of the new term. Boys were wearing shirts and ties and girls had all suddenly ditched jeans and dungarees for skirts. Shapely legs, some ending in high heels, had emerged to the delight of most of the boys. There were a few whistles and catcalls as girls entered the lecture theatre. After the nine o'clock pathology lecture they were to spend the rest of the morning on hospital wards. Half of the students only had to cross Middle Meadow Walk to reach the Royal Infirmary but Alison with the rest of her year made her way to Appleton Tower where coaches were waiting to take them to other hospitals around the city. Alison was to board the coach going to the Western General. She walked along with Robert who was sporting a crisp white shirt with a smart red paisley pattern tie and was bound for the City Hospital.

"What kind of stethoscope did you buy?" he asked her.

"A Littman," she replied.

"Very modern," he commented. "I went for the more traditional Sprague-Bowles. It looks like something Dr Cameron would use on *Dr Finlay's Casebook*."

Alison was amused. A lot of men seemed to be obsessed by having what they perceived to be the right type of equipment, be it a stethoscope, a music centre, a bicycle or a squash racquet. But was Robert becoming a bit of a poser?

"As long as you can hear the right things with it," she said.

On arrival at the Western General the students were directed to the Education Centre. The programme for their mornings over the next term was described. First, they would learn how to take a clinical history from a patient and next they would observe members of staff and be allowed to practice for themselves in small groups. By the end of two weeks they'd be expected to be able to take a proper history by themselves. As the term progressed, they would be taught how to carry out a clinical examination, taking a system at a time. To begin with they would examine each other before being directed to suitable patients on the ward. For the rest of the first morning Dr Robertson, one of the consultants, described a system for gathering information from a patient. He then demonstrated with one of his patients who had agreed to come into the lecture room from the ward. Alison scribbled down lots of notes. Before they left to catch the bus back to George Square they were arranged in groups of six and told which ward they were assigned to.

Tomorrow they were to report straight to their designated wards.

Back at the university Alison grabbed a quick sandwich for lunch before an afternoon microbiology practical. That evening she was invited to Linda's flat in Rankeillor Street for tea, so she set off after her lab. She stopped at a grocer's shop on Nicolson Street to buy some chocolate biscuits as a small contribution.

Linda had spent most of the summer at home in Chester working, but then had gone to Greece with Colin.

"We used the local buses to get around and ferries to the islands. Either we slept in our tent pitched on the beach or sometimes we found a room. Everything seemed very cheap and the scenery was amazing," Linda told her as Alison flicked through the pages of an album containing photographs of the holiday. "I was glad I was with Colin, though, as we met some girls travelling who were pestered a lot by the local men."

"Yes, Liz said something similar after her Euro-rail trip last year," Alison commented.

"I've been inspired to try and make you Moussaka for tea, so I hope it'll turn out OK," Linda said. "It should be ready in about half an hour."

"It certainly smells good." Alison had noticed the rich aroma on entering the flat.

"How are you getting on now?" Linda asked.

"A lot better now, I have to admit I had no idea how bad I would feel when we first broke up. It even seemed to affect my appetite and my concentration but I think they're back to normal now. They need to be because now that term has started, and also with working on Saturdays, I'm going to be really busy."

"So, I take it you've given up the badminton," Linda guessed.

"Yes, I decided I'd rather earn some money so that I can go to Paris."

"How's the job?"

"I love the deli. Just walking in through the door in the morning and inhaling all the wonderful scents is a treat. I'm working with other students, so there's a bit of banter and so far, no difficult customers. I suppose I'm used to a similar atmosphere in my Mum's shop, beautifully scented, quality produce and appreciative customers."

"You sound like an advert," Linda commented.

"Well I started out as one of their customers, so I was already converted."

Linda decided that they should go through to the kitchen to check on the Moussaka. It turned out to be a huge success and Alison was able to demonstrate her revived appetite by polishing off a very large portion. Linda chatted more about her summer and about the trials for the hockey team, she was hoping to be promoted to play in the firsts this year but the competition was steep. The teams were to be announced the next day and Alison wished her luck.

Alison enjoyed her new routine of mornings on the ward. There were two consultants who taught her group and their styles were contrasting. Dr Sutherland had a gentle, caring bedside manner and was very formal, calling all of the students "Miss" or "Mr" His hair was white and he was highly esteemed by staff and patients, Alison thought that he must be due to retire soon. Whereas Dr Wilson was younger and enjoyed a joke and some banter with the patients and called the students by their first names. In Alison's opinion, both seemed to be awe-inspiringly knowledgeable. Thankfully they were also benign and there was no humiliation inflicted on the students. According to other members of the year some consultants made it a ritual to pick on students and ridicule them in front of their classmates and patients.

At first, Alison worried that patients would find her a nuisance. But on the contrary, most of the patients that she went to see were in hospital for tests or well on the way to recovery from an illness and appeared to enjoy visits from students. Alison supposed that it helped to pass the time and she noticed that a lot of patients expressed pleasure that they were able to be helpful. The consultants stressed to the medical students that they should consider themselves to be 'part of the team' and not to be shy about approaching patients. Alison thought that it seemed to be a good idea to get plenty of practice with relatively well patients before trying to take a history from someone who was ill or in a lot of pain. She knew that by the middle of term she would be expected to come in to the ward on 'waiting evenings' to observe how acutely ill patients were treated and also to help the busy junior doctors to admit and process patients.

Third year gave an introduction to clinical skills but there were still formal lectures to attend every day and afternoons were generally spent peering down a microscope, either in pathology or microbiology labs. Alison began to feel dazzled by all the pinkish-purple blobs after an hour or so. Friday afternoons were quite different, being set aside for an introduction to psychiatry. Alison had to catch a local bus, or sometimes was offered a lift from a friend with a car, to Craighouse Hospital which was situated on the slopes of Craiglockhart Hill on the far side of Morningside. Alison was impressed by the grand scale of the buildings which were built of stone and sported towers, turrets both round and square and majestic chimneys. But it was the surrounding parkland grounds that took her breath away. There were acres of lawns, with shrubs and specimen trees. The views over the city took in the castle, Arthur's Seat and Blackford Hill. On a clear day, you could see across to Fife and well down the East coast. One would imagine that all this beauty might lift the spirits and aid recovery of people with mental health problems, but perversely the patients who inhabited Craighouse were the very chronic cases who in the past had not been able to be managed in the community. Many had been there for tens of years and there were no plans for their discharge.

In third year the students weren't expected to have much contact with individual patients. They were given a short lecture about a clinical condition from one of the consultant psychiatrists, which usually included a case history as illustration and then an introduction to the patient concerned. Even while just walking around the hospital Alison found that the patients' reactions towards her were unpredictable and could be very disconcerting. Many patients seemed blank-faced and apathetic. They often appeared to hug the walls, either shambling close to the corridor walls or sitting with their chairs ringed around the walls in the patient lounges. A lot of them seemed oblivious of their surroundings and of the people around them. They avoided eye contact and made no reply to greetings, but some occasionally muttered to themselves. In contrast, some individuals would rush up to her, often coming alarmingly close with no respect for conventions on body space. Their conversations could be random and nonsensical. One man who approached her kept stroking her arm and while to begin with it seemed harmless, he began to exert more and more pressure until the strokes were becoming more akin to hitting. Fortunately, a staff member noticed and led him away. Although she knew that the strange tics of face and limbs and rhythmical motions of tongues, heads and hands exhibited by many of the patients were long-term sequelae of medication, it all added to the strangeness of the environment. For weeks, she wondered if it was kindness or torture to give these people who were locked in, a spectacular panoramic view. Eventually she came to believe that for some it might give pleasure, and that the tantalising vistas would not trouble those others who were in actual fact imprisoned in their own minds.

After their psychiatry session, the students often met for a drink and a favourite pub nearby was 'The Canny Man's' on Morningside Road. A lot of them felt the need to let off steam and the atmosphere could be raucous. Some recognised that the ambience of the psychiatric unit had made them feel stressed while others used the excuse that it was Friday, the close of another busy week.

***

On a Thursday morning towards the end of November Alison and the other five students in her group were gathered on a side ward waiting for a tutorial to begin. They chatted amongst themselves.

"Does anyone know who's supposed to be taking us?" Grant asked after five minutes.

"I think it's the SHO," said David, just as a young doctor appeared in the doorway. His white coat was unbuttoned and he wore his stethoscope draped across his shoulders. His dark hair looked dishevelled and his tie was tucked into his shirt between the 3rd and 4th buttons.

"Sorry I'm late," he apologised. "I'm Dr Cooke. I think that today you're due to learn the examination of the respiratory system. We'll talk things through, then hopefully one or two of the male members of the group will allow us to practice on them before I let you loose on some real patients on the ward."

Alison recognised Dr Cooke. He had been one of Karen's doctors last autumn, and he'd been the one who'd stopped to help when she'd had that panic attack. She wondered if he would remember her, but thought that it was unlikely. She'd better pay attention now to what he was telling them. It was a lively session and the boys weren't too shy to volunteer to be examined. Once they had dressed again and the group was walking down the corridor to the main ward Dr Cooke caught up with Alison.

"Have we met somewhere before?" he asked. "Your face seems familiar."

"You looked after my friend Karen on C ten last autumn. I saw you when I was visiting."

"That'll be it, but I didn't know you were a medical student."

"No, well I've only just started clinical."

"And enjoying it so far?" he asked.

"Yes, very much."

"Well let's see if I can get you to hear some lung signs. I think Mrs McCormack over here should be a good person to start with."

He led the students up to a bed where a woman with brown curly hair was sitting. She was younger than the average patient on the medical ward.

"These are the students I told you about Mrs McCormack," he said. "Are you still OK with them examining your lungs?"

Alison was very pleased five minutes later that she had been able to hear the high-pitched wheezing rhonchi of asthma when Mrs McCormack breathed out. She thought she'd recognise that sound again. She wasn't always convinced that she'd picked up the sounds she was listening for, especially with heart murmurs. She probably wasn't destined to be a cardiologist. Sometimes she felt that she learned more when a junior doctor was in charge. She thought it was because the atmosphere was more relaxed. Much as she liked Drs Sutherland and Wilson, it definitely produced more performance anxiety in the group when the consultants were leading the teaching. She hoped that Dr Cooke might be sent to teach them again.

Fourteen

Dear Alison,

Thank you for your chatty letter with all the news from Edinburgh. It's hard to believe that I'll be home in another three weeks. The time here seems to be flying past, maybe because I have to concentrate so hard all the time on the language. I certainly sleep well every night – I'm so exhausted! I knew that it would be a challenge to communicate in French all the time but what I hadn't bargained for was the speed that the locals talk at. They tend to slur their words together and they use slang words that aren't in any dictionary. I suppose that coming from Scotland with so many different local accents and colloquialisms in a small country I shouldn't have been so surprised! Imagine learning the 'Queen's English' and then arriving in Glasgow for instance. I am surviving and it is getting easier.

I think that my spell at tutoring last spring has helped me with my work in school as it made me more comfortable around teenagers. Although a class full is different to one at a time, so far, I haven't felt that a class has been out of control. I try to pick subjects that I think are current and will be interesting and I think it's been working. I've also been doing small group work with some of the older pupils which is great fun. I'm hoping to get permission next term to go out of school for some of those sessions and perhaps visit museums or galleries with them.

I haven't had any visitors since Chris was here a month ago but there is plenty to do and see at weekends if I travel into the centre of Paris. There are also some other students that I can meet up with. The girl I spend most time with goes to Aberdeen University but actually comes from Shetland. She's trying to persuade me to come up and visit her there over the holidays but I don't think that mid-winter would be the best time to go, maybe next summer. I hope you'll be able to come over here next term. If you skipped a Friday and Monday off classes for the travelling, we would have the whole weekend for sightseeing. Keep saving up your pennies.

I do remember Dr Cooke from my time in the Western. He always seemed very nice. It's funny to think of you on the wards there amongst the huddles of white coats. To be honest I try not to dwell on my time there, too many frightening experiences. I'll be seeing Dr Wood when I get back and hope he'll be happy with me, I've certainly been feeling fine. Have you come across him at all?

I'd better finish now as I've got lessons to prepare for tomorrow.

Au revoir and love from

Karen.

Dear Karen,

I thought I'd better send you a letter to tell you my latest news even though you'll be home soon. I've been out on a date! In fact, two dates, with Dr Cooke — James.

I was really surprised when he stopped me in the corridor last Wednesday and asked if he could have a quick word. I thought it would be about a patient, but he asked me if I'd like to meet him for a drink. I didn't see why not, so I said yes and we arranged to meet at 'Bannermans' on the Cowgate that evening. You know it can get really busy there, with a queue waiting to get in, but being mid-week it was quieter. So, we were able to get a table and didn't have to shout at each other to be heard. I was a bit nervous but he was easy to talk to, so I did eventually feel more at ease. He's not an Edinburgh graduate. He was at St Andrews University and then Manchester for his clinical years. He didn't want to work down there, though, so he applied for his first jobs back in Scotland. Anyway, when we left he insisted in walking me most of the way home, to see me safely across the Meadows. Then he asked me if I was busy at the weekend. He has a car, so he picked me up on Sunday afternoon and we drove to Cramond. I'd never been there before, it's a wee village, and there's an island with a causeway that you can walk across to at low tide. However, the tide was in so we walked along the promenade and also up the River Almond — and held hands!

I'm trying not to get too excited — but I am! We can't see each other this week as he's on-call for two nights and at the weekend, it seems to come in clusters on the rota. But he's suggested going to the cinema together the following week.

Gordon and I were a couple for so long that it feels strange to be seeing someone else, but I feel ready to move on and I'm not going to rush into anything serious. Anyway, that's my news – I thought you'd be interested and I was bursting to tell you!

I am definitely planning to come to Paris next term, we can agree on the best weekend when you're home. I thought I'd ask my parents for money towards the journey as my Christmas present.

I don't have a lot of other news, although one of our group did a spectacular faint on the ward today. We'd gone with one of the registrars to watch a lumbar puncture. That involves inserting a very large needle [under local anaesthetic] into someone's back to take fluid from around the spinal column. I think a few of us were feeling a bit queasy but there was a sudden very loud thump as David keeled over and hit the floor. He wasn't out for long, but he'd bumped his head so hard when he fell that he split his scalp, so he had to be wheeled off to A+E to get stitched up. I don't know what the patient must have made of it all but David will take some time to live the incident down.

Looking forward to seeing you very soon,

Love from

Alison.

Fifteen

Alison gnawed on a sandwich made from a section of baguette with a filling of ham, chopped gherkins and gruyere cheese, pieces of the filling kept falling out onto her tray. She couldn't help thinking that although French bread was delicious it didn't really lend itself to neat sandwiches. She peered out of the window but could only see grey cloud far below. She was trying not to feel guilty about skipping today's and Monday's classes and her excitement was helping her to succeed. She had been to Brittany on two family holidays but had never visited Paris before. She began to feel pressure building in her ears and yawned to make them pop. They must be starting the descent. She delved into her bag looking for the piece of paper with the instructions from Karen written on it. She read it through again. In her distinctive purple ink Karen had directed her to take the linking train from the airport into the city centre. Then she recommended getting off at Chatelet Les Halles, where a lot of lines connected, and taking the yellow metro line to Concorde. That would take her to the bottom of the Champs- Elysees and Karen would meet her in Café Le Paris. The plan was that whoever arrived first should just relax and order a coffee, because that was what Parisian cafes were all about. Alison hoped that it would be nice enough to sit outside, although she realised that February was still a bit early to expect Spring-like weather.

When she arrived at Le Paris, she saw that quite a few people were sitting outside. It was dry and if she kept her coat on she didn't feel cold, so she settled down at a table and ordered a café noir congratulating herself on having managed so far with her half-forgotten school-girl French. There was a murmur of French conversation from the tables around her but she couldn't make out very many words. She was looking forward to being able to relax and let Karen do the talking once she arrived. There was a constant buzz of traffic noise from the thoroughfare and she was sure that there were more horns tooting than you'd notice in Edinburgh. She sipped the rich-roasted coffee and was considering whether to rummage in her backpack to find her book when Karen arrived. The friends hugged and kissed French style.

"You got here OK?" Karen asked once she'd ordered a coffee from the attentive waiter.

"Yes, I was amazed by how easy it was. The tunnels in Les Halles seemed never-ending, but it was quite easy to follow the colour guide. I've only been here for about ten minutes."

"Well let's enjoy our coffee and make some plans. I'm sure you'll have lots of things you want to see."

"Yes, but I don't want to drag you round all of the same places that you've already seen, so you should say what you want too. I think as long as I do the Eiffel Tower I'll be happy with anything else you suggest."

"OK. I thought we could have a wander, if your bag's not too heavy. Then maybe eat at a small restaurant near Rue St-Honore which is very reasonable. It's a must to sit at a café in the Champ-Elysees but I'd only recommend having a coffee or a drink. Eating is much cheaper if you just go slightly off the beaten track."

"That's fine with me." The girls finished their coffee and then set off towards the Tuileries gardens and the Louvre chatting as they went.

"How have things been this term so far?" Karen asked.

"Hard work as usual, but OK," Alison replied. "I think I'm getting more out of it now that I have contact with patients. It all seems to make a bit more sense."

"Well, that will help," Karen laughed. "And how's the delectable James?"

"Oh, he's fine," Alison smiled and blushed slightly. "We've been seeing each other once or twice most weeks, depending on our work commitments. I feel more comfortable with things now that I've moved unit this term. Once we started going out I felt a bit awkward when he was teaching us, not that I had any complaints about his teaching. I actually thought that he was very good at explaining things."

Karen hadn't managed to meet James during the time that she was back in Scotland for Christmas. Family commitments on both sides and James's work rota seemed to have conspired against it.

"So, since I only know him in his professional capacity, tell me what makes him tick?"

"Well, he's really keen on cooking, and likes trying out new recipes, so I'm being very well fed. And he likes cinema, not just the main-stream films, but foreign and arty ones, too. He's taken me a few times to the 'Filmhouse'. I'd never been there before. It's a new development of an old church on Lothian Road. So far, they've opened one screen, but I think it'll have more screens and a restaurant when it's finished."

"And what do you make of the arty films?"

"I liked a couple of them, but I have to admit others got tedious. But James has come along with me to the SNO at the Usher Hall and to one of Chris's concerts and he's never been a big fan of classical music, so we're both trying new things."

They stopped on the Pont Neuf to watch some barges float under them, then crossed onto the Ile de la Cite and continued walking towards Notre Dame. It was getting too dark to think of taking photographs, so they agreed they could come back this way again. Karen suggested heading towards the restaurant so they re-crossed the Seine and meandered along Rue de Rivoli then cut up to Rue St-Honore window shopping as they strolled along.

"My land-lady is very nice, but she only lets to female tenants and allows female guests. Probably because she's on her own. Anyway, when Chris came over we stayed in a small hotel near here and that's when we found this restaurant. It's just up this street and around the corner – here we are Rue St-Hyacinthe. The restaurant's just here and the hotel is at the other end of the street."

They went down a narrow staircase into a basement with whitewashed walls where they were greeted by the proprietor and led to a table. They chose dinner from the table d'hôte menu and ordered a bottle of claret. Alison's duck was delicious and Karen enjoyed a steak which looked too rare for Alison's taste. They both demolished a portion of tarte tatin and drank an after-dinner coffee. Feeling full they set off for Karen's lodgings in Le Pecq. They caught a train on the yellow metro line from Tuileries to Charles de Gaulle Etoile and were serenaded by a man playing the accordion for a large part of the way. Alison put a few francs in his up-turned beret. Next, they caught the RER to Le Pecq, a journey of thirty minutes. Karen didn't need to travel into the city every day as she spent three days a week at a school in the same suburb as her lodgings.

"Come up and see my garret," Karen invited Alison as they came in the front door of a large detached house into the hall. Her landlady Madame Dupuy must have heard their arrival and emerged from a half-glassed door at the end of the hallway to greet them. Karen introduced Alison.

"Aleeson I 'ope you af a good visit."

"Merci Madame," Alison replied then listened to a barrage of rapid-fire French between Karen and Mme Dupuy before escaping up the stairs to Karen's room.

"She was giving me advice on places to take you tomorrow," Karen explained as she showed Alison into the room.

It was under the eaves, but it didn't feel cramped as the ceiling was high and the floor-space must be almost half of the house. The wallpaper was crowded with roses and the furniture was of a solid, rustic style in dark wood.

"That couch over there pulls out to make a bed and Mme D. has left some bed linen inside the chest. She's a good sort, very friendly. She always takes foreign students and likes to mother us. The other girl staying just now, Casey, is from the States. She has the other attic room and we share the bathroom down on the half-landing, you passed it as we came up."

"It's a super room," Alison said as she started to pull out her bed and make it up. "I think I'll just topple in here and fall asleep, I'm so tired."

"If you want to do the Eiffel Tower, I think it's a good idea to get straight to bed and then out early in the morning to try and avoid the queues, it gets very busy."

"Fine with me," said Alison. "I'll just pop down to do my teeth then."

"Oh, I'd better warn you to watch out for cats. Mme D. has five of them and they sometimes appear in places you're not expecting. Occasionally I've had a sensation of being watched and discovered a hidden moggy staring at me. When she has to go away on business, she's quite high up in publishing; Casey and I are entrusted with feeding the cats."

"Right," said Alison. "I'll beware of les chats."

Next morning the weather was cold and crisp, but more important for their sightseeing and photography, clear and dry. As they journeyed into the city on the train, they agreed that for the best experience of the Eiffel Tower they should climb the stairs to the upper level. Once there a lift was the only choice.

"I've done the lift all the way with my parents, but I think it was much more of an achievement to use the stairs. That's what Chris and I did and you can have a rest and take in the scenery as you go."

"Yep, the stairs it is," Alison agreed, "I hope I don't get quadriceps failure, though. When I used to occasionally go hill-climbing with Gordon, my knees would be all wobbly on the way down because my muscles weren't used to the sustained exercise going up. And I've done even less exercise recently than I used to."

"He probably set a faster pace than we're likely to take, especially if you want to take lots of photos," Karen reassured her.

They had a very enjoyable visit and Alison was sure that one of the photos she took should come out very well – in it she had managed to line up the shadow of the tower so that it lay across the Pont d'Iena and the pool in the Trocadero gardens. The two wings of the Palais de

Chaillot should frame it beautifully. They spent a long time watching the miniature cityscape from their three-hundred-and-sixty-degree lookout spot. The sounds coming up to them were muffled and faint, but Alison was still convinced that Parisian drivers made a lot more use of the horn. On returning to the ground, without wobbly knees, the girls were famished, so settled in a nearby café where they ordered coffee and croissants with apricot jam. Then they decided to take one of the boats that cruise on the Seine back towards Notre Dame so that Alison would be able to take photographs there. As it was still quite cold and they had cooled down after their climb, they settled on the sunny side of the boat and watched the buildings glide past. Alison was impressed by the gilding on the statues of Pont Alexander III.

"I can't imagine anything as opulent in Edinburgh," she commented.

"No, it would be too showy. They're still under the influence of John Knox more than four hundred years on," Karen agreed.

They left the boat at Pont Neuf and spent the afternoon exploring Ile de la Cite, Notre Dame Cathedral and Ile St-Louis. Alison took lots of photographs hoping that some would come out well. Karen had arranged that they would meet up with Casey and two of the other students that she was friendly with in a bar near the Luxembourg gardens and then all go on to have something to eat. By five o'clock Alison's feet were beginning to ache, so Karen suggested they head for the bar early and establish themselves at a table.

"I haven't told you yet that James wants me to go on holiday with him in the summer," Alison confided as they walked along the Boulevard Saint-Michel.

"And? You're not keen?" Karen interpreted.

"Well. I'm not sure. We've only been going out for three months, it seems a bit serious."

"Could you not just leave it for a while to decide then?"

"It might be hard to book something at short notice, because I only get two weeks holiday and it's at the beginning of July which is quite a busy time. So that's why he's trying to plan ahead."

"Why not compromise and go with him for one week? Say you need to visit your parents for some of the time?"

"Then there's the money side of things. He's working, so money's no object, but I can't afford to spend much. I certainly couldn't manage to pay to go abroad." Alison seemed to be coming up with a lot of arguments against the proposal.

"If you don't want to go, then it's OK to say no. Otherwise, I'm sure you'll work something out between you. After all he must know you're not made of money and that you've got a Saturday job," Karen advised.

"I'll need to think about it for a bit longer," Alison decided.

"Here we are," Karen spotted the sign for 'Closerie des Lilas' bar. "Let's grab that table over in the corner.

You go and sit down and I'll get a carafe of white wine and some glasses." The others joined them over the course of the next hour and they had a very pleasant evening chatting about the city and their respective courses. Casey was from California, studying at UCLA with a year out at the Sorbonne. Kate was another languages student from Edinburgh University and Jayne was studying French at Bristol University. In the end, they were settled so cosily in their corner that they chose to eat there rather than move on. A pianist added to the atmosphere.

On Sunday morning Alison and Karen had a much more leisurely start. Karen prepared a breakfast of yoghurt with fresh fruit and crusty rolls with butter and jam in Mme D's large kitchen. While they were lingering over their second cup of coffee Alison met three of the five resident cats.

"What do you feel like doing today?" Karen asked.

"How about a visit to a gallery if they're open on Sundays? I can't come to Paris and not take in some culture."

"OK, but do you mind if it's not the Louvre? I've been there with my folks and with Chris. How about the Pompidou Centre? It's on my list of things to see. I'll pop up and get my guide book to check, but I think it's open this afternoon." Karen ran upstairs leaving Alison to stroke the remaining cat which had tortoiseshell markings, a white tummy and three white socks. It circled around her ankles, brushing against her bare skin and purred loudly when she scratched behind its ears.

The girls spent a happy afternoon in the modern art gallery. Alison particularly liked some of the sculpture and the textile exhibits and Karen was intrigued by glass wear in vibrant colours. They both agreed that while some of the art might not be to their taste, it certainly wasn't dull.

"I'm glad I've been, that was fun," Karen pronounced as they crossed the piazza after their visit. Today the weather was cold with a drizzle occasionally strengthening to serious rain. However, both girls felt like walking rather than using the metro, so put up their umbrellas looking out for an inexpensive Bistro as they went.

"I've decided I love Paris, I like its grand scale. It was definitely worth working on Saturdays and saving like mad to be able to come," Alison declared.

"I like it, too, although I think that Edinburgh is more dramatic with the castle rock and the hills," Karen gave her opinion. "But anywhere would be better than Peebles. I was so bored stuck there, I just feel more alive in a city."

Sixteen

The sun was low in the western sky and there was a pink tinge under the few wispy clouds, but it still seemed light as Alison walked down the drive away from Craighouse Hospital. She'd spent the evening interviewing one of the patients there in preparation for a case presentation to her tutorial group on Friday afternoon. Her assigned patient was called John Watson. He was lanky, dressed in trousers and a jacket that seemed at least a size too wide for him and had a thatch of thick white hair. She discovered from his notes that he was fifty-five years old. She'd been slightly nervous when she approached him in case he wouldn't respond well to her, but he wasn't uncooperative or aggressive. However, he did seem to find it difficult to sit still, squirming and fidgeting on his chair and on two occasions getting up and looking as if he would wander off until she called him back. His restlessness had seemed to be catching, she began to feel quite edgy herself. She found that his reaction to most of her questions was to screw up his eyes, turn his head to left and right and look around him suspiciously as if they might be overheard, and then say "Aaaye lassie, I canna tell ye that." In the end, she had to resort to his case notes for details. She discovered that he'd been diagnosed as schizophrenic in 1948 after various earlier breakdowns. When he presented to the psychiatric services, his main delusion had been that he was Napoleon, and to this day he still held that firm belief. Because of a poor response to the types of treatment that were available in the forties and fifties he'd been a patient in Craighouse since 1956. While she was in the duty room studying his notes one of the staff nurses came in and asked if she could help at all. Alison explained she was giving a presentation about John.

"Does he have any family or anyone who visits him?" Alison asked the nurse.

"Not that I know of. I've been here for about five years and I've not come across anyone visiting him. To be honest, very few of our patients have visitors," she replied.

"That's sad," said Alison.

"Yes, it is. Did you know that we're beginning to work with some of the more stable long-term patients with a view to moving them into smaller supported houses in the community?" the nurse asked.

"No, what kind of things are you doing with them?" Alison asked.

"Well some of the patients, like John, have never used decimal money or been in a supermarket, so we've been teaching them about money and taking them on wee outings to the shops."

"How do they react to that?" Alison wondered.

"Well John was amazing in the supermarket. He's usually so suspicious, restless and checking all around him, but he just seemed to be mesmerised by the variety of fruit and vegetables. He stopped in his tracks and just rocked on his heels, gazing at it all."

"Will he be moving from here?"

"Eventually they'll all be moving. This kind of hospital is very old-fashioned now, so it'll be closed. In ten years' time, we'll all be gone from here."

As she stood at the bus stop, Alison wondered how John and all of the other patients would feel about moving. After all, even if it didn't seem homely to her, he had lived on his ward for twenty-five years and possibly didn't remember any other home.

When she arrived back at the flat, she decided to have a snack of some biscuits and cheese as she'd rushed her meal earlier in order to visit John and was feeling peckish. One of the perks of her Saturday job was being given small end-pieces of meats and cheeses to take home, so she always had a good selection to choose from. She was rummaging in the fridge when Liz came up behind her.

"Alison, is that you in for the night now?" Liz asked.

"Yes, why?" Alison sounded puzzled.

"Well, I think we should tackle Elaine tonight." Both of them had noticed signs associated with the return of Elaine's bulimia, probably connected with her final law exams coming up next month.

"OK. If we hear her, we'll get together and wait outside the bathroom," Alison suggested.

"Fine. Can I have some of that blue cheese? What kind is it?"

"Bleu d'Auvergne, here put some on a cracker," Alison offered.

At half past eleven Liz and Alison were stationed in the hall outside the bathroom. Alison had alerted Liz when she'd heard retching noises a couple of minutes earlier. The toilet flushed and then they heard water running in the wash-hand basin before the door opened and Elaine appeared.

"Oh," she looked shocked to see them and then began to cry. "Oh, it's so disgusting, I'm sorry. I thought I was being quiet." Liz offered her a tissue and led her through to the lounge while Alison went into the kitchen to make everyone a mug of tea.

"It's the exams," Elaine confirmed when she'd calmed down a bit. She tucked her feet up under her on the armchair and wrapped her hands round the steaming mug. "I feel so stressed and yet I find it so boring and tedious having to study. That's when I start on the chocolate and I'm so podgy already; I can't afford to put on weight, so I feel disgusting and I make myself sick and I feel more disgusting, but at least I'm not going to get fatter."

"But Elaine you're not podgy or fat," said Alison. "You've got curves in all the right places, in as well as out."

"I need my clothes to fit me. I can't afford to replace them all."

"I can understand that," said Liz thinking of Elaine's extensive and expensive wardrobe.

"Have you tried working in the library?" Alison asked. "Or taking regular breaks?"

"That might work for a day or two but then I just sort of panic and shut myself up in my room again."

"How about trying raw carrots and celery instead of the chocolate?" Liz suggested.

"Or biltong?" that was Alison's idea.

Between the three of them, they came up with a plan for Elaine to spend different parts of her day in varying environments; including working in the flat's kitchen along-side one of the others since they had exams to prepare for too. She'd also try the healthier snacks and see how things went. Even if she occasionally gave in and had some chocolate, it was likely to be a lot less than before with the others helping her.

"And at least you can talk to us about it now if you're feeling stressed or have a craving and we can distract you," said Liz.

"Thanks, you're real pals. I don't know why I didn't tell you about it sooner, I suppose I was ashamed," said Elaine.

"You're going to be fine. And you'll pass those exams with no problem; you've always been near the top of your year." Alison gave her a reassuring hug. "Now I'm off to bed, goodnight." She felt shattered as she pulled her duvet up and switched off the lamp. "Well," she thought," between John and Elaine I've had quite an emotional evening."

The next evening Alison went into the ward for their on-call session. She was currently on a placement with one of the surgical units in the Royal Infirmary for her clinical experience. The students were expected to attend emergencies in order to see acute surgical problems and sometimes they were given the chance to assist in theatre. She accompanied the registrar to assess a patient who had arrived for a surgical opinion in the A and E department. His history of abdominal pain with diarrhoea and vomiting, and the site of the tenderness in his abdomen seemed to add up to appendicitis. Two hours later he was anaesthetised in theatre about to have an appendicectomy.

So far in this attachment Alison had gone into the operating theatre wearing the special pyjamas, hat, mask and clogs but had only watched the proceedings from a distance. Tonight, she was instructed in the method of thorough hand washing and scrubbing. Then she was assisted into a green gown and wriggled her hands into sterile gloves prior to joining the surgeon and theatre sister at the operating table. The sister reminded her that she could only touch things that were sterile, otherwise she'd be contaminated and would have to repeat the whole scrubbing routine. It was hot under the bright spotlights and she felt slightly smothered behind her mask, but she was pleased to be feeling neither faint nor sick. After cleaning the area for the incision with antiseptic the patient was covered with sterile drapes with only the small area over his appendix showing. The incision was made and Alison's job was mainly to hold instruments when asked, swab away excess blood and cut threads for the surgeon. It was very satisfying when the inflamed appendix had been removed and the patient was all sewn together again, his problem solved. Alison didn't think she could personally perform operations, but she could see the appeal of having a clean, surgical approach. Unfortunately, not all problems could be cured that way.

***

By the time that Thursday evening came around Alison felt that she deserved a break. She hadn't got back to the flat until after midnight the previous night and of course on Tuesday she'd been up late, too. She was in danger of nodding off while sitting on the bus as she made her way to James's flat for tea. She felt much more comfortable in her relationship with James now. He was so calm, and very relaxing to be around. She tried not to compare him with Gordon, but sometimes couldn't help herself. Gordon had always seemed restless, as if he was busy planning his next activity. Sometimes he did sit still to read a book but the subject matter would be bristling with daring and action; someone sailing solo around the world or climbing Mount Everest. James could happily chill out listening to some music, watching a film or reading a book with no apparent rush to be onto his next pursuit. Not long after her return from Paris he had raised the subject of the summer holiday and their relationship in general, and reassured her that he didn't mean to pressurise her at all. He didn't want her to be in awe of him because he was a bit older and he understood that she was not long out of another relationship. He told her that he enjoyed her company and found her attractive and that he hoped that the feelings were mutual. However, he wanted her to know that he was happy to keep things going at a leisurely pace if that was what she was comfortable with. A few weeks later she stayed overnight at his flat for the first time. In retrospect, she could see that some of her previous doubts were probably caused by nerves and tension about moving forward to a full sexual relationship with him. But now that they had she was actually much happier.

She got off the bus on Polwarth Terrace and crossed over to Harrison Road. She dawdled for a bit by the Union Canal and watched a mum with two young children throwing bread to the ducks. There was a great cacophony of indignant quacking as a barking dog ran up and scattered the birds. They flapped and splashed into the middle of the canal out of harm's reach and meanwhile the dog began to hoover up the bread that was left behind. The dog's owner apologised to the children who looked perfectly happy to turn their attention to petting the spaniel. She saw lots of other dog activity as she crossed the park to James's flat on Harrison Gardens, stopping to stroke a friendly Labrador on her way. James was the only person she knew who owned rather than rented their flat.

It was on the first floor of a stone tenement building and had a great view across the park towards the canal. He'd decorated using bright colours; the walls were turquoise in the lounge, yellow for the kitchen and coral in the bedroom. The furnishings were modern, light and simple and he'd hung framed posters from art exhibitions on his walls. Alison thought that the overall effect was bright but not too dazzling. Tonight, there was a delicious smell of curry spices when he opened the door.

"I'm trying a prawn biriyani, hope it'll be OK," he said as he hurried back into the kitchen after kissing her 'hello'.

"It smells good," she commented, following him. "Anything I can do to help?"

"No, just have a seat and tell me what you've been up to. Do you want a drink?" he offered, and brought her a glass of chilled white wine. They swapped stories about their respective nights on call as James finished cooking and they ate their meal. He had hardly managed any sleep the night before as he had been receiving medical emergencies and had been very busy. Alison described her first experience as a surgical assistant.

"It's so much messier than dissection was. I don't know how the surgeons cope when there's blood spurting everywhere, obscuring all the structures."

"Well hopefully they put a clamp on the vessel to stop it spurting," James proposed.

"Very funny. Anyway, I'm sure I'll never want to be a surgeon. That was delicious, a good recipe," Alison complimented him as she finished her curry.

"I think we both need some fresh air now," he suggested as he stacked their plates by the sink. "Let's go for a walk along the canal, then I'll give you a lift home so we can both get an early night tonight."

They set off hand in hand along the towpath in a westerly direction, the sun a pale orange disc ahead of them. The path was busy with cyclists, joggers and dog-walkers all making the most of the balmy, warm evening. Alison stopped and exclaimed over some fluffy, newly hatched ducklings bobbing erratically after their mother, their high-pitched peeping fading away as she led them into the cover of the reeds on the opposite bank.

"They're so cute."

"You're such a softie," James teased and gave her a hug. They walked half-way across the viaduct that carried the canal over the Water of Leith and paused to look down, the noise from the river and the white tips of the fast-racing current were a contrast with the calm canal behind them. Then they agreed to re-trace their steps back to the flat.

"I'm meeting Linda tomorrow at 'The Golf Tavern' after my psychiatry presentation. I think Colin will be there. Do you want to come?" Alison asked.

"Sure, I'll drop in. I might not be finished till about seven, though."

"That's OK. We'll wait for you. I think Linda is going to move into Spottiswoode Street next year. The rent is a bit higher than her current flat, but I think I can persuade her."

"That would be ideal, sharing with your two best friends," James commented.

"I know. Liz and Elaine have been fine to share with, but it'll be so great to be with Karen; and I hope Linda will come, too."

Seventeen

Alison used her thumb to smudge the soft black pencil where she'd drawn clouds. She was attempting to sketch the view from the cottage on the east side of Coniston Water looking towards the Old Man of Coniston. She wasn't very happy with the standard of her work but was content to soak up the afternoon sunshine. James came out of the cottage behind her and kissed the top of her head while examining her effort.

"Not bad," he commented and placed a glass of cloudy homemade lemonade with ice-cubes tinkling on the table beside her pad.

"It's well seen I've not done any drawing for the past five years, I'm really out of practice," she complained.

"I don't have an ounce of talent to begin with, so I think it's good," James plonked himself onto the bench beside her. "What do you want to do for the rest of the afternoon? How about taking the rowing boat out?" he suggested.

"Well, then you'll have to do most of the rowing because I tend to pull squint and go round in circles," Alison admitted."

"That sounds like an excuse to get out of some exercise," he teased her. "Maybe you just need some expert instruction."

Alison was happily spending a few days in the Lake District with James. After she had completed her exams and had seen on the notice board that she had no orals or re-sits, she'd headed up to Oban to stay with her parents for the first week of her summer break. Apart from five days over Christmas she hadn't been home since the previous summer. At Easter, she'd stayed in Edinburgh and had been able to pick up some extra shifts at the Deli as some of the other student helpers had taken a break then. When she arrived back in Oban, she realised how much she'd missed seeing Jess, and she enjoyed being pampered by her mum. She'd been worried that she'd feel constantly on edge but, apart from taking action to avoid places where she thought she could bump into anyone from the McRae family, she'd managed to relax. Next, she'd gone to Glasgow to visit Helen and Neil. James drove through from Edinburgh on the Sunday to join her at Helen's and met her sister for the first time. She and James had set off for the Lake District on Monday morning. They were staying in a cottage which belonged to James's Great Aunt Lizzie who was currently in Canada visiting her daughter and family in Toronto. So, there was no rent to pay which made the break affordable for Alison. James had spent childhood family summer holidays here, so was familiar with the area, but hadn't visited since leaving school. After their drive and settling in yesterday they'd opted to spend today around the cottage. Once their juice was finished they ambled down the track to the lakeside taking the oars for Aunt Lizzie's boat with them from the garden hut. They had to shed their shoes and socks and paddle into the water to launch the boat, Alison was pleased that at this spot the lakebed was fine gravel as she had an aversion to mud and weed squelching up between her toes. The water wasn't too chilly and once they'd clambered in James installed himself to begin rowing.

"Which way do you want to go?" he asked. "Up towards Bank Ground Farm or down to Brantwood?" Alison voted for the Brantwood direction and they set off. They hadn't gone far when their boat was rocked by the wake of the Gondola which was steaming back to Coniston Pier from Brantwood with quite a crowd of passengers. It was an unusual looking vessel with a golden snake peering over its high pointed prow

"Wow, that's the way to travel. Have you ever been on it?" Alison asked.

"No, I think it's really old but it was out of commission for years. The National Trust re-furbished it, and it only began sailing again last year. Once the water has calmed down again I think you should have a go at rowing." Alison's uncoordinated rowing style had them zigzagging through the water as she over corrected and then lapsed to her usual lop-sided method. They were also both overcome by laughter which didn't help with the steering or their progress. Eventually they took one oar each and James was able to apply compensating strokes to keep them on an even course.

"What do you want to do tomorrow?" he asked once they'd eventually landed the boat back by the cottage.

"Well I think we should tackle the Old Man as long as the weather is OK for it." Alison was up for a challenge.

"OK, then maybe on Thursday we can take a drive down to Windermere and have lunch there."

"Sounds good. On the subject of food, will we barbeque those steaks for tonight?"

"Yeah, I'll get the coals going now, so we'll be ready to cook in about an hour. You could do the marinade." They climbed companionably back up to the cottage and set about preparing their evening meal, hungry after the outing on the lake.

On Wednesday, the weather was fair again and they took the car round to Coniston village then set off by Church Beck carrying their picnic lunch and plenty of water in a small rucksack. They followed the tumbling stream until the path struck off to the left up towards the Low Water. They planned to have a rest there before pushing on to the summit. Alison felt that she was coping quite well with the ascent until, as they were paused by a style over a stone wall preparing to climb over, to her astonishment a man came running down the hill, leapt over the style and ran on down the mountain.

"A fell runner," James explained.

"He didn't even look young," Alison complained, and it was true that the wiry athlete had definitely been grey haired. A bit put off by this display of extreme physical fitness they continued at a steady pace up to the tarn where they stopped to drink some of their water and share a Mars bar between them. Then they pushed on to the summit and were rewarded by a fantastic view over the lake including the Gondola in miniature. They sat under the cairn, feeling as if they were on top of the world, and ate their sandwiches. Alison pointed out and identified a buzzard gliding below them in the thermals, its wing tips fanned out. Its mewling call wafted up to them. Apart from that and some sheep baaing in the distance it was very quiet and peaceful.

"I thought it would be busier up here, especially in the summer," James commented. "Maybe it's more popular at weekends." They felt lucky to have the mountain to themselves. Their guidebook described how they could continue on to more adventurous walks, taking in several other peaks. But they decided to go back by much the same route with a slight detour to see the remains of old buildings from the copper mining era. When they reached the village, they bought ice cream cones and licked them while sitting on the edge of the wooden pier with their lower legs and feet dangling out over the water.

The next day they certainly encountered lots of other holidaymakers. The town of Bowness on Windermere was very busy and seemed to be a spot where coaches dropped off their tour passengers to spend an hour or two browsing round the shops. James had treated them to lunch on the terrace of the Old England Hotel where they looked out over the lake and watched the boat life as they ate. After lunch Alison wanted to shop for a 'thank you' gift to leave for Aunt Lizzie, but was now regretting the suggestion as they struggled along the crowded streets. They went into a craft shop and she was pleased to find a small painting of a local scene on silk with overlying embroidery and appliqué work which she thought would look good in the cottage's dining alcove. Having completed her purchase, which the assistant gift-wrapped for her, she and James decided to return to the hotel for their car and then escape from the crowds. As they came out from the shop doorway, Alison heard a very familiar voice which she recognised instantly.

"Alison is that you?" Her heart gave a massive thud. Sure enough, when she turned to look behind her, there was Gordon. He looked so handsome, wearing a white T-shirt with navy shorts and deck shoes which showed off to advantage his muscular, tanned limbs. His dark blond hair had natural sun bleached ends and his deep blue eyes were assessing her companion. Alison stuttered through introductions and Gordon shook hands with James.

"We're just here for a few days on holiday," she explained.

"I'm down at the Ullswater Centre for the summer. Today's my day off and a few of us came down here for lunch. It's always very busy, but there are some good spots that are quieter once you get to know the place."

"How's the job going?" she asked.

"It's good. I've been made full instructor now. I like it at Loch Eil best, it's almost like home, but it's a great centre that they have down here too. How about you? You must be about to start fourth year."

"Yes, on Monday. I've got General Practice first. I'm looking forward to it."

"Well I'd better let you get on, enjoy the rest of your holiday," he said and, after shaking hands with James again, he carried on past them along the pavement. Alison was trembling but tried not to let James see that she'd been upset. She should have known better though as James was well tuned in to her emotions.

"A bit awkward," he commented, taking her hand and leading her gently back towards the hotel car park.

"I can't believe that I spent a week skulking around the streets in Oban in case I came across one of his family and then I walk into him down here. I'd forgotten there was an Outward Bound Centre in the Lake District, but even if I'd remembered I thought he was safely up in Fort William."

"Yes, I think I'd prefer it if I thought he was safely out of the way, too," James remarked.

The next two days passed by quickly. On Friday, they took a walk through Grizdale Forest where the trails featured sculptures, many from wood, stone and other naturally occurring materials. James commented that a lot more pieces had been created since his last visit. On Saturday, they stayed around the cottage and took the boat out on the lake again, not really wanting to be in a car since the next day they would drive home. Although they were relaxed in each other's company Alison felt that their idyll had been spoiled by her meeting with Gordon. She recognised that he still exerted a strong effect on her, but she doubted that his outlook and priorities in life had changed any.

***

Monday morning was upon her very quickly marking the end of her holidays. Alison took the bus to Corstorphine, a suburb on the west side of the city where she was attached to a GP's surgery for the next month. On her first morning, she sat in on consultations with her tutor, Dr Crawford, and then went out with him on his house visits. She estimated that Dr Crawford was probably about the same age as her parents. He dressed in a smart but casual style, wearing a sports jacket, shirt and tie, and cords. She had noticed that some of the other GPs were more formal in suits. She was amazed by the variety of problems that they were presented with over the morning, from a very small baby with an infected umbilicus to an eighty-five year old lady who had fallen while out in her garden and had to be admitted to hospital as they suspected a fractured hip. She enjoyed spending the afternoon with the practice nurse who seemed very keen on health promotion. Most patients left her having had advice, and often clutching an information leaflet in their hand, about their diet or stopping smoking; even if they'd attended for something apparently unrelated, perhaps to have their ears syringed.

On Wednesday during morning surgery Dr Crawford received a phone call between patients.

"Tell her I'll be there immediately after surgery," he instructed. "That's about Mr Green, the patient with terminal lung cancer that we saw yesterday. His wife has just phoned to say he's passed away, obviously not unexpected. You can come with me later, worth seeing the procedure after a death," he told Alison.

When they arrived at the house, an hour later Mrs Green's face was tear-stained.

"I'll leave you with him," she stated and showed them into the sitting room where a temporary sickroom had been set up. She retreated to the kitchen and Alison could hear a low murmur of conversation from there, obviously someone had come to keep her company and offer support. The sitting room seemed incredibly quiet compared with yesterday's visit when the rasping sound of Mr Green's coarse, laboured breathing had dominated the proceedings. They approached the bed and Dr Crawford opened his case.

"You may think it's obvious that someone is dead, but it always has to be confirmed by a qualified doctor. It's as well to have a system to go through, because it'd be embarrassing to make a mistake and have someone wake up at the funeral home," he said.

He took out his stethoscope and ophthalmoscope. "I can do three things at once here: one, listen for a heartbeat, two, feel for the carotid pulse and three, observe the chest wall for any movement indicating respiration. I do this for two minutes." He opened the top buttons of Mr Green's pyjama jacket and applied the stethoscope over the left side of the chest wall while placing his fingers on the neck under the angle of the jaw. Alison thought that the skin had already acquired a waxy appearance. The two minutes seemed to last longer.

"Next I check for any pupillary reflexes." Dr Crawford turned on his ophthalmoscope light, then lifted Mr Green's upper lid and shone the beam into the eye. The pupil was unreactive and Alison could see that the front surface of the eye no longer looked clear but thickened and cloudy. The test was repeated on the other eye.

"This is an expected death, so we don't need to look for any signs of foul play and will be happy to issue a death certificate. If someone dies suddenly and it's unexplained or unexpected, we'd have to inform the police or the procurator fiscal."

"That must be upsetting for the relatives," Alison commented.

"It can be, but they usually appreciate the need to be thorough, and that a death has to be taken seriously. It's helpful at this stage to ask the relatives if they've planned on a burial or a cremation as we need extra paperwork and a second doctor's opinion if it's to be a cremation. So, we'll go and speak to Mrs Green now." He re-buttoned the pyjama top, carefully brushed both eyes closed with the palm of his hand and tucked the sheet up under Mr Green's chin.

"Best to remove any heavy bed-clothes, turn off heaters and open a window if you think there'll be any delay in getting an undertaker to come," he advised.

They knocked on the kitchen door and he went in to speak to Mrs Green and her daughter to learn that they'd already contacted the local undertaker's firm and had decided on a burial. Refusing offers of tea or coffee he told them that the death certificate would be ready for collection at the surgery by the end of the afternoon. He also offered to contact the district nurse who would arrange for the equipment in the temporary sickroom to be removed, allowing their lounge to return to normal. She climbed into the car with Dr Crawford and they set off towards the address of their next visit, a nine-year old boy with prolonged vomiting and abdominal pain.

"I'm happy for Mr Green," Dr Crawford told her. "He wanted to die at home, he was comfortable at the end and the process wasn't too protracted. There can be satisfaction in helping patients to have a good death." Alison was impressed by his attitude and realised that it had grown from understanding and caring about his patient.

By the end of her first week attached to the practice Alison was even more able to appreciate the extent of the GPs' knowledge about their patients. Frequently one of the doctors would make a comment which displayed the connections they made between patients;

"Ah now this patient we're about to see, Mrs Brown, remember the baby with the terrible nappy rash we saw yesterday? That's her grandson, his Mum's her youngest daughter." She was also surprised at the interest the patients obviously took in their GP's lives. Dr Crawford was asked at least once per surgery about how young Sheila was getting on at university or whether Douglas had heard about his exams yet. A few patients also asked after his dog. It certainly seemed quite different to the relationship that patients in hospital had with the consultants. When she mentioned this he explained,

"Well I've been working here for over twenty years and I live locally. Because we're on call from home for evenings, overnight and at weekends I don't want to be too far away. I suppose patients will have seen me out at the park with the kids when they were younger or going around the hill with the dog."

She enjoyed meeting all the members of the primary health care team, going on rounds with the district nurse, attending the baby clinic with the health visitor and doing antenatal checks with the community midwife. She was given a project to complete over the attachment which would involve visiting three diabetic patients of different ages, a child, a young adult and an elderly man to compare their experiences and treatments. She thought it would be interesting and had phoned to arrange suitable times to visit each of them in the next week.

On her way home by bus on Friday she thought about her original vision when she started medical school of being a GP and working in Oban. She had come to feel since living in the city that small town life was less attractive. She could now imagine that being a GP in a small town might be too claustrophobic for her, but maybe a city practice would be OK. She had liked the range of different problems she'd seen this week and being able to get out visiting patients at home added to the variety.

From her seat on the left side of the bus she could see the entrance to the Zoo as they passed, and then as she caught sight of the Murrayfield Hotel her thoughts turned to the visit that her parents were planning in three weeks' time to coincide with her twenty-first birthday. They were going to be staying at the Murrayfield. They'd asked her where she'd like to go for a special meal on her birthday and Helen, Neil, Karen, Chris and James were all invited. She should phone tonight to let her Mum know she'd decided on Denzlers Restaurant in Queens Street. Elaine had been taken there for lunch after her graduation and had recommended it highly. She also needed to confirm her booking for Nicky Tams for her party. She was having it on the Saturday after her birthday so it was only four weeks away now. James was working tonight so she didn't have a date and wasn't in a hurry. She could call in to Nicky Tams on her way home. Once she got off the bus in Princes Street and climbed the Playfair steps by the art galleries her route took her past the top of Victoria Street, so it wouldn't be out of her way.

Eighteen

Alison's twenty-first birthday fell on a Wednesday. By then she had moved on from General Practice to her first week of a four week block in Care the Elderly. She went in to the Royal Victoria Hospital as normal on the morning of her birthday but planned to leave early if possible. When she arrived in the ward office one of the consultants, Dr Shore, asked if she would like to go out on a domiciliary visit with her. Geriatricians were one of the few hospital consultant groups who visited patients at home, believing that it gave them more insight into what were often very complex problems. Today they were going to visit a lady who at the age of one hundred and six was still living at home but was almost completely confined to her bedroom, only moving between bed, a commode and an armchair.

"The problem is that the daughter, who is her main carer, is now aged eighty-two so elderly herself. She really needs to have hip replacement surgery carried out for bad arthritis and so obviously won't be able to look after her Mum. We need to try and work out a care plan for the old lady," Dr Shore explained as she drove them towards Trinity, a smart area by the Firth of Forth. When they arrived at the house, they were greeted by a white-haired elderly lady with a marked limp.

"I'll take you through to meet mother," she offered. They followed her into a room where a tiny figure was propped up in bed on multiple pillows. Her scalp was bald but for a few wispy, white hairs. Her skin was so thin that it almost appeared to be transparent and her multiple wrinkles showed that it was now several sizes too large for her frame. She peered in their direction with watery blue eyes as her daughter introduced them, speaking in a very loud voice.

"Mother, it's the doctor," she said.

"I've no need for doctors," was the feisty reply. "There's nothing wrong with me but old age and my daughter Margaret looks after me fine."

"Well her mind seems sharp enough," Alison thought. She didn't envy Dr Shore's task of persuading the old lady that perhaps Margaret needed a rest. Eventually they came to an agreement that she would go for 'a holiday' in a local Nursing Home while Margaret had her operation.

"I do feel slightly guilty," Dr Shore admitted on the drive back. "We purposefully didn't mention that Margaret isn't likely to be fit to have her Mum back home."

"I think she might have guessed that," Alison said. "She seemed sharp enough mentally."

"Yes, and hopefully she'll like the Nursing Home once she's settled in; there will be more company for her. And I think we're doing Margaret a service as she's probably been looking after her 'old Mum' for twenty years or more. I'm sure she's earned a rest."

"I hope she looks at it that way and doesn't feel guilty," Alison commented. They arrived back at the hospital at lunchtime and Alison decided to head for home as she had nothing pressing scheduled for the afternoon. There were only ward rounds, which might be interesting but didn't involve her directly.

When she arrived back at the flat, Karen rushed to greet her.

"Happy Birthday," she yelled and enveloped Alison in a large hug. "Come and open all your cards, the postman's been and you've got flowers, too."

"I think I need something to eat first, I haven't had lunch yet," Alison headed towards the kitchen.

"Well I put everything on the table through here anyway. You sit down and I'll get you a sandwich," Karen offered.

It was great to have Karen here with her in the flat. When she first arrived back from the Lake District, she'd been on her own as Liz and Elaine had both graduated and moved out. Linda was back in Chester for the summer and Karen, though back from France, was at a boarding school near Perth working with Chris at a residential music summer school. She had just returned at the weekend and moved in to what had been Liz's room at the front of the flat, opposite Alison. The girls had agreed that it seemed daft for Alison to move all her belongings in order to vacate Karen's original room. Karen was just as happy in her new room which was actually a bit bigger and Alison was enjoying her company, though she didn't see her in the mornings as she had to be up and out early to get to the hospital and Karen could sleep in.

She munched on a cheese and pickle sandwich as she opened a pile of envelopes to reveal cards with good wishes from family members, friends from Oban and university friends too. Karen produced a card and a brightly wrapped gift.

"It's from me and Chris, it'll go well with the present from your parents."

After consultation Alison's parents had bought her a new music centre with a turntable, cassette player and radio. James had set it up in her bedroom for her but so far, she didn't have a lot of music to play on it. She unwrapped Karen's gift to find a selection of cassette tapes; Mahler's 1st symphony, Gershwin's Rhapsody in Blue, a Corries collection of Scottish folk songs and a Joan Armatrading album.

"We know you like all sorts of music, so these should cover most moods," Karen explained.

"Thank you," Alison gave her a hug.

"I put your flowers in the bath," said Karen. "There are two bunches."

"Two?" Alison looked puzzled, expecting that James might send a bouquet.

"Do we have two vases?" she asked as she went through to the bathroom to retrieve the flowers. One bouquet was of pink and white roses and the card read, 'Happy Twenty-first Birthday with Love from James'. The second was a yellow and white creation with a mixture of roses, carnations, chrysanthemums, gerbera and baby's breath. The card was in an envelope, it seemed to be tricky to get it out. Eventually after much fumbling the card emerged, she opened it and read, 'I couldn't forget your special birthday. Congratulations and have a Very Happy Day. Best Wishes from Gordon.'

"Wow, he's resurfaced again," she thought. "That was nice of him," she commented to Karen as they divided and arranged the flowers between two vases and a milk jug and placed them around the lounge. Alison also made a display of her cards on the mantelpiece. Karen wasn't fooled by Alison's seemingly cool façade as she had previously been taken into Alison's confidence about the meeting in Bowness.

Alison spent the early afternoon relaxing in her room listening to some of her new music selection. Then she had a soak in the bath, washing her hair and shaving her legs and armpits. She always reckoned that it took about three hours to prepare for going out. After bathing she massaged in body lotion and used the hairdryer to tame and style her hair. Next, she applied nail varnish to her fingers and toes. She listened to more music as it dried. Then she was ready to don the purple silk two-piece which she'd made from a Vogue pattern with Elaine's sewing machine, which she would miss. Make-up, perfume and jewellery were her finishing touches. She'd found a bracelet and earrings set of silver and amethyst to match her outfit at Galerie Mirages in Stockbridge and bought it, knowing that she was guaranteed to receive some birthday money from her aunt and grandmother.

She heard the jangle of the doorbell just before six o'clock and, pleased to be ready on time, rushed to let her parents in. Mr Scott had two bottles of Bollinger grasped by the neck in each hand. He placed them on the hall floor in order to give Alison a large hug which lifted her feet off the floor.

"Happy Birthday," he greeted her after kissing her on both cheeks. "Can we store these in the fridge until the others arrive? Oh, hello Karen, you can show me where your glasses are so we're all prepared." He headed off into the kitchen with the bottles and Karen followed. Alison's Mum greeted her more gently and complimented her on her smart dress. They went through to the lounge together.

"What a beautiful display of cards and flowers," her Mum remarked and proceeded to the mantelpiece to see who the senders were. "Oh, Auntie Sally remembered, that's good, and here's one from Fiona from the shop. And who's Morag? One of your medical student friends? I like this one from Helen. Oh, did Gordon send flowers?" she turned to look at Alison.

"Yes, the yellow ones," she could feel herself begin to blush under her Mum's scrutiny. "We've not been in touch at all. Oh, there's the door again, I'd better get it," she escaped out of the lounge and was greeted by Helen and Neil when she opened the front door. James and Chris weren't long in arriving to complete the gathering. Then Mr Scott made a ceremony of opening the champagne and toasting the birthday girl. Alison appreciated the effort that they'd all made to be there and opened two more gifts. The first was a small package from Helen which contained a silver leaf-shaped pendant, intricate with details of veins and texture and sprinkled with small faceted peridot stones representing dew drops.

"Oh, it's beautiful, thank you," Alison said while fastening the chain behind her neck.

"I wanted to get you something that was your birth stone, but not too traditional. I'm glad you like it," Helen said looking pleased. James's gift was much larger and out of the packaging emerged a framed watercolour painting by Ken Lochhead. It showed a misty Edinburgh skyline with silhouettes of famous landmarks, the crown of St Giles Cathedral, the dome of the Bank of Scotland and the castle.

"Thank you, James; it'll look great in my room. It's certainly a lot more grown up than my old posters. Oh, and for the flowers as well."

They had ordered two taxis to arrive at seven fifteen and ferry them to the restaurant for dinner. As they clattered down the close stairs, Alison was bringing up the rear with James. She grabbed his hand to stop him a step below her and pressed up close, kissing him warmly.

***

At Nicky Tams James and Alison were in a tight embrace dancing to the strains of Sheena Easton's 'For Your Eyes Only', the theme from that summer's Bond film. Alison's skin was moist with sweat from the exertion of a night of dancing and the muggy heat in the low-ceilinged cellar venue. She was bare-foot and dancing on tiptoes as her high-heeled sandals had started to hurt her feet half way into the evening. The party was going well and she felt that her friends must be enjoying themselves; as although it would soon be closing time most of her crowd was still around her on the dance floor. She grinned as the music changed to Stevie Wonder's single "Happy Birthday". She'd lost count of how many times the track had been played during the party; and of course, everyone made sure she danced each time. Then the beat changed again getting even faster. It was a very new release "Happy Birthday, Happy Birthday" by Altered Images. The song was so infectiously bouncy that even though everyone had seemed tired, now they all jumped up and down in time. That was the last song and they gathered their belongings, including shoes, and clambered up from the cellars to the street.

"It was great to end with a lively number," Karen yelled as they began to walk up George IV Bridge towards home.

"You don't need to shout anymore," Chris commented. "We're all right next to you."

"My ears are ringing, though," said Alison. "You don't realise how loud it is till it stops. Thanks for coming back specially," she added, linking arms with Linda. "Oh, I'm a bit wobbly on my feet. These sandals are killing me."

"Nothing to do with all the drink, then?" Chris asked.

"Don't be cheeky," Alison retorted.

"I was happy to have an excuse to come back up early." Linda continued on the previous theme. "Now I'll be able to take in a bit of the festival, I've always been in Chester when it's on."

"Yeah, last summer was the first time I was around for the festival; and I thought it was great. I'll still try to see some things this year, but I've got quite a lot of work to keep up with," Alison sighed. Now that her birthday celebrations were over she'd have to concentrate on preparing a case presentation for the team at the Royal Victoria next week and then she'd be moving on to the Andrew Duncan Clinic for her psychiatry block after that. However, it was still Saturday night, or rather early Sunday morning, so she wouldn't dwell on work and spoil the party spirit. She gave herself an internal shake and patted the statue of Greyfriars Bobby as she came level.

"Hey, I've got some champagne in the fridge that I got as a present, will we pop it when we get back to the flat?" she suggested.

"I think I might rather have some hot chocolate," Karen said. She'd never quite regained her taste for alcohol after having chemotherapy, usually only having one or two glasses in order to fit in with the crowd.

"We can do both," Alison agreed.

"And is there anything to eat," Chris asked. "I'm famished."

"Nothing new there," Karen laughed. "I'm sure we'll have some cheese, but don't get too excited it's probably just cheddar. We miss Alison's freebies from the deli now that she's given up her job."

"Yeah, it's a shame, but I just felt I'd need the weekends to study now that I'm in final phase. I'll have degree exams every four months. Oh, why do I always keep talking about work? I suppose it's because the rest of you are all still on holiday," she complained.

"Not me," James reminded her. He'd been very quiet on their walk, and she realised he was probably exhausted as he'd been on-call on Friday overnight and had to stay for a Saturday morning ward-round, only grabbing a few hours of sleep before her party.

"I know you're used to sleep deprivation, but do you just want to crash when we get in?" she asked him.

"Oh, I might manage some of that champagne first, it sounded good," he replied. "All this fresh air's wakening me up." They were crossing the Meadows now and the night was clear enough to allow a view of stars to peep through the trees. "At least we don't have an early start tomorrow."

"No, we can have a last lazy day," Alison agreed.

Nineteen

The wind was swooping up piles of leaves and swirling them into mini-tornadoes as Alison crossed Bruntsfield Links heading back to the flat on a Friday afternoon in late October. The gale was causing her hair to escape in tendrils from her scrunchie and flap around her face. She usually walked to and from the Andrew Duncan clinic, but on her way home today a bus was approaching as she came round the corner onto Morningside Road. She'd run to catch it, thus escaping some of the stormy weather. She hurried up the path towards the flat and let a few leaves blow past her into the close hallway before she could shut the front door.

"Phew," she thought, "I don't really feel like going out again tonight."

However, she knew that she should go to the FYC disco or she'd feel guilty for not supporting it. Each year-group over the span of their course held fund-raising events to make money for their graduation ball and year-book. As is the way of such things, the organisation usually fell to the same group of people, which didn't include Alison; but she felt bad if she didn't at least back their efforts. Tonight, it was a Halloween themed disco at the Americana. Alison was planning to go as a ghost. She had borrowed a cream skirt from Karen and was teaming it with an off-white blouse, cream tights and white gym-shoes. She was going to brush talcum powder through her hair and had bought some white face paint from the toy shop in Morningside. She'd arranged to meet Robert and Alastair at the Golf Tavern before going to the venue. James wasn't on-call for his unit tonight, but he was currently studying for his Membership exam which he needed to pass in order to progress up the career ladder. He was also honest enough to say that her FYC events made him feel a bit ancient since he was at least four years older than everyone else there. Alison was going to try to persuade Linda to accompany her. Colin had broken up their relationship on his return to Edinburgh a month ago as apparently, he'd met someone else over the summer break. Linda had been glum since then and Alison thought a night out might cheer her up.

When she came into the flat, she could see into Karen's room as the door was ajar.

"Hi," she called. "You still here?" She pushed the door open a bit farther to see Karen stuffing toiletries into a small suitcase.

"Yeah, I'm running a bit late if I'm to catch the five o'clock train. Can you lend me your green hat? I've got nothing that goes with this jacket and my head will be freezing in this wind, that's one disadvantage of short hair."

"Sure," Alison went into her own room, found the hat and placed it on Karen's head, pulling it snugly down over her ears. "Off you go then. Say hello to Chris."

She followed Karen to their front door and waved to her as she clattered down the stairs. Karen and Chris were spending a second year apart as Chris had accepted a place at the Royal College of Music in London for a two-year Masters course in musical performance. It was a great chance for him to progress and Karen was beginning to talk about moving to London herself next year after her graduation. However, they had yet to live through another year of snatched weekends, letters and phone-calls. Alison thought that if they were still together by the end of this year then they were likely to survive as a couple.

She went into the kitchen and put the kettle on to make coffee, then wondered if Linda was in and might want a drink. She found her in the lounge reading a heavy textbook.

"Want a coffee?" she asked.

"Mmm, that'd be good," Linda replied, glancing up momentarily. When Alison returned with the coffees, Linda put her book aside and asked about Alison's day on the ward. She'd shown quite an interest in her experiences during this attachment as there was some overlap between psychiatry and her own psychology course.

"I went with one of the patients for his ECT session," Alison reported. "I'm not sure what I think about it really," she admitted.

She explained that Bill, a balding middle-aged man, had already been on the ward when she arrived there nearly two months ago. He could usually be found slumped in a corner seat of the patient's lounge apparently gazing into space, hardly even blinking. If spoken to, he seemed to re-surface from a great depth taking a very long time to respond and his answers, although not unhelpful, were slowly spoken and often mono-syllabic. He didn't take part in any of the therapeutic group sessions unless someone asked him a direct question; which generally was avoided as he took so long to respond. Occasionally Alison had noticed a trail of tears running down his face unchecked. From his case notes she'd discovered that he was married with two children and until recently had worked as a manager of a supermarket. His illness seemed to have been brought on by the death of his father nine months previously. He began to retreat into himself, finding everyday tasks more and more difficult until he'd just seemed to stop functioning. He didn't eat or drink unless helped and stopped washing or changing his clothes. Unfortunately, he hadn't responded to the anti-depressant drugs that his GP had prescribed and eventually he came into the ward because his wife became unable to cope with him. On the ward, a higher dose of medication was tried with little effect and the nursing staff had to cajole him into eating, drinking and showering. The professor described his condition as depression with severe psycho-motor retardation and three weeks ago had suggested ECT treatment as an effective option for Bill. Alison had been surprised, she hadn't realised that ECT was still used and, like a lot of people, had the impression that it was a rather barbaric blunderbuss procedure. However, there was no doubt that after having had twice weekly ECT sessions for the past three weeks, Bill seemed to be much improved. So, given the chance today Alison had accompanied Bill to the ECT suite.

"Wasn't it gross seeing someone have an induced fit?" Linda asked.

"It wasn't so bad, he was given an anaesthetic and a muscle relaxant, then once he was asleep he had the electrodes applied to his scalp and the current was administered. It really only made him twitch a bit because of the drugs, but it did still seem unpleasant."

"Does he complain of any side effects?" Linda wanted to know.

"Yeah, he feels a bit muddled for the rest of the day. But he's so much better – yesterday he spontaneously said 'hello' to me and he's got some expression back on his face. It's hard to describe the improvement, it sounds minimal, but it seems huge."

"I'll need to read about it," Linda decided. "It sounds as if it has a role but got a bad press in the old days because they over used it."

Alison decided to begin on her campaign to get Linda to go out with her that night.

"You're not really going to do any more reading tonight though, are you? D'you want to come to the FYC disco with me?" she asked. "After all you were a member of the year for a term; you'll know lots of people."

"Oh, I don't know. I'm not sure about the fancy dress," Linda replied. Alison thought this was encouraging, not an all out "no".

"I'm sure we could think of something simple. You could be a ghost like me, or a vampire or zombie is quite easy," she coaxed.

"Mmm, well if you help me to put a costume together I'll come," Linda agreed. The friends went into their rooms to rummage through drawers and wardrobes for suitable gear.

At the Golf Tavern it was easy to spot Robert as he was dressed in a black cloak and a top hat. Given that he was already over six feet tall he stood out from the crowd.

"I don't think Count Dracula had red hair," Alison greeted him.

"Well I wasn't going to the extreme of hair-dye," he replied. "Can I get you both a drink? Nice to see you Linda, are you the ghost of a hockey player?"

"Yes, well spotted." Linda had managed to find white shorts and polo-shirt, added white socks and trainers and borrowed Alison's idea of talc and face paint. She'd brought along her stick wrapped in white bandages. "A half of cider please."

"I'll have the same please. Is Alastair not here yet?" Alison asked

"Nah, he's out at Bangour doing obstetrics, so thought he'd be running a bit late." In final phase, the students could be placed in hospitals across the Lothians, over in

Fife or down in the Borders as well as in the Edinburgh wards.

"How've you been getting on with surgery?" Alison asked Robert when he came back from the bar with their drinks. "Still think it's for you?"

"Yeah, it's been great. I got to do a fair bit of stitching last week, Mr Roper's cool."

"Are you on your elective next?" Linda asked. "I find it hard to keep track of what you're all up to." The last two years of the medical course, or 'final phase' consisted of six blocks of clinical experience in rotation, but students could start off at any point on the cycle. Robert had started with surgery, so next he had his elective period of four months when he could choose a subject that interested him, and also where to study it, with no exam at the end. Lots of students took this opportunity to go abroad if they, or their parents, could fund it.

"I'm going to Canada. My uncle lives in Toronto, so I can stay with him and I've arranged an attachment at Mount Sinai Hospital, two months in A and E and two months in general surgery."

"Will you be there over Christmas?" Alison asked.

"Yeah, but that'll be OK, I'll still be with family. I've met my Aunt and Uncle and cousins a few times. They've been back here to see my grandparents and we had a holiday in Canada when I was about ten. I'll get on with them fine. I'm quite looking forward to all the snow over there."

"It sounds good. I do my elective last, so I haven't even thought about it yet," Alison commented.

"Wow, you're one of the lucky ones, you get all of your exams out of the way early," Robert was envious.

"Yeah, that's OK as long as I pass them," Alison quipped. "Can't say I'm feeling over confident for the ones coming up next month. I think this'll be my last night off, I'll have to start studying."

"You'll be fine," Robert reassured her. "Hey, look what that daft bugger dressed up as!" This as an apparition made its way towards them.

"You're assuming that's Alastair. It could be anyone," Alison giggled. The person was wearing a rubber facemask which also had hair. Its complexion was greenish with bulging, jaundiced eyes and thin, whitish lips. The hair was long, straggly and grey. On his body, he was wearing a loose tunic-like garment which appeared to be made out of sacking and was given a waist by a piece of rope tied as a belt. The bare legs were hairy (yes, it was definitely a man) and he had sandals on his feet.

"Well, given that it's not actually Halloween until tomorrow, and we're the only people in here wearing costumes, I'd bet on it being him," Robert stated. "Hey, you'll need a straw to drink your pint, man," he called to Alastair.

"I hadn't thought of that," came a muffled reply. Then Alastair's features were revealed as he tugged the mask off.

"You look a bit red in the face," Alison commented.

"It was hot, smelly and a challenge to breathe," he admitted. "Where's that pint you mentioned Robert?" Robert went up to the bar to buy a drink." I think I'll only be wearing the mask for my grand entrance," Alastair decided.

"What are you actually meant to be?" Linda ventured to ask.

"A mad monk, of course," was the answer.

After a few drinks, the friends decided to make their way to the disco. They attracted a few glances and comments as they walked along Leven Street and past the King's theatre towards Toll Cross.

"Did y is jist come aff the stage?" one joker suggested. Alastair also got a few jibes about his legs. "Yer a bit old to be guising, it's for the weans," a woman at the bus stop commented. They turned left after the Cameo cinema into Thornybauk and soon saw the old Meat Market building, now converted into the Americana nightclub ahead of them. Once they were in past the door, Alastair with his head-gear back in place, they could hear that the DJ had selected a seasonal hit. "The Monster Mash" was booming out. They were enveloped into the dancing crowd of witches, vampires, ghouls and other strange creatures.

***

Two weeks later Alison was writing furiously to finish her answers on the care of the elderly exam paper. She glanced up at the clock at the front of the hall, five more minutes. She'd been nervous this morning hurrying along Chambers Street towards Adam House. Although it was a familiar venue, she'd been there for end of term exams over the past three years; because today's was a final degree exam, this seemed more serious. The morning paper for psychiatry had been multiple choice and she thought it had gone OK. But there were five marks for this last essay question about possible pitfalls in prescribing for elderly patients and so far she'd only managed to think of four points. Oh, it came to her, memory problems leading to muddled compliance, the use of dosette boxes. She scribbled on as quickly as she could and was just finished as the invigilator asked them to put down their pens.

"Whew, just made it," she thought, flapping her right wrist around and massaging her thumb to ease the writer's cramp. She tidied her pens and ruler into her pencil case, retrieved her coat and scarf from the back of her chair and followed her classmates out of the hall and downstairs. The fresh air as she emerged onto the street was welcome after the stuffy, overheated building. She caught up with Callum, who'd been one of the other students at the Andrew Duncan clinic.

"We're going to Bobby's Bar for a few drinks. Want to come?" he invited her.

"Sure." They set off along Chambers Street towards the pub.

Twenty

From her seat behind the consultant, Dr Osborne, Alison listened as he took the patient's history and watched as he carried out an examination. It seemed strange to only have a weekend off after exams and then be straight back into a new attachment. There were no holidays due until Christmas. She'd need to go across to the medical school at lunchtime to see if the results list was up. The good thing about her current block in medicine was that it was twice as long as all the others, so there would be no more exams for eight months.

"Miss Scott would you like to take some blood off for me? A red, brown and yellow tube should be OK. Oh, and an ESR please."

Alison was jolted out of her day-dreaming and at once her stomach started to churn. She'd been warned that students were often asked to take the blood samples at outpatient clinics, but she hadn't tried again since that day in physiology when she'd fainted, and she didn't want to make a fool of herself. She went across to the equipment trolley and picked up the tourniquet.

"Can I see your arms please Mr Thomson?" she asked. The patient was still shirtless after his examination and she was relieved to notice that he had slim arms and veins that she could see even before applying the tourniquet. She put it on his left arm above the elbow and pulled it tightly. Then she went to collect the syringe, needle and tubes. Her hands were shaking as she lined up the needle with the protruding vein, but she managed to force it in and saw a flash-back of blood. She pulled back on the plunger steadily but felt her hand slipping a bit with nervous sweat. She was in danger of pulling the whole thing out before she had enough blood. Thankfully she managed to steady the base of the needle with her other hand and complete the task. She removed the needle and applied pressure with a piece of cotton wool.

"Just press hard on the cotton wool to stop the bleeding," she instructed the patient. She decanted the blood into the different coloured tubes for each test, heart hammering. Then she went back to check that the bleeding had stopped and applied a plaster.

"Thank you, Miss Scott," the consultant said. She was still feeling panicked but thankfully not faint. It was good that she'd managed OK, but now she would be sitting for the rest of the morning worrying about having to take more blood, and what if the next person had difficult veins?

By the end of the morning she had successfully taken blood from four more patients. When she'd obviously been having difficulty finding a vein on either arm of a plump woman patient, Dr Osborne had come to her rescue without belittling her.

"Mmm, this one's a bit tricky," he agreed. "Let me have a look, I think we might need a smaller needle and attempt from the back of the hand. Want me to take over?" he asked and Alison had thankfully acquiesced.

After the clinic had finished she made her way out of the hospital at the east gate then crossed Middle Meadow Walk and entered the medical school quad by the vennel there. She always hated the moment of checking the list on the notice board. She crossed the quad, pulled on the heavy wooden door and entered the hallway. In contrast to previous occasions it was deserted; no wall of bodies and heads to peer over. Maybe she was too early, but it could just be that the students, instead of arriving straight out from a lecture en masse, were now spread about at different locations. She could see that there were white pages up on display, found the relevant list and saw her name amongst the passes. She gave a sigh of relief and, feeling a weight lift from around her stomach and a sudden burst of hunger, went to buy some lunch.

After lunch, she went to her ward to ask the houseman if there were any new admissions that she could help clerk in. The unit accepted general medical admissions on their on-take days but otherwise specialised in gastro-intestinal problems.

"Oh, could you take Mrs Ford? She's come in for investigation of blood in her stools. I've done her bloods and sent them off, but if you could do her admission that would be great."

The harassed junior doctor handed her a case file and indicated a thin, pale woman, two beds down the ward.

"Then you could present her at the ward round tomorrow morning," he suggested. "Dr O. likes students to be hands on. I'd suggest you think carefully and maybe do some reading tonight. He'll expect you to come up with a reasonable differential diagnosis." Alison headed onto the ward to admit the patient, thankful for this advice and already beginning to feel that she was a useful addition to the medical team. She thought that she would enjoy this unit.

***

The week before the Christmas holidays Alison was feeling miserable with a bad cold. She'd taken the day off in case her sneezing and constantly running nose passed on the virus, causing more problems for patients on the ward who were already ill and run down. She sat in the lounge wearing her pyjamas, with a crocheted blanket wrapped around her. Despite dosing herself up with aspirin, a hot lemon drink and having the electric fire turned full on she still felt chilled. A run of arpeggios came drifting from Karen's bedroom as she practised her flute. Alison balled another sodden tissue and aimed for the waste-paper basket. Then their doorbell gave its clattering ring.

"I'll get it," Karen called.

Alison could hear voices but hadn't worked out who the visitor was when Liz came into the lounge with Karen.

"Hi, there. Sorry you're not so well. I've brought mince pies, interested?"

"Mmm, I love mince pies, I'm not that ill," Alison replied. "What brings you here?"

Liz explained that she was in Edinburgh attending accounting lectures but had popped over on her lunch break to see if anyone was home. Karen, returning from putting the mince pies in the oven to heat, asked her how her job was going.

"Oh, I'm enjoying it. So far, I've been sent to about six different firms to audit their accounts. I go with one of the partners or a more senior apprentice, so they basically tell me what to do. The jobs are all quite different though, I've done a butcher's, a golf club and a decorating firm. Some weeks I'm just in the office preparing accounts and I've got quite a lot of course assignments to hand in, too."

"Sounds busy," Karen commented.

"It must be nice to be earning a salary. Did you have a splurge with your first pay packet?" Alison asked.

"I bought the most expensive pair of shoes I've ever owned," Liz admitted. "They're gorgeous, but not very practical."

"Are you going to be one of these shoe fetish ladies with cupboards full of them?" Alison asked.

"Not likely on my apprentice salary," Liz commented. "I'll get a substantial pay rise when I pass my exams, though, and a few of us are planning a big trip to California for a holiday then. What're you doing for Christmas, going home?" she asked.

"I'm going through to Glasgow to Helen's then going up to Oban for Christmas with her and Neil. I'll be back here for New Year cos James doesn't get much time off. Karen's going to be back for New Year, too," Alison said.

"Yeah, I'm going to my parents for a few days at Christmas, otherwise I'm here. Chris is coming up for New Year."

"I'll maybe come over then, too," said Liz. "Would there be any floor space?"

"I don't think Linda will be around, I'm sure you could have her room, and there's always the couch if she changes her mind," Karen offered.

"OK, you're on," Liz decided. "But I'd better be getting back to lectures." The visit from Liz had cheered Alison up and she'd enjoyed two warm mince pies with her lemon drink.

***

A clock began to chime and the restless crowd erupted into cries of 'Happy New Year'. People were embracing, kissing and passing bottles around, drinking a toast to good luck in the coming year. A couple of youths had climbed on top of a bus shelter and were dancing a jig there while two policemen were encouraging them to come down in case they hurt themselves. The throng of revellers, including the police who had been noticed greeting people with a handshake, seemed to be in a relaxed and genial mood. It was Alison's first time at the Tron for Hogmany, and although she wasn't a fan of big crowds, she felt up-lifted by the collective good spirits. It helped that it was a crisp, dry night with stars brilliant above them. She and Karen had cooked a simple dinner of haggis, tatties and neeps followed by trifle. They'd been joined by Chris, James and Liz for a cosy evening in the flat before crossing the Meadows and walking up to the Tron for the bells.

"Happy New Year," Karen gave Alison a hug. After a few minutes, the crowd slowly began to disperse, parties would be starting up all around the city.

"Where exactly is your friend's flat?" Alison asked Chris. They had been asked to join a party held by one of Chris's musician friends. They'd been warned that everyone would be expected to contribute, by playing, singing or, if not musical, reciting a poem. Chris and Karen had their instruments with them.

"It's just off the top of Leith Walk, so if we go down the Bridges and then onto Leith Street we're almost there," Chris directed. They had to wiggle a path through milling bodies to the corner of North Bridge, but then the going was easier and they set off at a brisk pace towards Princes Street.

"Hey, did you get my cold?" Alison asked Karen, noticing that she was coughing.

"Yeah, I had a cold over Christmas when I was back home. I think it's nearly gone, probably just this frosty air catching my throat," she replied.

"Wrap you scarf round your mouth and nose then," Chris advised and began to demonstrate. This turned into a joke as he enveloped Karen in his own scarf in addition, and then pulled her hat down low so that her eyes were covered, too. She played along, miming, arms out straight, hands feeling for imaginary objects while she took exaggeratedly small, tentative steps, staggering slowly in a zigzag course along the wide pavement.

"Come on," Alison and Liz grabbed an arm each. We'll never get to the party at this rate." They whirled Karen off between them.

The party was in full swing when they arrived. There must have been around twenty people and Alison could count three violins, two guitars, a flute and a bodhran played by various musicians. They were jamming, playing mainly Scottish folk tunes in keeping with the occasion. Alison was able to enjoy herself better once she'd got her 'piece' out of the way. She'd decided on Burns but hadn't been able to rely on her memory, reading from a collection of his poems.

Then let us pray that come it may,

As come it will for a' that,

That sense and worth, o'er a' the earth,

May bear the gree, an' a' that.

For a' that, an' a' that,

It's coming yet, for a' that,

That man to man, the world o'er,

Shall brothers be for a' that.

James gave her hand an encouraging squeeze as she finished to a small applause and a few cheers, and now she was humming along to a rendition of 'Westering Home'

"I used to know all the words to this in Primary school," she said, sipping from her glass of wine.

"I hope I can remember all the word to my poem, it dates back to primary school days, too," James replied. He'd chosen a very relevant poem 'Ring out, wild Bells' by Alfred, Lord Tennyson and when his turn came he gave a near perfect recitation.

"I think it would've been easier just to have brought a tambourine and joined in with the musicians," he commented afterwards.

"Maybe, but I think our poems added a lot to the atmosphere," Alison averred, alcohol accentuating her emotions.

"Well I'm about to lower the tone," said Liz, and then went on to lead them all in a jolly performance of

Coulter's Candy, musicians played along and everyone joined in on the chorus:

"Ally bally, ally bally bee,

Sittin' on yer mammy's knee,

Greetin' for a wee bawbee,

Tae buy some Coulter's Candy."

The party kept its momentum for hours and it was nearly six o'clock by the time the friends climbed up the stairs of the Spottiswoode Street flat, quiet now as they were all weary. Karen's cough echoed off the tiled walls.

***

Karen continued to cough and three days later when Monday came around Alison tackled her about it.

Don't you think that you should go to see the doctor with that cough, it doesn't seem to be getting any better?"

"Oh, don't make a fuss; it's just the tail end of a cold. I'm not going to the doctor about every sniffle," Karen sounded cross. "I've got a mother at home who wants to molly-coddle me. Don't you start." Alison was surprised by Karen's aggressive tone so she backed off, but didn't feel happy about it.

Coming back to the flat two nights later after seeing a film with James she could hear a strange noise as she closed the front door behind her. It was a rhythmic

217

squeaking, a bit like a record left running on a turntable but higher pitched. It seemed to be coming from Karen's room so she knocked and stuck her head round the door. Karen was propped up on pillows in bed, her breathing fast and shallow and her eyes closed. The noise was produced by every exhalation.

"Karen, are you OK?" Alison asked anxiously. Karen's head flopped on the pillow and her eyes opened slightly.

"Oh God, what am I going to do?" Alison tried to think clearly. She recognised that Karen needed medical help but, since Linda was still on holiday, she was on her own in the flat with no phone. "Maybe the neighbours have a phone," she thought. "It would be quicker to try that than going to the phone box. But should I phone 999, or just the doctor – oh I wish James had come up with me, he won't be home yet either after dropping me off, so no use phoning him." She grasped Karen's wrist and could feel her pulse hammering; the rate must be well over a hundred but she didn't stop to count.

"Karen I'm going out to phone." She decided to try the flat across the hall; she knew it was owned by a couple that the friends jokingly called the yuppies, they were sure to have a phone. She rang their bell and hoped they'd be in. She could hear footsteps coming and was relieved when the male yuppie opened the door.

"Hi, I'm from across the hall. D'you think I could use your phone? My friend is really ill, she can hardly breathe and we don't have a phone."

"Sure, come away in, it's just here in the hall."

Alison had decided on 999 after feeling Karen's pulse rate. She gave all the details to the controller on the other end of the line and thanked her neighbour. He offered to go down to the front door to look out for the ambulance and Alison went back to sit with Karen until it arrived. Witnessing Karen's every laboured breath it seemed to take ages for help to come, but it must only have been around ten minutes when she heard heavy footsteps and voices on the stair. She was relieved to give over responsibility to the ambulance crew who had brought oxygen and a chair stretcher. They wrapped Karen up in blankets and strapped her into the chair before setting off down the stairs with her. Alison grabbed her handbag and keys and followed them; she'd need to phone Karen's parents from the hospital.

Twenty-one

Alison rode along in the back of the ambulance accompanying Karen to the Western General hospital. When they arrived, she was shown to the waiting area of the A+E department while Karen was wheeled through to the clinical area to be assessed. After about an hour, when she was just starting to doze off despite the uncomfortable plastic chair, a doctor came to inform her that Karen had pneumonia so would be admitted to a ward. She helped to fill in some of the background personal and medical details as Karen was unable to hold a conversation and her notes weren't likely to be available until the morning. She offered to phone Karen's parents, thinking that the news of her admission would be alarming but that it might be less frightening to hear her voice than that of a stranger. She found a payphone at the entrance to the department and looked for some change in her purse. It was now around one o'clock and the phone at the Douglas's house rang for a long time before it was picked up.

"Brian Douglas," a thickened, sleepy voice announced. She slotted some money into the phone.

"Mr Douglas, it's Alison here, Karen's friend. I'm sorry but Karen is back in hospital, she has pneumonia."

"Oh, do we need to come now?"

"Well, they're about to move her up to the ward. She's on oxygen and they've started IV antibiotics, so she's stable. I'm heading home now, I think you could probably wait until the morning to visit. Maybe phone the ward in a few hours to check, it's the same one she was on before. I've given them your details."

"Thank you, Alison, it's a bit of a shock, although she did have a cough and a cold at Christmas. Do you know any more? What about the Hodgkin's?"

"I think they'll be doing tests over the next few days for that."

"Yes, well we'll give them time to get her settled and then phone the ward. Will you take a taxi home please? I'll pay you back for it later; don't want to have to worry about you wandering around the city at this hour."

"Oh, right, thanks Mr Douglas. I'll probably see you tomorrow," Alison hung up and went back to find Karen in her curtained cubicle. Her breathing was still very rapid, but didn't seem quite so noisy and her colour had improved. She picked up Karen's right hand in both of her own and rubbed it lightly.

"Karen, I've let your Dad know you're here. I think you'll be going up to the ward in a minute, so I'll go home now. I'll come in tomorrow."

The response was a slight nod of Karen's head and a weak squeeze of her hand. Her eyes didn't open. Alison disengaged her hand, collected her jacket and handbag and went to the A+E reception to ask them to call her a taxi.

It wasn't easy for Alison to get news of Karen's progress. When she visited the ward next day, Mr and Mrs Douglas were both there. They told her that tests had been scheduled but didn't give her any details of what those were or if there were any blood results back yet. Alison assumed a scan and bone marrow biopsy would be needed. Karen's condition seemed unchanged since she'd left her earlier, so she kept her visit brief.

"It's frustrating," she told James later when she called in at his flat to fill him in on the news. "I'm not a relative, so the staff won't tell me anything, her parents seem a bit shell-shocked so I don't know if they have information they're not telling me or if they just don't know. And Karen isn't responsive, only concentrating on breathing. She seems really weak."

"It can be difficult as a medic to adjust to being on the sidelines because you're used to having all the information available at your fingertips. But it's confidential and you'll just have to be patient until people want to share things with you."

"D'you think this infection means she's having a relapse?" Alison wanted to know his opinion.

"Chances are high I'm afraid," he acknowledged.

Chris arrived at the weekend; he'd only been back down in London for four days. Alison had managed to leave him a message about Karen's admission via his department and he called in at Spottiswoode Street before visiting the hospital.

"So, she's had some tests, but you don't know the results?" he clarified.

"Yes, she might know, or her mum and dad. But I'm not in the loop for passing on information and Karen hasn't been well enough to talk to me," Alison explained.

"Is she getting over the pneumonia yet?" he asked.

"I thought her breathing was easier yesterday. I wish I'd made her go to the doctor at the beginning of the week."

"Well, you did suggest it and she made you back off. It's not your fault," Chris reassured her. "I'll report back to you later. Want to meet for a drink?"

"Yeah, OK. Where do you suggest?"

"How about the Bailie? I could probably get there for about half eight after visiting finishes, and then later I'm dossing down with my old flat mates in St Bernard's Row. Is James about?"

"Yeah, I think he's free, I'll ask him."

A hum of voices could be heard as Alison and James went down the stone steps to the basement from the corner of St Stephen Street. The volume rose and a great puff of heat and cigarette smoke hit them when they opened the pub door.

"Saturday night, it's busy," James commented as they squeezed past a group of men to the bar. "I'll get the drinks; can you see Chris?"

"Can I have a half of cider? I'll have a look round for him." Alison wriggled and pressed her way through the crowd keeping a lookout for Chris's curly dark hair. She'd made a circuit of the room and was just returning to where James was at the bar when she saw Chris come in the door. She waved to attract his attention and pointed to James so that Chris would know to get his order in. Eventually the three found a small space to stand in, wedged between two table-ends.

"How're things with Karen?" James asked after taking a sip from his pint.

"She's not good," Chris replied. "It seems that the Hodgkin's is back, though they don't know the extent of it yet. Her chest is improving but it was really hard to get her to talk to me. She'd just answer with a word or two and she seemed really down. I think she's lost hope."

Alison had tears in her eyes listening to this description of her friend.

"What else can they do?" she asked James.

"Well, it depends on the staging but she could have more chemo, or maybe radiotherapy," he replied.

"It must be a real blow to her, it's not surprising she's down," Alison reasoned. "But maybe her mood'll pick up, you know she's always had a lot of faith in Dr Wood."

"I hope so. I've never seen her like this." Chris replied.

"How long can you stay?" Alison asked.

"I'll have to get back to London on Monday, there's a concert coming up on Thursday so a heavy rehearsing schedule this week."

"Well if you're going in again tomorrow, I'll try to go on Monday," Alison proposed. "Are her parents still here?"

"They weren't there today. I think they're coming back at the beginning of the week to meet with Dr Wood. Maybe there'll be a treatment plan by then. Look I don't mean to be anti-social, but I think I'll head off now. I'm pretty shattered."

"Oh no, that's OK." Alison reassured him as he drained his glass. "Can you give me a phone number in London to get hold of you? And do you have James's number? I wish we had a telephone at the flat, it's hard staying in touch with people."

Chris gave her shoulder a squeeze.

"Don't worry, I'll keep in touch."

Alison rummaged in her handbag and tore the end pages out of her diary. The men wrote their respective telephone numbers with a pencil stub that she'd also produced and exchanged pieces of paper.

"Will we just head off, too?" Alison asked James. He nodded and they followed Chris to the door. They were surprised when they exited into a flurry of tiny snowflakes and the ground was sparsely speckled with white.

"Wow, snow," Alison exclaimed. "D'you think it'll lie?"

When she woke up on Sunday morning, the light in Alison's room seemed very intense, so that at first, she thought she must have slept in very late. Then she remembered the snow. She drew her curtain open slightly and was dazzled by the white blanket lying five or six inches deep. It had the effect of making the individual gardens meld into one large space. So far it looked almost unmarked. There was only a small trail of paw-prints curving round the upper left of the area which she thought would have been made by a cat. She pulled on her dressing gown and a thick pair of socks and went into the kitchen to make a mug of tea. The room was a mess, despite being on her own since Wednesday she'd been rushing in, snacking and just leaving the debris. So, there was a tower of washing-up to be done and she really should sweep and wash the floor too. She ignored things for now and went into the lounge where there was a pile of ironing waiting to be done. Tomorrow she'd be back on the wards and be expected to look neatly turned out. When she opened the shutters, the brightness seemed to suddenly show up dust coating the mantelpiece and coffee table. Linda would be back on Tuesday and it wouldn't be very welcoming for her to come in to a dirty flat. She'd have to motivate herself to do some cleaning.

However, she couldn't help feeling down. She remembered snowy days at home in Oban and how much Jess loved to chase snowballs and then eat them. And last year when it snowed one evening she'd gone with Liz and Elaine in the dark to build a huge snowman on the Meadows. They'd all felt a bit childish, but it had been fun and later back at the flat they'd made mulled wine to warm up. But today she was on her own. James needed to study. Her sigh made a steamy film on the window. She gave herself an internal shake and talking to. She shouldn't really be feeling sorry for herself; after all she was fit and healthy not lying in a hospital bed like Karen. She'd do the tidying and then have a soak in the bath with some of her Christmas bath oil. What she needed was some invigorating music. Five minutes later, changed into jeans and a sweatshirt, she was tackling the kitchen cleaning while singing along with the Beatles to 'Here comes the sun.'

***

When she walked home from the Royal Infirmary across the Meadows on Monday evening, there were still remnants of snow on the grass but the paths and pavements were mainly clear, or slushy. She stood well

227

back from the traffic flow while waiting at the pedestrian crossing to avoid being sprayed with dirty slush. She was surprised to see a light shining from the fanlight window as she came up the last stairs and approached the front door. She'd phoned Linda from the call box around the corner last night to let her know about Karen. Linda had been upset at the news and had confirmed her plan to travel back to Edinburgh on Tuesday. Alison was even more surprised when in reply to her shouted greeting Mrs Douglas appeared in the hall from the kitchen.

"Oh, Alison dear, hello, I hope I didn't give you a fright. I've decided to make the flat my base for the time being. It's a bit dicey on the roads with all this snow; you know it lies for longer with us in the Borders. And Karen's room is lying empty. This way I can be handy for the hospital and I can cook some proper food. That hospital cafeteria is all stodge."

"Right, good idea," Alison replied politely meanwhile feeling very relieved that she'd done the cleaning yesterday. But she also thought that it might be a bit awkward sharing a flat with Mrs Douglas, and what if it wasn't just her.

"What about Mr Douglas?" She asked.

"Brian has gone back down to Peebles just now for the beginning of term. His headmaster is very understanding, so I'm sure they'll try to arrange cover for some of his afternoon classes to let Brian get away early. That way at least he's not having to do all of the driving in the dark. You see we don't know how long Karen will be staying in hospital."

"No," Alison began to unwind her scarf and slip her coat off. "Is there any more news?"

"Why don't you come and have a bite to eat with me and I'll explain. I've made a risotto and salad, enough for two."

"OK, that would be very nice." Alison accepted the offer. Maybe there would be advantages to having Mrs Douglas as a flat mate in terms of good food and access to information. She dumped her outdoor clothes and arrived in the kitchen after a visit to the toilet. From closer up she noticed that Mrs Douglas had red-rimmed eyes. She sat at the table and allowed Karen's Mum to serve the meal.

"So, were you meeting with Dr Wood today? Chris mentioned something about it."

"Yes, but the news isn't good and there aren't many treatment options," Mrs Douglas swiped at her eyes with the back of her hand. "The Hodgkin's seems to have come back just as aggressively as before. So, they can try what they call salvage chemotherapy. But if it didn't work the first time there's no guarantee it'll be a cure. Plus, they have to try to build Karen up a bit first, so clear up this infection and give her some transfusions."

"So, she'll be in for a while?"

"Yes, probably all of this week. Then they might let her out for a bit before the chemo."

"And how's Karen taking the news?" Alison was finding it quite hard all of a sudden to chew and swallow any food.

"Oh, she's very upset, and angry. It's hard to talk to her. I don't know how we're going to manage."

Now Mrs Douglas was openly tearful and Alison felt dreadful; sick and totally inadequate in knowing how to respond to Karen's Mum. She couldn't really think of anything to say. She reached out and with her hand covered Mrs Douglas's hand where it lay on the table.

Twenty-two

During the next week Karen's antibiotics were swapped from IV to oral but her drip stayed up giving her blood and platelet transfusions. Alison visited on two evenings, both times coinciding with Mr Douglas who'd driven up from Peebles. Karen was passive, seeming to listen in to the conversation between Alison and her dad but not contributing. Alison and Linda were getting used to encounters with Mrs Douglas in the mornings. Wearing a quilted blue dressing gown, she'd be sitting in the kitchen drinking a mug of tea as they grabbed a quick breakfast. She was usually out, visiting at the hospital, when they got back home in the late afternoon and tended to spend her evenings at the flat quietly in Karen's room. On Friday morning, she announced that she'd be taking Karen home to Peebles that day.

"So when will her treatment start?" Alison asked while munching on a piece of toast.

"It depends on her blood counts. Our GP is to check them on Thursday with a view to possibly beginning the treatment the following week."

"And she'll stay in Peebles until then?" Alison clarified.

"Yes, you could maybe phone."

"OK. I've got to dash now, it's my last day on this unit and I'm down to give a presentation at the clinical meeting. Want to check my overheads before it starts." As she went downstairs, Linda caught her up.

"It doesn't sound like Karen's being given the choice of staying in Edinburgh," she commented.

"Maybe not, but she's just not like herself," Alison explained "When I've been there, she hasn't expressed any opinions or shown any spark of interest in anything. So, she's probably just going along with the plans they're making for her."

Alison used the phone at James's flat twice to phone Karen during the following week. To be told on both occasions by Mr Douglas that Karen was sleeping and to maybe try another time.

"Do you think she's really sleeping? It's as if she's avoiding me," Alison complained to James.

"You've got to remember she's not well, and she's going through a lot just now. Maybe she doesn't know what to say to you," he commented.

"We were always able to talk about all of this before. I feel really cut off."

James chose his next words carefully.

"Alison, you do realise that Karen is probably going to die." Alison looked stricken.

"That's what she's facing up to." He came and sat next to Alison on the couch, putting his arm round her shoulders. "From my time working on that ward I reckon if her disease has come back so aggressively and so quickly the chemo's not likely to do much. In fact, she probably won't tolerate much of it." Alison turned her body towards his; sobbing and he held her and stroked her back soothingly. "I wasn't sure if you were blocking it out or being brave." He murmured into her hair.

"I think I didn't want to admit it, because then it might happen," she whispered. "What can I do to help her?"

"You've already helped her a lot by being a good friend. There might not be any more that you can do for now except keeping yourself available if she wants to talk to you. But you have to come to terms with not being able to fix everything. As a friend or as a doctor you can only do your best. You'll wear yourself out if you don't recognise that some things are beyond what can be mended."

"It feels like giving up, letting her go."

"No, you can still be there as a human, a friend. That can be harder than all the busyness of curing and treatment." They sat together quietly for a few more minutes and then James suggested making mugs of tea. They decided against going out to the cinema as they'd originally intended.

The next week Alison tried to throw herself into her attachment at the dermatology department, but she found that the skin rashes and lesions were quickly beginning to look very similar to one another and confusing her. There had been no sign of any member of the Douglas family, so she assumed that Karen's blood counts hadn't recovered sufficiently to start chemotherapy. On Wednesday, she received a post-card with a picture of two Scottie dogs and a Peebles postmark. It was written in purple felt-tip pen:

'Dear Alison,

Still very tired and my counts are low. Might be back in Edinburgh next week, Karen.'

"I wish we had a phone," she complained to Linda that evening. "James is on call so I can't go to his flat and I can't be bothered going out in this rain to the phone-box."

"I think maybe you should just leave it for now. Or why not send a letter or post-card in reply?" Linda suggested.

"Good idea. I think I'll do that. I got some nice notelets from my auntie at Christmas," and she went to her room to compose a note to Karen.

On Monday evening of the following week Alison and Linda got together to cook a pasta dish with chicken. They also prepared a side salad and were sitting in the dining alcove tucking in, when they heard the sound of a key turning the lock of the front door. Could it be Karen?

"Hello, we're in the kitchen," Alison called. The tapping of high heels on the polished wooden floor told her before anyone appeared that it wasn't Karen but the return of Mrs Douglas.

"That smells good girls," she commented as she entered the kitchen.

"Sorry we can't offer you any, we only cooked enough for two," Linda replied.

"Oh, that's OK, I'm not very hungry. I'll make a cup of tea though; it's always so hot in the ward I get really thirsty." She went to fill the kettle with water.

"So, is Karen back at the Western?" Alison asked.

"Yes, they've cautiously started some chemotherapy. So, she has to stay in for monitoring in case her counts fall. Do you both want some tea?"

They took mugs of tea through to the lounge to drink.

"Chris came down to see us at the weekend. He seems to be getting a lot out of his course in London; it's a great experience for him. He brought along his violin but Karen didn't feel up to playing any duets. I was able to accompany a couple of his pieces on the piano, it was very pleasant."

Alison felt an unexpected stab of jealousy as the seemingly cosy scene was described. But then she thought guiltily that it couldn't possibly have been a very comfortable visit for Chris.

***

Alison was aware of butterflies stirring in her stomach as she made her way down the hospital corridor to visit Karen on Wednesday afternoon. She knew from Mrs Douglas that neither of Karen's parents would be there and it was now nearly three weeks since she'd had a chance to speak to Karen on her own. She had to acknowledge that she was nervous. But that was silly, when had she ever had any reason to be nervous of her friend before? She pushed open the swing door into the ward. Mrs Douglas had explained that Karen was being isolated to protect her from potential infections, so was in one of the single rooms close to the ward entrance. Alison was approaching the first door when she overheard a furious voice.

"No, you can't bloody try again. I'm sick of being jabbed by needles and it's not my fault if you're incompetent. It's all a waste of time anyway. Just leave me alone." Although the tone was low and hoarse the meaning was pointed and a flustered doctor hurtled out from the room almost bumping into Alison, causing her to recoil. Wow. Alison wasn't sure whether to admit that she'd overheard, but decided to wait a moment before entering the room pretending that she'd just arrived. She took a deep breath and advanced towards the door again.

"Hi," she announced herself. Karen turned her head and Alison was immediately shocked by the change in her appearance. She'd obviously lost weight, her face gaunt with sunken cheeks. There was a yellowish hue to her complexion and her lips were swollen and pitted with open ulcers.

"Yes, I look like hell and feel like crap," Karen stated, croakily.

"I didn't know what to bring you. Your Mum said you couldn't eat much and your eyes have been hurting so you're not reading much, anyway I thought you might manage a magazine." Alison thought that she was babbling as she deposited the latest copy of 'Cosmopolitan' onto Karen's bed.

"Can't imagine I'll have much need of the latest fashions and tips on dating," Karen commented.

"No, maybe not," Alison felt awkward. Karen's tone was icy; there was no friendliness or joking in her voice.

"Bit of a miscalculation, but I'm sure you had good intentions. Just take it back. I won't look at it." She batted the magazine away with the back of her hand and Alison scrambled to pick it up from the floor where it had slithered down off the edge of the bed.

"Is there anything else you'd like?" She was red-faced.

"Yes, I'd like my life back if you can arrange that. I'd like to not have this fucking disease. Not to be pumped with chemicals and stuck in this shit-hole." Somehow the angry words seemed to carry into every corner of the room despite being hissed at low volume. Alison supposed it was the venom in their delivery that propelled them.

"I'm sorry Karen," she whispered beginning to feel tearful.

"And don't start crying over me. I... can't—stand—it." Karen's last words were punctuated by coughing which then built to a crescendo, shaking her frail body and making her eyes and nose run. Alison offered a glass of water with a straw and a tissue but both were batted to the side by Karen as she curled up into a ball coughing furiously into her knees. Alison rang on Karen's alarm and stuck her head out into the corridor. A nurse was approaching in response to the buzzer.

"She's having a coughing fit and can't seem to get a breath," Alison explained.

"Probably talking too much," the nurse commented and Alison watched as she propped Karen up and applied an oxygen mask. Karen's eyes were now closed and her head lolling, exhausted by the exertion of the coughing fit.

"I'd better just go then," she said quietly. Neither Karen nor the nurse seemed to notice her departure. She walked out of the ward head down, trying not to cry. That was awful; she'd been totally unprepared for Karen's anger and hadn't really known how to cope with it. Not only that, she'd prompted Karen to almost kill herself with that coughing fit. She just missed colliding with a compact, burly, white-coated figure coming in the opposite direction.

"Ah, Karen's friend the medical student, were you visiting her?" It was Dr Wood, looking dapper as usual; today his shirt was pale green and his tie royal blue with tiny matching green dots.

"Sorry, I can't remember your name."

"Alison Scott." He took in her red cheeks and tearfulness and guided her, with his hand on her elbow, to a bench seat in a window alcove set back from the corridor. They sat down side by side.

"Not easy to deal with the angry ones," he commented." Although, it surprises me that more patients aren't angry, really. We've let them down. The ones who are very grateful for what you're doing when you and they both know it isn't working are difficult too, in a different way."

"There isn't much hope for Karen is there?" Alison asked him.

"I think not, but in medicine there can always be unexpected outcomes, nothing is ever one hundred percent certain. Why don't you sit here for a wee while and regain your composure? I'm expected on the ward."

"Thank you for speaking to me. I feel better to know that you struggle with things too."

"We all do." He nodded then gave her a brief salute as he disappeared along the corridor towards the ward.

Alison checked her watch, four forty. She wondered if James might be free to go home soon. Linda would be socialising after hockey and she didn't want to be on her own in the flat. Or it might be even worse if Mrs Douglas was there. She wouldn't know what to say to her. How on earth were Karen's parents coping with this? She decided to go along to the renal ward to look for James. When she got to the doctor's room, the houseman was there writing up a new admission.

"I think James is probably down in the dialysis suite. Do you want to phone and check?" he nodded to the phone on the desk. "The number's on that list on the notice board."

"Thanks," she eventually spoke to James after a nurse had fetched him to the phone. He suggested that she stayed in the office as he was almost finished with his tasks but needed to come up for his jacket.

"Hope I'm not in your way," she checked with the houseman.

"Not a problem, and if you made me a coffee you'd be a life-saver. Milk no sugar, kitchen's next door." Knowing the busy long hours that the junior doctors put in, Alison didn't mind fetching coffee and made one for herself, too. She'd almost finished it when James appeared in the doorway.

"Ah, I see Pete is entertaining you, or knowing him, he probably got you to skivvy," he commented while shrugging off his white coat and swapping it for his outdoor jacket from the coat rack in the corner of the room. Pete winked at her and she gave him a wave as she left. She'd found his absorption and quiet acceptance of her company soothing.

"I suppose you've been to see Karen," James guessed, taking her hand as they made their way out of the hospital to the car park. She began to tell him about her afternoon visit and her talk with Dr Woods.

"You should try not to take her anger personally," James advised. "She's angry at the whole world, not just you."

"I know you're probably right, but it was hard to cope with. She looked so frail, as if a breeze would blow her away. I don't know where she got the energy for the fury she was expressing. It seemed out of all proportion."

"Mmm, maybe it's what's keeping her going, you never know. I've got an arrangement to meet with Eddie and Sandra for pizza tonight. Do you want to join us? Or I can cancel if you don't feel up to it." Alison wasn't sure. She'd feel guilty making James change his plans because of her, especially as it was hard for him to meet up with his friends when they all worked different rotas. Also, she found Eddie and Sandra, his former flat-mates from medical school, a bit intimidating. Although they tried to make her welcome they had that aura of a ready-made group with in-jokes and shared experiences. James was picking up on her uncertainty.

"I really don't mind cancelling."

"No, I'll come. As long as they don't mind if I'm a bit quiet."

"They'll understand, anyway we often rattle on about ancient stuff. You can zone out." He put his arm around her shoulder and hugged her against his side as they

241

reached the car. "None of us will want a late night since we all swap over jobs on Monday. I've got lots of tidying up to do over the next two days. Glad I'm not on at the weekend."

James was referring to the biannual rotation of junior doctors that happened on the first of February and the first of August. There was a joke that you certainly didn't want to fall ill on those days as most of the staff were inexperienced and settling into new jobs. James was due to swap from his current job in renal medicine to the neurology unit at the Northern General hospital.

"Do you want to come back to mine after?"

"No, it's OK, Linda should be in later. I just didn't feel like being on my own. But I'll need to get my things organised for tomorrow. I'm in the treatment room at dermatology. I might get to help, or even do some of the lumps and bumps excisions."

"That would be good, more interesting than just watching." James released her and unlocked the car.

***

A bell was ringing in the distance. Alison struggled groggily up from sleep trying to orientate herself. Her room was still dark, but it was Saturday so she hadn't needed to set her alarm. The clock said eight fifteen. The ringing was repeated and she now recognised the doorbell. Wondering who was calling so early at the weekend, she worked her feet into her slippers and grabbed her dressing gown from its hook on the back of her bedroom door. As she stepped into the hall, she noticed Linda's door was open and that she'd beaten Alison to the front door.

"James. Come in," Linda sounded surprised. Alison hadn't made an arrangement to see James this morning so she was puzzled, too. Then, as he came close she could see how grim he looked. He grabbed her hand as he passed her in the hallway and led her towards the living room.

"I'm sorry, there's no easy way to tell you this. Karen died last night." Alison was stunned.

"But?" she whispered in protest as her knees sagged and she collapsed onto the settee. Linda started to sob. James crouched down in front of Alison holding on to both of her hands now.

"Her Dad phoned me and asked me to come and tell you. Do you want to know more?" Alison nodded numbly as tears began to roll down her cheeks. James explained that Karen had suddenly developed pain in her abdomen around teatime on Friday. Then she began to vomit blood and it became obvious that she'd had a bleed in her stomach. Unfortunately, because of her anaemia and low platelet count the transfusions weren't able to keep pace with the haemorrhage. She died just after midnight.

Twenty-three

A raging wind was sweeping dark, purplish clouds across the sky from the west and their car was battered by heavy sheets of sleet. Icy drops exploded noisily on the windscreen then trailed lazily down towards the bonnet. The noisy weather contrasted with the silence inside the car. After a few miles, the cloud had scudded past and they were dazzled by low sun and its reflection on the wet road. Alison's eyes were gritty from a combination of crying and lack of sleep. She closed them against the glare, glad that she wasn't driving.

James had been taking care of her over the past week. He'd stayed with her for the weekend, encouraging her to rest, eat and take some exercise at the appropriate times. On Monday, he'd contacted her university supervisor and negotiated two weeks off from classes. She wasn't really sure where time had gone, it was already Friday and she'd done nothing. She remembered meeting Chris. Was that on Tuesday or was it Wednesday? Obviously, Chris was devastated but he was full of plans for a musical memorial service for Karen that Alison found difficult to concentrate on. She envied his busyness as it gave him fuel to keep going. She felt adrift. Today James was driving Alison and Linda to Karen's funeral and then tomorrow he had arranged to take her home to Oban. She had gone along with everything numbly; still part of her disbelieving that Karen had gone. She was always so full of life, even on that last, most recent visit when she'd been raging. Alison didn't like to remember that afternoon and she found it distressing that her final contact with Karen had been such a disaster. She wished that they could meet again to try and make amends.

She understood now that Karen had developed a duodenal ulcer. Some of the chemotherapy medications could have been to blame, but in addition the stress of her illness probably had a large part to play. The ulcer had perforated and bled catastrophically on that last Friday night. It sounded final. Maybe the ritual of the funeral would make it seem true.

"OK, Karen's dad said, we're best to drive past the church and cross the river to park, it's only a short walk back," James said and broke the silence. Alison opened her eyes to see that they were driving along Peebles High Street towards a church with a crown on its tower. James turned left onto a bridge crossing the River Tweed and then left again into a car park.

"We've made good time despite the weather," Linda commented.

"Yes, twenty to eleven. We'd probably be best just to go now though, the church might be quite busy," James suggested.

They donned coats, scarves and gloves and James collected an umbrella from the car boot, although currently the sun was shining. They battled against the freezing gale, crossing the bridge to the Old Parish Church. Once in the door they were greeted by a man in a black suit who handed them each an order of service and asked them to fill the pews towards the front of the church. Soft organ music was playing and there was a low hum of conversation. The main body of the church was already half-filled. James led the girls to a pew on the left side of the aisle six rows from the front.

Alison sat down, clutching the paper that she'd been given. There was a photograph of Karen on the front taken before her chemotherapy when her hair was long. As she gazed her eyes began to fill, her tears blurring the image. It was how Karen had looked when Alison first met her. She blinked, stared up at the stained glass windows and took some slow, deep breaths trying to pull herself together. At the corner of her visual field she saw Mr and Mrs Douglas passing the end of her pew being led towards the front of the church. Mr Douglas wore a dark suit and was holding his wife by her upper arm, he was looking straight ahead and she had her head bent. Both were avoiding any eye contact. Next a minister wearing a black cassock advanced up the aisle to the front of the church and requested that the congregation should stand.

The organ music changed to play a strong and haunting melody. Alison bit her lower lip which was quivering and held tightly on to James's hand as six pall bearers passed along the aisle carrying a pale wooden coffin at shoulder height, walking slowly in time to the music. They carefully deposited their burden onto a low bench in front of the communion table then all stood together facing forward and bowed respectfully to the coffin. Alison concentrated her gaze on the floral display on the coffin lid and gave herself the task of trying to name the various flowers, aiming to stop thinking of Karen's body lying there in the box. She'd counted and named twelve different kinds of white flowers by the time the men joined Mr and Mrs Douglas in the front pew and the minister announced the first hymn. It was the 23rd psalm to the familiar tune of 'Crimond', but Alison found she couldn't produce more than a wavering squawk, so proceeded just to mouth the words silently. The service continued with prayers and bible readings. Alison let the words skim over her as she didn't really believe in an afterlife and as far as she knew Karen hadn't either. But maybe Karen's parents were religious and if these words were offering help or comfort to them, then Alison felt that the ceremony was worthwhile. She did listen carefully when one of the pall bearers, standing at the golden eagle-shaped lectern, talked briefly about Karen's life. Struggling to keep his emotion in check he told stories about Karen's childhood and referred to her growing talents for languages, music and sport. He finished by urging everyone to remember most of all how she loved to throw parties and have fun. Checking her order of service Alison read his name, 'Paul Douglas'. She thought he was one of Karen's uncles and was grateful that he'd brought some of the essence of Karen into the service. She struggled through another hymn, 'All things Bright and Beautiful', then the minister gave a blessing and they remained on their feet as there was a reprieve of the processional music which Alison identified as 'Nimrod' from the service sheet. The casket was borne back out of the church followed by Karen's family. Chris walked after them accompanied by an older couple that Alison presumed were his parents.

"You OK?" James asked her softly as they gathered their belongings to leave the church. Alison nodded.

"Are you sure you want to go to the cemetery? We could go straight to the hotel where the reception will be if you want."

"No, I'll go to the cemetery. I might regret it later if I dodge out. How about you Linda? Can you manage to carry on?" Alison was flanked by James and Linda as they emerged onto the street.

"I'm coping so far," Linda replied. Like Alison she had red-rimmed eyes and she was clutching a paper hankie.

Although it wasn't very far to the cemetery they went to collect the car because of the likelihood of more sleet and the subsequent journey to the hotel.

The cemetery was large and flat. They passed an ancient stone-roofed tower surrounded by a scattering of very old worn gravestones on their right as they walked to the more modern area of the graveyard. Here everything was tidier, the headstones regimented, close-packed, straight and shiny with clear writing. Snow lay in patches of longer grass and had blown into west-facing crannies among the monuments. The sky was blue overhead but there were thick grey clouds approaching on the wind. The funeral party was gathering round the prepared plot but Alison deliberately hung back, she didn't want to be too close. There was only a short reading and a prayer and then the coffin was being lowered into the hole. Alison kept her gaze high above the heads in front and realised that she was looking at a golf course on the adjacent hills. No golfers to be seen today and icy drops started to batter the mourners. Alison's teeth were chattering as the trio retraced their footsteps to the cemetery car park. No one was lingering. In the car James turned the heater and fan up high.

"I hope we get a hot drink at the reception, I'm absolutely freezing," Linda complained.

"You know. I think I understand Chris and his memorial service better now," Alison commented. "Earlier in the week I couldn't get why he was so obsessed by the idea, apart from maybe giving himself something to keep busy with. But today was all about what Karen's parents wanted to do. Chris needs to acknowledge Karen's life in his own way."

"I think it's a good idea. Plus, because it's going to be in Edinburgh a lot more of Karen's friends will be able to come," Linda gave her opinion.

"Yeh. I couldn't help feeling at the cemetery that Karen's really stuck in Peebles now and she was always trying to get away. She loved cities and crowds. I think she'd rather have been cremated and her ashes scattered somewhere."

"I don't think you could scatter them in a crowded place," James objected.

"No, and it's not up to me anyway. Probably I'm expressing my own preferences. It seems to me that funerals are really more for the people left behind than for the person that died. I can see why her parents want to keep her close by."

"I thought it was good that someone from her family spoke about her at the service," Linda said.

"I think that was her uncle. I'd like to try to talk to him at the reception, and to Chris," Alison replied.

At the hotel they were offered sherry, whisky or a soft drink and directed to a table laden with sandwiches and sausage rolls. Both girls accepted a glass of sherry thinking it might help to generate some warmth. James decided he could risk one whisky, as he wouldn't be driving again immediately. They made their way across to where Chris was standing and were introduced to his parents.

"Are you one of Chris's musical friends?" Mrs Thomson asked Alison.

"No, I was Karen's flat mate and badminton partner. But Chris, I wanted to tell you that if you need a hand with the memorial at the Edinburgh end, I'd be willing to help. It might be quite hard for you to arrange everything from London."

"Thanks Alison, I might take you up on that. I'm aiming for the beginning of the summer term. Don't want to get tangled up in holidays or exams. I'll try to speak to some people and get them to commit over the weekend, before I go back down south."

***

Alison hadn't realised how comforting it would be to arrive back in Oban and be cosseted by her parents. She realised how much James had done, caring for her and seeming to know what she needed. She thanked him before he drove off on Sunday morning.

"It's fine. I'm glad I was able to help a bit. Let me know which train you'll be on next week and I'll meet you." She waved until his car was out of sight.

Alison spent a lot of her time out of doors taking Jess for long walks. She relished the brisk weather and enjoyed watching Jess dash along the beach chasing seagulls and small waves. The wind which tangled her hair into knots seemed to have the opposite effect on her mind, helping to unravel her reflections.

Recent events had made her forget that this week was one of the busiest of the year for florists, the run up to St Valentine's Day. So, she was co-opted into the shop to help. It was while sorting out flowers and preparing bouquets with her Mum that she was gradually able to tell her about the last weeks. She described Karen's initial passivity and then her fury. She listed the twelve types of flowers that she'd identified in the floral tribute on the casket. She remembered that in her first year in Edinburgh St Valentine's Day had fallen on a Wednesday and that Karen had insisted that everyone wear only red and pink clothes for the badminton team social night. She'd also ruled that they could only drink red or pink liquids. Alison had stuck to red wine, but two of the team had felt decidedly unwell after experimenting with Campari.

On Saturday, the Scott family settled down to a late evening meal after the shop had closed and all of the deliveries had been made. Alison's Mum, experienced from past rush times, had heated up a pre-prepared pasta dish from her freezer.

"Are you sure you feel up to going back tomorrow?" Mr Scott checked.

"Yes, I'll be OK. I've got Linda and James to talk to, and I really don't want to miss any more time off from Uni. It'll already be hard to catch up. Also, I've said I'll help Chris to organise a musical memorial event. So, I'm going to be quite busy."

"Well you know you can come back up any time you want to," her Mum reminded her. "Or I'm sure you could pop through to see Helen."

"I might do that one weekend soon."

"I've been meaning to ask you if you have any ideas yet about your elective," her Dad asked.

"No, not really."

"It's just that I'm due to write to my friend Harry MacDougall, the guy that emigrated to Australia. He sent a note in his Christmas card and I really should reply. He's a surgeon in Perth and I'm sure he could help you to arrange something if you were interested in going there. We'd be happy to pay for the travel." Mr and Mrs Scott had been hatching this plan to encourage Alison. They felt it would give her a boost to have something new and exciting to plan and look forward to. Alison was surprised, she had never expected her parents to offer money, enabling her to go abroad.

"Well I hadn't been considering going that far afield but if you're writing to him maybe you could ask. I don't think I'd want to do a surgical specialty. Maybe a medical attachment or A and E. I think you can sometimes stay in hospital accommodation to keep costs down."

"I'll see what he says."

***

When Alison stepped onto the platform at Waverly station the next evening, she was greeted by James proffering a pink and white bouquet.

"Happy Valentine's Day. I wasn't sure if you'd be scunnered with flowers, so I asked my Mum and she advised that no woman is ever offended by a gift of flowers," he greeted her.

"She's right. Thank you, they're beautiful." Alison accepted the flowers and his hug and kiss.

"I've booked us a table at 'The Magnum'. I think we should just go straight there now, we'll be slightly early but we can have a drink first. I hope you're hungry."

"Yes, I am, starving. There was no buffet carriage on either train because it's Sunday and I had no food with me cos I'd planned on buying a sandwich." James took her hand and they set off towards the station exit.

Twenty-four

"Is the level moving with respiration?" the registrar asked.

Alison lay on her side on the linoleum of the ward floor where she'd been asked to examine the water seal jar under a patient's bed. She could see the water level oscillating in time with the rapid breath sounds coming from above.

"Yip."

"And can you see any air bubbling in through the tube?"

"Yes."

"OK. Thanks, you can get up now, it should be OK. We'll get another X-ray to check."

Alison stood up, dusting herself down. She'd been helping the registrar to insert a chest drain for a young man with a large pneumothorax.

"How are you feeling?" she asked the patient.

"It's a bit nippy, like, and my breathings still hard."

"You should feel it gradually improving," the registrar reassured him. "I'll write you up for some painkillers. Once the local anaesthetic wears off the drain might be a bit uncomfortable and, as we explained, it's likely to be in for a few days. The porter will be coming to take you down to X-ray and I'll see you again once you're back."

Since her return from Oban, Alison had been based on a respiratory ward. She was enjoying being back into the swing of work and found the ward interesting. She'd formed the opinion that a visit here would be a good deterrent against smoking, and was glad that she'd never started. Apart from some asthmatics and the man with the pneumothorax nearly everyone else had smoking related diseases, either chronic bronchitis, emphysema or lung cancer.

She was getting lots of practice at reading chest X-rays and when the patient returned to the ward with his film she was able to see that the drain she'd helped to insert was lying in the correct position. She went to tell him that it was all fine and was pleased that he could tell her that he was already beginning to feel the benefit of the analgesics he'd been given. She believed that she'd been helpful this morning. Engaging with patients and seeing them improve was definitely a boost to her morale. Obviously, this wasn't always the outcome for her patients, but she was aware that she should try to dwell on positive experiences at present. It would be easy to become morose and depressed and so she was working actively against that.

Getting involved with Chris in arranging the memorial was turning out to be a good thing too. Alison didn't know much about music, but Chris was organising all of that. He'd asked her to borrow musical scores from the music library. She'd never even noticed its entrance before, next to the Central Library on George 1V Bridge then down a flight of stairs. Thankfully the librarian was very helpful and Chris had sent her a comprehensive list of his requirements. Some of the music had to be ordered so she was currently waiting for it to arrive. Then she'd have to contact the musicians, another of Chris's lists, to come and collect their scores. The venue was to be the Reid Concert Hall. This was another new tucked-away place that Alison hadn't previously visited. She'd walked past it almost every day as it stood between the medical school and Teviot Row Union, opposite the McEwan Hall. Inside was a beautiful space, long and high with a honey-combed effect ceiling and rows of windows along its upper half. Chris said that the seating capacity was three hundred people and she was currently making a list of sporting and university friends to be invited. The date they'd set for the event was Saturday 25th April, after the Easter break, and Chris was planning to come up next weekend for a first rehearsal.

Alison was thinking about this as she walked home, hoping that all of the music would be available from the library on time for the rehearsal. Although she'd noticed that Chris seemed quite relaxed about it, saying that he could work with what they had. He explained that the musicians would practise and get up to speed in their own time. When she came through the front door and into the hall, she was surprised to find a pile of boxes and suitcases stacked along the wall and blocking the door to her room. The door to what had latterly been Karen's room was standing open. The boxes were filled with books, records, cushions and she could see a desk lamp poking out from one.

"Hello?" she called and Mr Douglas appeared from the front bedroom wearing jeans and a sweater and looking rumpled, his hair unusually out of place.

"Hello Alison. We're moving Karen's things out. Oh, we've blocked your door, let me move those boxes."

"That's OK. I don't need in right now. Do you need a hand?"

"No lass, not an easy job, but we're almost done. A cup of tea might be nice though."

"OK I'll put the kettle on." By the time she'd made the tea and set out mugs, milk and biscuits Mr and Mrs Douglas had joined her in the kitchen. Mrs Douglas, always thin, had lost weight and looked haggard with dark shadows under her eyes.

"This is very welcome," Mr Douglas sighed after taking a long drink from his mug. "Maybe you could give us a hand with taking things down to the car after tea?"

"Yes, of course," Alison agreed.

"Now we don't want you to worry about the rent for Karen's room. We'll pay it until the summer as was agreed."

"Oh, we hadn't really thought about that," Alison admitted.

"Well, if you did know of someone who wanted the room sooner and who'd fit in with you and Linda, then obviously we'd be happy to let them have it," Mrs Douglas added.

"I don't know of anyone. People don't usually move in the middle of a year but I'll ask Linda. I suppose we'd be looking for someone for next year anyway." Alison had genuinely never considered yet that they'd need to look for another flat mate.

Once their mugs were drained she propped the front door open with a hefty text book and helped to carry boxes down to the pavement. Mrs Douglas brought the car from farther along the street and double-parked by the stair entrance. Mr Douglas was just packing the last of the boxes into the boot when Linda approached, walking from the direction of the Meadows.

"Mr and Mrs Douglas have been collecting Karen's stuff," Alison explained, unnecessarily.

"Well, I think that's the lot," Mr Douglas pushed down the hatchback door firmly. Mrs Douglas was still in the driver's seat.

"Will you be coming to the memorial?" Alison asked, unsure if Chris would already have issued an invitation and, strangely, not wanting to let Karen's Dad leave just yet.

"We haven't decided. I'd like to come, but at the moment Margaret doesn't think she could face it. Given that it's another two months away she might change her mind. I don't know if I could come on my own without her. Will you keep two seats for us, just in case?"

"Of course. I think it would mean a lot to Chris if you came, and I'm sure Mrs Douglas would enjoy the music, if she felt up to coming."

"Yes, she'd get a lot of pleasure from it, but it would be bitter-sweet without our lass playing there too. I'll work on persuading her."

"I'll phone you nearer the time," Alison promised giving him a hug and a peck on the cheek, "or sooner if we find anyone for the room." She and Linda stood as he lowered himself into the front passenger seat and then waved until the car turned the corner into Warrender Park Terrace.

"It's funny, but I didn't want him to go without knowing we'd be in touch again. I'm not sure I feel that way about Mrs D," Alison commented as they climbed up to the flat.

"No, she's harder to relate to. He's just so warm and open. Must've been hard for them clearing her room,"

"Yes, and I suppose they have a lot of things in Peebles to sort through too. Really hard."

"What were they saying about the room?"

Oh, that they'll pay up until the summer unless we can find someone, but not to worry. D'you know anyone who might be interested?"

"Mmm, maybe. There's a girl on the hockey team, Suzy, that I know is unhappy in her current flat. But I don't know if she's committed to paying rent for the rest of the year. I don't suppose she could afford two places."

"Is she nice? Would we get on with her?"

"Yeah, I think so. D'you want me to sound her out a bit?"

"Could do. Maybe she could come round for a coffee."

***

The next six weeks seemed to fly past for Alison in a routine of ward work and evening study. She spent a weekend visiting Helen and Neil at the beginning of March and had a deliciously memorable Indian meal with them at a restaurant close to the Mitchell Library. Occasionally she had days of feeling very down and gloomy. She found then, as she had on her recent week up in Oban, that if she could get out and walk in the fresh air it seemed to help. One of her favourite walks was close to her first year accommodation at Pollock Halls. If she went up into the Queen's Park from there and climbed to the south end of Salisbury Crags, she could go through 'the Gutted Haddie' to Hunters Bog under Arthur's Seat. She liked it there in the valley, enclosed by the hills. From certain places, there were no buildings to be seen at all and she could imagine herself to be out in the countryside. Sometimes she sat and perched on a rock, stopping to enjoy the peace. With very little traffic sound encroaching she could hear the slightly squeaky twittering of wagtails from the gorse bushes beside her. Previously they'd been dipping and zigzagging along the path in front of her as she walked. On one afternoon, she heard long drawn out mewling calls from far above and then spotted a pair of buzzards circling in the thermals under Arthur's Seat. She looped round to climb a higher path running along the side of the hill and her ascent took her level with the birds. She enjoyed watching their lazy circling and gazed north across the Forth to Fife and then south to the streak of Hillend ski-slope on the Pentlands. She missed the company and busy antics of Jess that she'd had on walks at home but generally headed back to the flat in a more positive frame of mind.

At the end of March James suggested that she accompany him on a visit to his family home for Easter weekend which was in two weeks' time. Alison had met James's Mum the previous autumn when she'd been down to Edinburgh to do some shopping. James had prepared one of his famous Sunday roast lunches which Alison had come to share with them. Mrs Cooke, or Maddy as she'd asked to be called, had an enormous appetite and did justice to the roast lamb and trimmings followed by lemon meringue pie. She was a larger than life character, broad and bouncy and dressed that day in a shimmering magenta and purple swirly-patterned kaftan, accessorised with a heavy gold and amethyst necklace and matching dangly earrings. Alison found her easy to talk to and enjoyed her sense of humour, but felt rather pale and quiet in comparison. She hadn't yet met James's father who was a farmer and apparently didn't often stray far from the farm. She agreed to the trip and so Good Friday morning found them driving north out of Edinburgh over the Forth Road Bridge. It was a sunny day and even this early in the season a few yachts were using the breeze, tacking to and fro between the bridges. They had breakfasted on coffee and toasted hot cross buns, but Alison already had some hunger pangs and there was an audible rumbling which caused James to comment.

"Hungry already?"

"Yes, I seem to be. Can we stop somewhere for a snack?"

"Did I warn you that my mum will have cooked for the equivalent of an army and expect you to put away generous portions?"

"Mmm, well maybe just a coffee would do."

They found a roadside café just after they passed Perth where their route turned east to follow the River Tay towards Dundee. James's family farm was beyond Forfar, so after coffee they skirted Dundee and carried on to the north. Then they turned off the main road and into a network of gradually narrowing country roads and lanes, and eventually in at a driveway between two tall stone gateposts each topped by a mossy stone sphere. In the field to their left was a group of bullocks. They all raised their heads from cropping the grass and looked curiously as the car drove past. The field on the other side had been ploughed and was corrugated into tidy brown ridges. They pulled up into a gravelled parking area in front of a two storey stone farmhouse with walls half hidden by creepers. The door opened and Maddy appeared to greet them. Alison was taken by surprise, not sure that she'd have recognised this woman as the same person from that Sunday lunch six months ago. She was dressed in ancient corduroy trousers of a very faded green colour and a moth-eaten pinkish jumper with at least three large holes visible and liberally covered with whitish dog hairs. The owner of those hairs now appeared in the shape of a large woolly Retriever, tail wagging.

"Hello, there," Maddy greeted them. "You've made good time and I'm sure you'll be hungry. Don't worry, lunch will be soon. This is Joe, he's a big softie."

As Alison turned to Joe and greeted him with a pat and a rub, she appreciated that it wouldn't really make sense to wear wafty, silky clothes on a farm. Maddy obviously had made an effort to dress up for her trip to town. This seemed to be the case as all weekend she wore a similar collection of faded trousers and well-worn jumpers. Mr Cooke joined them for lunch. Even if she hadn't known, Alison thought she'd have guessed that he was a farmer. He was tall and broad with a ruddy complexion that stopped sharply over sandy-coloured eyebrows, mid-forehead at his cap-line. Above that his forehead was pale and he had a halo of coarse, thick white hair but was completely bald on top. He was dressed in worn-looking comfortable cords, a woollen jumper and a tweed jacket. He smiled at Alison and shook her hand firmly but during the meal said very little, concentrating on packing away large quantities of a tasty shepherd's pie followed by apple crumble. Maddy made up for her quiet husband with constant chatter.

"I suppose you're wondering where James gets his looks from," she ventured. Alison had no time to reply before Maddy continued. "Well he's tall like Jim but neither of us has a slim build or his dark colouring. We reckon he must be a throw-back, but to which generation we couldn't say. When you meet Malcolm on Sunday you'll see much more of a resemblance, more similar in character too. Not that we're anything but proud of James, he's so brainy and doing so well for himself. But we know that it'll be Malcolm who'll come back and take on the farm." Unusually James, renowned for his calm, unflappable manner, looked slightly uncomfortable. Alison knew that Malcolm, his younger brother, was studying agriculture at Aberdeen University. James had previously told Alison that he was perfectly happy for him to take on the responsibility of the family farm. Whilst he loved his parents and liked visiting the farm, James had no inclination for a rural lifestyle or to be a farmer.

After lunch James explained farther as he showed Alison round the farm. She was enchanted by the ginger-haired Tamworth pigs, their ears standing to attention, and cooed over the most recent litter of piglets as they suckled from their mother. There was also a batch of newly-hatched fluffy chicks in the barn, penned off, their pastel yellow accentuated under a warming light.

"It all looks very nice on a sunny day with daffodils and cute baby animals," James commented. "But I used to feel so trapped in the middle of winter up to my knees in mud or snow, thank goodness for the library in Forfar. I got through my three-book allowance every week. And the cute animals grow up and go to be slaughtered. I suppose I always felt I was the odd man out."

"Well it's good that Malcolm is interested, it's let you off the hook. You can do what you want and your parents are proud of you."

"Yes, I suppose it has been liberating. Speaking of which, I'm afraid my mum isn't very modern and will have assigned you a separate bedroom."

"Don't worry, my mum would do the same," Alison laughed.

Over the weekend James took Alison exploring locally; they walked along the beach at Montrose, taking Joe with them for a run, wandered through the estate grounds at Glamis castle and were intrigued by the camera obscura at Kirriemuir. The images were surprisingly vivid, and it was amusing being able to 'pick up' a few sheep in the palm of your hand. Neither of them had visited the Outlook Tower by Edinburgh castle where there was another camera obscura and they planned that they should go there soon. Maddy fed them very well and Alison thought that James had inherited his mother's cooking skills if nothing else. Mr Cooke seemed to overcome his shyness later in the day, perhaps aided by a couple of drams. He played a competitive hand of whist and beat everyone at Scrabble. When Malcolm arrived on Sunday, he proved to be a perfect amalgamation of his parents. Tall and broad, with a mop of red hair he was chatty and good-humoured, entertaining them with tales of his university escapades.

On Monday afternoon as James drove them south they were laden with baking, jars of jam and even home-made Forfar bridies. Alison was singing along with U2 on the car's cassette deck when she experienced a jolt of guilt, realising that she hadn't thought about Karen for the whole weekend. But after that initial reaction she acknowledged that this was probably a healthy sign and continued to sing.

Twenty-five

The cacophony from the orchestra tuning up was jarring and, in combination with her anxiety about how the event would go, it was threatening to give Alison a headache. Thankfully it began to quieten as the starting time approached. She was sitting in the front row between Chris and James. Although he was the organiser, and had composed a piece of music for today, Chris had wanted to be in the audience rather than taking part. Alison looked around and spotted Karen's parents on the aisle seats of the back row. Mrs Douglas had agreed to come on the condition that she could sit near to the exit and make a quick get-away. When Alison had phoned Peebles to check on their attendance, Mr Douglas had explained that his wife didn't feel up to socialising or talking to people yet but wanted to support Chris's memorial.

There was a hush as the conductor, a post-graduate music student who'd studied with Chris, came from a side door to stand in front of the orchestra. He raised his baton and the music began with a huge organ chord, the opening of the fourth movement of Saint-Saëns's organ concerto.

Chris had been keen to make use of the Reid Hall's organ and also wanted to begin with something rousing, even if it was usually a finale. He'd remembered that Karen had liked the pop song 'If I had words to make a day for you' based on the Saint-Saëns's theme, hence his idea to start with this piece. As the orchestra joined in and the theme built up, Alison felt her tension ease and she began to relax. The programme lasted for an hour comprising of short pieces or excerpts. Chris thought that this would help to make the event more accessible for those who didn't usually attend classical music concerts. He and Alison had co-written a sheet to explain the relevance of each of his choices to Karen. There was a concerto for two flutes by Vivaldi to mark Karen's own instrument. Then Chris's former string quartet, with a new player at first violin, played an arrangement of Paul McCartney's 'My Love' which was Chris's song for Karen. Next came five Bagatelles for clarinet and piano by Gerald Finzi, a composer who had died of Hodgkin's disease in 1956. Chris's own composition had a folky feel. It was for flute and violin, representing his partnership with Karen. Alison recognised the two girls who were performing from the party she'd attended at New Year. She found it hard to believe that Karen had been singing and playing with them then; supposedly healthy just a few months ago. The final piece was sung by two girls with the orchestra backing; a version of 'Bridge over Troubled Water' Karen's favourite song. Alison was in tears by the end of it but loved the way that the cymbals crashed to represent waves, making her shiver. At its conclusion, she turned to give Chris a hug and saw that she wasn't the only one who was crying.

That evening Alison and Linda were relaxing back at the flat after a lot of chat in the hall following the concert, which had then led on to an informal gathering for a substantial number of the crowd at Teviot Row Union. They were curled up on armchairs in the lounge drinking mugs of hot chocolate and Linda had unearthed a packet of chocolate digestive biscuits.

"I don't suppose we'll see much of Chris now. He'll be based in London and won't have much to bring him up here anymore," Alison commented.

"I get the impression that he'll be OK, though. I think he'll bury himself in his work, but the music helps him to express himself," Linda said.

"When I look back he's changed a lot. Remember he used to do all those funny voices? I didn't notice when he stopped, but I haven't heard him do that in ages."

"Maybe Karen being ill made him grow up faster, but he'd probably have dropped it anyway."

"One day he'll be a famous violinist and we'll be able to say we knew him."

"Or he might be a composer. I really liked the thing he wrote. Are you going to hog all the biscuits?" Alison passed her the pack.

"What time is Suzy coming round tomorrow?" she asked.

"I suggested eleven. We should probably save some of these for her." Linda screwed up the top of the biscuit pack and put it up on the mantelpiece.

"You think she might be keen?"

"Yeah, she's definitely looking for a new flat. She'd have moved in straight away if she could have afforded it or got someone to take on her old flat, but it's not easy half-way through the year."

"What went wrong in her current flat?"

"The other two just seemed to gradually exclude her from things, give her the cold shoulder. She doesn't seem to know why; they'd all got on OK in Pollock. I think they both study geography and they seem to do everything together, Suzy's a chemist. Anyway, the atmosphere hasn't been good so I think she just goes out a lot; she's got good friends on her course and in the hockey crowd."

"Oh well I'm sure I'll like her if you get on with her OK."

"Don't feel pressured to say yes, though, if you don't feel she'll fit in. I don't know about you, but I'm pretty bushed, think I'll head to bed. Want me to wash your mug?"

"Thanks." Alison drained the last of her now cooling chocolate and handed up the mug. "I might read for a bit. G'night."

***

271

Alison was in the doctor's office on the ward writing up the case-notes of a patient she'd just clerked in. She smiled to herself; it was funny when patients got medical terms mixed up. The elderly man had been quite emphatic in telling her several times that every time he passed water he got 'epistaxis'. When she enquired gently what exactly he meant by this, it turned out to be haematuria, blood in his urine, not a nosebleed. She was thinking through the differential diagnoses and trying to work out which tests they should be ordering to investigate him. She wouldn't be the one to make any decisions, but this was learning on the job. She was expected to take each case as far as she could and to read around subjects that she was unsure of.

"Hey, Alison," Fred, the houseman, came into the doctor's office. "You look a sporty type, I'm sure you'd love to play hockey on Thursday for us."

"Well I'm better at badminton, but I'll give it a go."

"Know anyone else that could play? Sandy, the reg. says we still need another couple to make up a team."

"My flat-mate's in the Uni hockey team. I could ask her."

"Ace! We don't take it too seriously, but this match is against Simpsons and some of those midwives are brutal. Six o'clock on the Meadows, by Middle Meadow Walk."

That evening James had offered to cook a meal at Spottiswoode Street for Alison and Linda.

"Mmm. You can come back and cook any time," Linda complimented him as she swallowed her first mouthful of pork in a creamy Dijon mustard sauce.

"Glad you approve," James replied. Alison brought up the subject of the ward hockey team.

"Yeah, I can help out," Linda agreed.

"I'll warn you, it won't be what you're used to," James told her. "The goal-posts will be a pile of jumpers and there's no goalie. Not everyone knows the rules and some folks get a bit over-enthusiastic."

"I'm sure I'll cope. Oh Alison, did you see there was a letter for you? I put it on the work-top over there." She pointed and Alison went to retrieve the letter. She returned to the table weighing the bulky envelope in her hands.

"It's hefty and it looks like my dad's writing. Unusual for him, it's normally Mum who writes." She opened the envelope and scanned its contents. "It's about my elective. He's enclosed a letter and some information from his friend in Australia. It looks good. I'd be based at the Royal Perth Hospital and I'm to let him know which specialties I want to be attached to, he suggests maybe two eight week placements and he's given me a list of the units that could take me. I'll need to have a closer look and think about it."

"What did you do for your elective?" Linda asked James.

"I was in London at St Thomas's on a general medical unit. I loved it; the experience I got on the unit was great and just being in the middle of London with everything going on was amazing."

"You know, I've never been to London," Alison commented.

"Well why don't we go in the summer? I've been meaning to ask you what you'd like to do for holidays."

"Yeah, that might be fun. I suppose we should be thinking of organising something, it's not so far off, is it? I'd probably want to go to Oban too for a visit but I'm not sure what my folks are up to over the summer. I'll check. Oh, I'm getting excited already, we could visit all those places I've read about and seen in films, and maybe go to a show."

"I'll look into trains and possible hotels then. Do you have any summer plans yet?" James asked Linda.

"I might try and get a holiday job up here. I'm a bit fed up with summers in Chester, though I know Marks and Spencer will always take me back. Then if I've saved enough I could have a holiday before term starts."

"Wouldn't the M&S here take you on?" Alison asked. "You must know all their systems; I'd imagine all the stores are much the same."

"Good suggestion. I might pop in and ask them."

***

Gasping for breath and with a stitch in her left side Alison raced up the makeshift hockey pitch trying to reach the ball ahead of one of the midwives who was just by her shoulder.

"Here Alison," Linda shouted as she managed to gain a few feet. She passed the ball across and let Linda take it on to the goal. So far, they were winning, but Alison hadn't realised how unfit she'd become since giving up badminton. She bent over, leaning on her stick to regain her breath before trotting back into position at a more relaxed pace. After the match, they congregated in 'The Mortar' pub, a favourite gathering place for medics, just across the road from the medical school and the Royal Infirmary.

"That was fun, but I thought I was going to need resuscitation at one point." Alison recounted. "I haven't been doing any sport recently."

"I don't think we'd have won without your friend," Fred commented.

"I thought she was going to explode once or twice when people didn't play to the rules."

"I lost count of the number of penalties after a while and then I just stopped caring cos no-one was listening to me at all," Linda said.

"Well done anyway, you're our star player. Can I buy you a drink?" Fred asked.

"A half of cider, thanks."

"I think I'm going to have to take up jogging to get fit again. I loved badminton, but with studying and having to go in for on-call nights I can't really commit to a team. It'll only get worse once I'm qualified; the rotas for the first few years are pretty killing. Anyway, I'm not sure it would be the same without Karen." Alison commented.

"Well it would be easy enough to run around the Meadows or the Links from the flat," Linda encouraged her. "Oh, thank you," as her drink arrived. "How often do you guys play hockey?" she asked Fred.

"There are matches most weeks over the summer, but I can't always make it if I'm on call. About six of the medical units in the Royal play, then some surgeons, the orthopods, Simpsons, A+E, we all try to play each other once. Some of the other hospitals play, too, like the Deaconess and the Eastern. Are you not a medic then?"

"No, I gave up after a term and then swapped to do psychology."

Alison got drawn into a conversation about the forth-coming exams with the other students from her ward, but she noticed that Fred and Linda seemed to be engrossed in lively chat. Later as they dawdled home across the Meadows Linda asked,

"How do you get on with Fred?"

"I like him, he's usually cheerful even when he's busy and you can ask him things without him making you feel stupid. Why? Did he ask you out?"

Linda blushed. "Yeah we're meeting at the Botanics on Sunday afternoon."

"That's great."

"Well don't make too big a thing of it just yet. Oh, I forgot to tell you, I went into Marks on Princes Street and when I said I'd worked for them in Chester they were quite encouraging about a summer job. They gave me a form to fill out."

"Will your parents be OK about you staying up here?"

"I don't think they'll mind, we've got to pay the rent for the flat over summer anyway, so I might as well be living in it. I'll probably go to see them for a week at the start of the holidays and then maybe towards the end, too. I'm trying to get them to come up during the Festival, they'd love it."

"It'll be so much better for me if you stay, otherwise I'd be on my own. If they come for the festival, your folks could stay in the spare room. Suzy isn't going to move in until the end of summer, is she?"

Alison had liked Suzy when she came to visit for coffee. She was chatty and seemed to have an open, friendly manner. She described herself as being a tomboy and her clothes, jeans and a Led Zeppelin T-shirt under a black leather jacket, advertised her love of rock music. She made a point of checking that Alison and Linda wouldn't mind her practising guitar in her room as she hoped to get into a band next term. They reassured her that they were used to music rehearsals and it was agreed that she'd take on the unoccupied room.

Twenty-six

The holiday week in London that James had planned came around at last and Alison and James were enjoying being tourists. Their base was a hotel on Russell Square and each day they set out in a different direction, trying to see as much as possible. Today they'd got up early and gone directly to Madam Tussauds in order to beat the queues. Alison was delighted and spooked by how lifelike the exhibits were, and James took her photo beside the Beatles dressed in their Sergeant Pepper uniforms. She discovered that he was a Doctor Who fan when he asked to have his photo taken beside Tom Baker as The Doctor. Their legs became achy after wandering slowly through the galleries so they made their way to the Planetarium and took their ease, sitting back to view the light show. It took a minute for their eyes to adjust when they emerged from the darkness onto a dazzling busy street, but it was only a short walk to Regents Park where they flopped to lie prone on the grass, soaking up the sun.

"That was my favourite," Alison sighed.

"You said that yesterday about the Tower of London and also the day before about Hampton Court Palace," James laughed at her.

"Well, it's all great. Can we get something to eat and then hire a rowing boat?" she suggested.

"The lake looks quite busy and I remember your wonky rowing from last year. We'll have to be careful not to have a collision – it's not the dodgems," he teased.

"I don't mind being a passenger and letting you show off your expertise," she smiled at him as he gave her his hand and helped to pull her up onto her feet. "I think we passed a sandwich place as we came in, we won't need more than that if we're meeting Chris for Chinese tonight."

They spent a lazy afternoon in the park; after their picnic lunch and uneventful rowing they wandered round the rose gardens and then across to Primrose Hill. They admired the view but both agreed that it was a bit tame compared with Arthur's Seat. Alison said it was another place to tick off from her list.

"We used to sing a song in primary school that began: 'I saw a black bird on Primrose Hill.' I can't remember the rest of it," she laughed as she sang.

They decided not to visit the zoo as they'd both been to the one in Edinburgh, so they settled down on a tree-shaded bench to read the books they'd brought with them.

"Doesn't it feel decadent to read a novel instead of a text book?" Alison asked gleefully as she immersed herself in her Mary Higgins Clark crime mystery.

An hour later and feeling re-energised they retraced their footsteps to Baker Street tube station. They had arranged to meet Chris at a Chinese restaurant close to Leicester Square and successfully managed to navigate the Underground and subsequent warren of small streets that made up Chinatown. Chris was already sitting at a table when they arrived and stood up to greet them.

"Great to see you both," he and James shook hands and he gave Alison a hug.

"Hope you've not been waiting long," she checked with him.

"No, I just got here a minute ago. How is the holiday?"

"It's so exciting to see everything and the weather's been great."

"Been to the theatre yet?"

"We've booked for *Cats* tomorrow, thought it would be nice to do something special on our last night."

"You'll love it," Chris predicted. "Let's order and then catch up. This place is famous for its dumplings and dim sum." They concentrated on their menus and put in an order. When the food arrived along with three packs of chopsticks, Alison started to giggle.

"Oh, I know I'll be hopeless at this." Both Chris and James demonstrated to her but her technique was fairly hit and miss, making her giggle more. "I'd definitely be thin if I had to use these all the time," she commented.

"I'm sure you'd improve quickly if you had to rely on them," James predicted.

"It's delicious," she managed to guide a dim sum into her mouth. "I'm sure I'm getting better already and if you two stopped watching me it would help. Tell us what you've been up to Chris."

"I was really busy last month with end of term concerts and assessments, and I got good grades, thankfully. Things are a bit quieter now but I've had some paying work, which is encouraging and will help cover the rent. I'd rather have musical jobs than have to pick up bar or shop work."

"You've got another year here at college, yeah?" James asked

"Yes, and over the summer I've got an orchestra tour of Wales coming up and I might be in Edinburgh for a bit of the festival. How are you getting on Alison? I take it your exams went alright?"

"Oops," Alison dropped another mouthful; luckily it landed back in her bowl. "Yeah, I got through the medical exams, they were pretty scary though. I move onto obstetrics when I get back. I'm looking forward to it, but apparently it can be tricky to get enough deliveries cos the student midwives are after them, too."

"How many do you have to do?"

"Five and we're only there for eight weeks and at gynae during the days for half of that time."

"I ended up going in at the weekends, there was less competition then," James commented.

"Might be a good plan," Alison agreed. She steeled herself to move beyond small talk. It would be easy to coast along like this but she felt she owed it to Karen to at least attempt to check how Chris was coping. "How have you been in yourself Chris?"

He was quiet for a moment.

"Not great a lot of the time," he eventually admitted. "I felt very flat after the memorial was over and it was hard to motivate myself to get up some days, but I know it's better if I keep busy. A lot of the people I meet here didn't know Karen or about what's happened, that can be helpful 'cause they just treat me normally, no kid gloves. But I get lonely, too."

"I don't know how I'd have coped without James and Linda for company," Alison said. "But I'm sure that Karen would want us to get on with things and live life to the full, so I'm trying to do that."

"Yes, I'm grabbing any opportunities that come along. I'm hoping to get some tours abroad next year, might as well travel while I'm young free and single."

"I'm going to be travelling, too." Alison told him about her plans to go to Australia for her elective and that she'd decided to ask to be assigned to the haematology and care of the elderly units. "I'm going to write back to Mr MacDougall when I get home."

"Are you sure that haematology is a good idea?" James asked.

"Yes, I've thought about it carefully and I am genuinely interested in the subject. It might be because of what happened to Karen, it probably is. I know I've got a lot of other specialties to experience, but at the moment it's something I'd consider doing longer term."

"I wouldn't like to think of you being down when you're half-way around the world from home," James told her.

"I don't think it'll upset me. Anyway, I think it's worth spending a bit more time on a specialised unit, and it's probably better if it's not the Western General right now."

"Australia sounds magic and I wouldn't worry, I'm sure you could swap units nearer the time if you changed your mind." Chris reassured her.

***

Alison couldn't stop herself from grinning as she walked up to London Road to catch a bus. She'd just left the labour suite after witnessing her first delivery. She'd had no idea that it would make her feel so elated. At first, she'd worried that she might faint. The room had been very warm and the obvious pain and distress of the woman in labour was beginning to wear through the clinical shell that Alison had learned to raise as a shield in difficult or distasteful situations. There was also something that she found disturbing about the rhythmic whooshing and hissing of the nitrous oxide that the mother was inhaling from a cylinder as her anaesthetic. Maybe Alison had subconsciously changed her breathing pattern to match it, effectively hyperventilating; she definitely began to feel slightly dizzy. She even wondered if some of the gas was escaping into the room and making her woozy. Then her attention was grabbed. After a huge amount of effort and pushing she could begin to see the baby's head at the perineum, a little more clearly with every push until, with a massive heave, the whole head was protruding, looking down at the bed. The midwife gently wiped away some blood from around the mouth and nose. On the next push, a shoulder came out and the midwife pushed gently until the other one came clear and then a complete baby girl emerged, still attached by the umbilical cord. Once the cord had been safely clamped the baby's dad was given the chance to cut it. He'd looked flustered and declined, so the midwife let Alison do it. It was much bigger and thicker than she'd expected, like a greyish, knobbly hosepipe. It spurted a bit as she cut it. Then she watched as the baby was quickly swaddled in warm towels and presented to her mother who was now smiling and crying simultaneously. Alison had never seen a new born baby before. She watched, fascinated, as the mother encouraged the tiny girl to suckle on her breast and thought she'd never seen anything so perfect, despite still being streaked with blood and vernix.

"Come and see us tomorrow," the Mum had invited her and Alison had promised that she'd look in at the post-natal ward in the morning. She didn't know how to express the deep sense of privilege that she felt at having been allowed to share in their experience.

"Anyone seeing me will think I'm mad," she thought, feeling that she was floating slightly above the pavement as if on a magic carpet.

She got off the bus on Princes Street at the Scott Monument and crossed the busy road. She'd arranged to meet Linda after her shift at Marks and Spencer and, still in a euphoric mood, she regaled Linda with all the details of the birth.

"Mmm, sounds like the sort of thing where you have to have been there to appreciate it fully," Linda said doubtfully.

"I'm dying to go and see wee Beth again tomorrow. The only scary thing is that I'm meant to do the hands-on of a delivery myself next time. But I know there'll be a midwife scrubbed up alongside me to keep me right, and no doubt take over if I get into difficulty."

"No offence, but I'm glad I'm not about to give birth any time soon."

"Cheeky besom, just think how encouraging I'd be. Anyway, have you thought which film you want to see?"

The girls had decided to have a night out together as James and Fred were on call for their respective wards.

"I heard that there's a new Steve Martin film that's meant to be really funny, *Dead Men Don't Wear Plaid*. It's on at the Cameo."

"Haven't heard of it, but a comedy sounds good. What time does it start? Could we get some pizza at Dario's on the way past?"

"Yeah, we've got loads of time so that should fit in fine." The friends began to walk along Princes Street towards Lothian Road indulging in a little window-shopping on their way.

The humorous film kept Alison's spirits high and she was still full of amusing banter as she and Linda crossed Bruntsfield Links on their way home. It was one of those Scottish summer evenings that seem to be everlasting, still light and warm at ten o' clock. They passed lots of other people out walking or sitting chatting in groups, making the most of the long day. They clattered up the stairs and into the flat. Alison picked up a bundle of mail lying on the doormat as she came in. She flicked through them as she walked down the hall and then stopped so suddenly that Linda bumped into her. She waved one of the letters at Linda.

"What?" Linda asked.

"It's Gordon's writing."

"Oh! Well you'd better sit down and read it then."

Alison went into the lounge and slit the envelope open with her index finger, making rather a ragged mess of it. She skimmed quickly through the two sides of writing and then began to read it again more slowly. Linda had come into the room behind her and looked at her enquiringly.

"He's been up in Oban and he met my mum. She told him about Karen and he wanted to write to me because he got a terrible shock about it and he knew I'd be badly upset. Also, he'd met Karen a few times and really liked her. That was considerate of him. But this next bit's weird; I can't believe it. Mum must have told him I'm going to Australia. How long was she talking to him for? Anyway, it turns out that he's moving to Perth in September and staying for a while. So, he'll be there at the same time as me. He's put an address in case I want to meet up."

"How likely is that?" Linda asked.

"What, him being in Perth or me wanting to meet up?"

"Well, both."

"He'll be going there for the sailing – yip the address is care of the Royal Perth Yacht Club. But I suppose there are a lot of other places in the world that he could go to for sailing. As for meeting him, well I might. We should be able to be civilised friends after all this time."

"Sure, I can see that you're totally over him by your reaction to his writing on an envelope."

"It just took me by surprise. I'm quite settled with James now."

That night Alison dreamed about sailing. The dream definitely didn't seem to be set in Scotland. There was very bright, hot sunshine and she was wearing a T-shirt over a swimming costume, enjoying the cooling spray that flew up. The figure at the tiller was wearing a white T-shirt with navy shorts and deck shoes, showing off muscular, tanned limbs. His dark blond hair had natural sun bleached ends and his deep blue eyes were gazing at her. It was Gordon, just as he'd looked last summer at Lake Windermere.

The next morning Alison decided to put the dream and the letter out of her mind. She didn't need to make a decision about whether or not to meet up with Gordon for months. She set off for Elsie Inglis, keen to visit baby Beth. Maybe she'd be allowed to hold her today.

Twenty-seven

On Monday morning, there was a surgical list at the gynaecology unit and Alison was in theatre to observe. She'd watched a hysterectomy and a pelvic floor repair and now the last case was to be a laparoscopic dye test. She tried hard not to yawn behind her surgical mask. Last night she'd been very late home after sitting all day with a woman in labour to attain her fourth delivery. The woman was a 'prim', so everything took a long time and the baby didn't emerge until after midnight. Then Alison had to deliver the placenta and ask one of the SHOs to come and supervise while she repaired the episiotomy she'd made to ease the delivery. Even after all of that she'd felt she couldn't rush off, so stayed and accompanied the new Mum and her baby boy to the post-natal ward and saw them settled in. She'd treated herself to a taxi home, but probably only managed to get three or four hours of sleep. She'd been exhausted after the long day but had trouble winding down, her mind still buzzing with the excitement and stress of being in pole position for the delivery. Even with back-up in the form of a very experienced midwife right at her shoulder, she'd felt an incredible weight of responsibility for the whole event. Luckily her gynaecology attachment was at Bruntsfield hospital which was only two streets away from the flat, so she'd been able to set her alarm for eight o'clock and maximum possible sleeping time. Of course, when the radio came on she was deeply asleep and it was a struggle to surface and get going.

"Alison, come a bit closer. I want you to have a look down this laparoscope," Dr Martin, the consultant, beckoned to her. She had to stretch, stand on tip-toe and lean across to see through the instrument without touching anything that was sterile. He held and moved the eyepiece at the top of the tube that he'd inserted into the patient's pelvis through an incision at her umbilicus. Alison had a view of the top of the woman's womb which looked like a pink dome. She could see a fallopian tube with frilly ends emerging at each side above the ovaries which were oval with surfaces raised by multiple small bumps. They reminded Alison of the sago pudding her Granny used to make for her.

"Now this lady and her husband have been trying to get pregnant with no success. Her day 21 progesterone levels indicate that she's been ovulating over the past three cycles. So today we're checking if her tubes are patent. Sister is about to inject some blue dye through the vagina and I want you to watch out for it appearing from the fallopian tubes through the laparoscope. You keep looking and let me know what you see." Alison kept looking and after about two minutes could see a puff of blue begin to gather at the frond-like ends of each fallopian tube and then increase in volume to a trickle then a steadier flow.

"There's plenty of dye coming, both sides," she reported.

"Good, that means her eggs should be getting through. Can I have a quick squint? Not that I doubt you, but I'd like to see. Beautiful!"

After the procedure Alison changed out of theatre pyjamas back into her clothes and then went to the hospital dining room for lunch. She saw Paul, her fellow medical student, and went to his table to join him.

"How're things?" she asked

"OK. I was in the clinic this morning, had to take some of the case histories. You girls have such an advantage here; I can't get to grips with asking women all these details about their periods. It makes me feel pretty uncomfortable."

"Not cut out to be a gynaecologist then? How're you getting on with your deliveries?"

"I've got them all, thank God. You?"

"Still one to get and this is our last week before we swap to paeds."

"Awful about that stillbirth last Friday."

"Yes. It must have been terrible to have to go through labour knowing that the baby had already died."

"He wasn't really overdue or anything and apparently he looked perfect. There'll be a P.M. of course."

Alison had learned now that in addition to the joyful experience of most deliveries there were also intensely sad times when babies were born with serious problems, or as had happened last week, were born dead. The whole hospital had changed atmosphere, everyone grieving for the baby and wondering how the bereft parents were going to cope. She and Paul ate in silence for a few moments. Paul finished his macaroni cheese and wiped up all of the remaining cheese sauce with his chips until his empty plate gleamed.

"What's the programme for this afternoon then?" He asked.

"Lots of admissions to the ward I heard. They'll be looking for us to help with clerking in."

"I'll meet you up there then. I'm going to need a fag if I've got to ask about periods again. I'll go for a wander on the Links." Left on her own Alison decided that she'd need a coffee to fortify her and help keep her awake for the afternoon. She went up to the counter to order one.

Later on, the ward she took responsibility for admitting two of the pre-op cases for the next day, a lady with an ovarian cyst large enough to make her abdomen look very swollen and another young woman for infertility investigations. She decided after that to head for home, intending to go out for a run round the Meadows before a bath and early bed. She had been trying to stick to her intention of regular running to keep fit and was slowly increasing the distance of her route.

On Tuesday, she and Paul swapped roles, with Alison going to the outpatient clinic and Paul to the operating theatre. They met up again at lunchtime; today Paul was demolishing a huge plate of mince and potatoes.

"You did well to stay out of theatre today," he commented.

"Why?"

"That woman you admitted with the ovarian cyst, Dr Anderson only went and punctured it and the stuff sprayed all over me, I got drenched and everyone thought it was hilarious."

"Oh," Alison couldn't help letting a small chuckle escape. She didn't know him well, but Paul was thought to be a bit of a poser. He had a sculpted-looking haircut and a neat Van-Dyke beard and moustache. He favoured waistcoats and even occasionally wore a bow tie. She'd have liked to have seen his face when he got soaked.

"Did Dr A. say whether he thought it looked benign?" she asked, drawing the focus away from her giggle.

"Yeah, he thought so, and there was no sign of any metastatic tumours."

"Oh, that's good, my lady will be so relieved. I'll maybe pop up to the ward and see her later in the week. What's your case for the role play tomorrow?"

On Wednesday mornings, the students on this block went as a group to the reproductive biology department for lectures on psycho-sexual problems. Tomorrow they were going to act out scenarios that might present to the clinic. They'd each been given a case as a 'patient' and would have to take turns at pretending to be the doctor.

"I've got trouble with gender identity and want a sex change."

"Tricky. I've got to play a woman who wants her husband checked out cos they haven't managed to consummate their marriage. He's got erectile dysfunction."

Paul snorted. "Who's your husband?"

"Richard."

"Ace! Well I hope you get him sorted out. What are you doing this afternoon?"

"I think I'll head over to Elsie's to see what's going on, try to get my last delivery."

"OK, well good luck."

***

James looked up from the 'Scotsman' as Alison clattered into his flat. They had arranged to eat together but she was earlier than expected and a glance at her face told him something was wrong.

"What's up?" he asked.

"We've got this wee boy on the ward with leukaemia and they're taking samples from him to try and get a match for a bone marrow transplant. If no-one in his family is close enough, there's a register of donors in London. Why couldn't they have tried that for Karen?" She sounded angry.

"Come and have a seat." He put his newspaper down and tried to settle her down with him on the settee. But Alison was worked up and agitated. She perched on the edge of the couch's cushion and snatched her hand back from him, not responding to his attempt at a hug.

"OK. Well, you see all the work-up takes quite a long time. You're right that theoretically it is a treatment that could have been used. But Karen seemed to have responded to her first treatment and be in remission, so there was no obvious reason to consider it at that stage. Then when she relapsed everything just went downhill so fast there wouldn't have been an opportunity to look for donors."

"Being an only child would mean less chance of a family match I suppose." Alison was following his explanation.

"Yeah and there's no guarantee of a match on the register. I've heard of it, the Anthony Nolan Register named after a wee kid. His Mum helped to set it up, but it's only been going for a few years and I think it's still quite small."

"Does it work?"

"You mean bone marrow transplants? Yes, they can be a big success, but they're not without risks and complications. D'you want to read up a bit about them? I'll have some articles somewhere that I read for my exam, I'll look them out for you if you'd like."

"Thank you, I'm sorry I exploded on you. Somehow it just brought it all back." Alison was on the verge of tears.

"Which is one of the reasons I worry about you choosing to do extra haematology on your elective."

"I know," she bent over, put her palms flat over her eyes and shook her head. "Maybe you're right. I'd thought I was doing so well, but even quite small things can still push me over. I'm not totally committed yet to which units I work on, I could still change."

"Think about it," he decided that she needed some space, so let the subject drop. "Want to help me in the kitchen?"

"As long as you don't comment on my chopping techniques again."

"OK. I promise not to."

"What're you making tonight?"

"Beef stroganoff."

"Yummy, sounds good." She followed him through to the kitchen where he provided her with a wrap-around apron, a knife, chopping board, two onions and a pile of mushrooms.

"You do the veg and I'll do the meat."

Alison took her board over to the sink and turned on the cold tap before beginning to peel and chop the onions. She could sense James looking at her and turned to see that his eyebrows were raised in enquiry.

"My Granny always told me that this stopped your eyes from nipping. You're supposed to run the cold water over your wrists."

He laughed at her as tears began running down her face despite her precautions.

"I wasn't going to comment," he teased "but I guess it must be a genuine old wives' tale."

"Well I suppose I might be worse without the water." She was giggling as she finished dicing the onions. "There you can have these." She gave him the board with the pile of diced onions, collected another board and began to peel and chop the mushrooms. "I've decided I definitely don't want to specialise in Paeds," she announced to him.

"Any particular reason?"

"I just find it too difficult being around ill kids. They can't understand what's going on. Either they're scared and screaming the place down which is distressing, or they're quiet and being brave, which I think might be worse. And the parents are hard, too; it's like having to deal with three stressed patients instead of one. I'm not saying that an adult's relatives can be ignored or are always easy to deal with, but somehow with kids all of that angst is magnified."

"Oh well, that's another option scored off from your list."

"Yeah, I'm much better at saying what I don't want to do than knowing what I will do. No burning ambition."

"I'm not sure many people are sure at the outset, and a lot change their mind when faced with the reality of a specialty. Knowing your limits is important."

"Yeah, we're not all like Robert, programmed from day one. Here you are, veg. ready for cooking." She handed over her chopping board with sliced mushrooms and accepted a glass of red wine in exchange as James continued cooking.

After they'd eaten James disappeared into his box room and emerged with a back-copy of 'Medicine', a monthly journal that he subscribed to in order to keep abreast of the latest in medical practice and some British Medical Journal articles.

"You can take these home with you to read up about bone marrow transplants. Want a lift?"

When they drew up outside the flat on Spottiswoode Street, Alison was initially surprised to see a collection of boxes and bags lining the pathway up to the close door. Then she remembered that Suzy was due to move in this week, she'd popped in to collect her key at the weekend. These must be her belongings.

"I'll park the car and give a hand with her stuff," James offered when she explained. When they'd struggled up three flights of stairs, James bringing a heavy box and Alison two bags full of pillows and bed linen they discovered Suzy and her parents in the front bedroom.

"Oh, hi Alison thanks for helping. This is my mum and dad." Alison introduced James and they shook hands all round. With five of them it didn't take many more journeys on the stairs to have all of Suzy's belongings brought up. Then Suzy's mum helped to make up the bed.

"I want to know you'll be comfortable tonight," she insisted while inserting the downie into its cover. Once that was achieved to her satisfaction Suzy's dad suggested taking them all out for a drink.

"Where's your local?" he asked.

"We usually go to the Golf," Alison replied. It was a warm evening and she enjoyed the stroll across the Links to the pub. They settled at a table and James went up to the bar with Suzy's dad to order.

"I'm so pleased to meet one of Suzy's new flat mates," her mum said to Alison. "We were worried about her last year with those other nasty girls." Suzy looked at Alison behind her Mum's back and rolled her eyes.

"Don't worry; we'll look after her Mrs Cameron. It's a pity that Linda isn't here, too, but maybe you've met her. Do you ever get along to support the hockey team?" Alison asked.

"No, it's a bit too far to come down from Perth, especially on a week-day. We used to turn out regularly for her school matches, though." Mrs Cameron then proceeded to prattle on at length about Suzy's talents for hockey and music, going into great detail about school musical productions from the past. Alison leaned into James when he sat down beside her and let the chatter wash over her. There was something about the family atmosphere and the proud maternal monologue that was very soothing. Snuggled up beside James she felt secure and content.

Twenty-eight

As she stepped down from the train onto the platform at Queen Street station, Alison's ears tuned in to the buzz of conversation in the distinctive Glasgow accent. She'd know where she was even with her eyes shut. It amazed her that you only needed to travel a few tens of miles in Scotland and everyone sounded completely different. She emerged from the cover of the station's roof, walked along Queen Street and turned into St Vincent Place at the corner of George Square. Despite the tickle of smirry drizzle on her face she was feeling incredibly light-hearted today. Maybe it was cold, and a bit wet and drab but another set of exams was over, passed and under her belt. Now she only had the surgical block to go and then no more exams, she'd be on her elective. She turned left onto Buchanan Street heading towards Frasers where she'd agreed to meet Helen. Her sister was buying lunch as a post-exam treat. As she neared the shop entrance, she craned her head trying to spot Helen.

"Hey, here I am," she felt a tap on her shoulder, whirled round and discovered that Helen had been right behind her. Helen was snuggly dressed in a cherry-red coat; she had a jaunty black beret perched at an angle on her head and a matching scarf elegantly draped. Alison admired and was envious of Helen's style; she'd always thought that being an airhostess suited her sister. They laughed and hugged.

"Will we go into Frasers for a coffee and a catch up? Then we can have a look around some shops and work up an appetite for lunch," Helen suggested.

Once they were settled with coffee and scones Helen congratulated Alison on passing her exams.

"You're nearly there now," she said.

"Yes, that's just what I was thinking. It's hard to believe there's only one more lot to go. It feels like I've been studying and sitting exams forever."

"So, what comes next?"

"My surgical block, which includes A and E and anaesthetics."

"Where are you based for that?"

"I'll be out at Bangour General which is like an old army hospital, lots of wooden huts. It's in the middle of the countryside just a bit west of Edinburgh airport. I'll probably stay there during the week unless I'm lucky and someone else has a car and can give me a lift. It's a bit far to travel every day."

"So, do they give you a room?"

"Yeah we get a room in the doctor's residency and the staff canteens are usually very reasonable. So how are you and Neil?" Alison was rewarded by a huge grin from her sister.

"Guess what? I'm pregnant."

"Wow, that's great." Alison was genuinely surprised. "When are you due? How are you? Oh gosh, I've just done my obstetrics; it's a bit scary to think of you as a mum-to-be."

"I'm fine, just a wee bit of nausea so far. It's still really early; I'm not due till June. So, we're not announcing it generally yet, but I wanted to tell you."

"So, do Mum and Dad know?"

"No, I thought we'd wait until Christmas to tell them."

"Keeping up the tradition of the big Christmas announcement?"

"Yeah, well I should have had my scan by then and be past the risky early weeks."

"I just can't believe you're going to be a mum and I'll be an auntie. Would it be bad luck to go and look at some baby things?"

"I think it'd be OK to look, but we shouldn't buy anything."

"Let's go then." So, the sisters headed off to the baby department and had great fun researching the equipment that Helen would need and planning the future nursery. Then they wandered into other departments trying to get inspiration for their Christmas shopping. Eventually Helen admitted to feeling hungry again.

"I'm trying so hard not to over-eat, but I find I start to feel sick if I leave off eating for too long."

"Not a problem," Alison reassured her. "I'm perfectly happy to have some lunch. Where are we going?"

"I thought Sloans; it's just around the corner." The sisters left the cosy cocoon of the department store and hurried down Buchanan Street into Argyll Street. The historic Sloans restaurant was only a block away and was warm and welcoming, which they appreciated even though they'd spent only a few short minutes on the wet street.

"I'm going to have the fish and chips," Alison told the waitress after studying the menu.

"I think I'll have scampi. You're allowed a glass of wine if you'd like, Alison. I'll stick to water."

"I'll go for a glass of Chardonnay, then, thanks." The waitress departed with their order. "Have you thought what you're going to do about work once you've had the baby?"

"I hope I'll still be able to work part-time, maybe a couple of days a week. It should be possible, as I've only ever worked domestic flights. But if I can't keep flying then I can probably get a place on the ground crew, you know doing the check-in desk and stuff like that. They'll probably move me there once I get obviously pregnant anyway."

"You don't want to be a full time mum then?"

"I don't think so, but you never know I might change my mind once the baby's born. When do you start applying for jobs?"

"Just after New Year. I'll have to get sorted out before I go to Australia. I can't exactly pop back for interviews."

"Yeah, Mum told me about your big trip. It sounds great."

Alison recounted the details. "I was really surprised that Dad suggested it."

"They're not so bad, our parents," Helen grinned. Their food arrived and there was silence for a few minutes while they attacked it hungrily. Then Helen asked Alison if she knew yet what she wanted to specialise as.

"Not yet. I keep joking with James that I have a huge list of things I don't want to do and a tiny one for things I might be interested in. But sometimes I get a bit worried about it."

"What about James? Didn't he just pass some big exams too?"

"Yeah, his membership exams. So now he can start applying for senior reg. jobs. He wants to carry on in hospital medicine and specialise in endocrinology."

"Which is?"

"Oh, things like diabetes and thyroid disease. But he says he probably needs to make a move away from

305

Edinburgh for a while. He's been advised that it's a good thing for his career to move and get different experience."

"You won't be so keen for that."

"He seems to think it might just be for one or two years. He's not planning on selling his flat, says he'll just rent somewhere wherever he ends up. In fact, he suggested I could move into his place and he'd only charge me minimal rent. That way he could still stay there if he comes up for weekends."

"Are you tempted?"

"I'm thinking about it. I don't think I'd want to stay on at Spottiswoode Street once I'm working. Linda's likely to move on once she graduates and it would be weird living there with other students."

"Neil and I have started looking at houses. We'll want somewhere with a garden, and it sounds ridiculous but we're already thinking about which areas have good schools. To be honest it makes me feel I'm turning middle-aged already." Alison laughed, as her sister still looked fresh-faced and could be mistaken for a teenager.

"Lots of changes ahead, that's for sure. So, are we allowed pudding?" She opened the menu to peruse the desert selection.

**

Bangour General Hospital was set on a hillside in a field adjacent to a farm. A ground frost had set in during the night so Alison had to step carefully as she left the hut designated as the doctors' residence to walk to the canteen for breakfast. Her breath was clouding in front of her as she picked her way along the frozen path and there was a distinct odour of manure in the air. The residence was on the edge of the site and she could see a donkey grazing alongside the fence. When she opened the swing doors to the canteen, a wall of hot steamy air hit her and the farmyard smell was replaced by the scent of toast. She loaded her tray with cereal, toast and a mug of tea, payed and looked around for a suitable table. She spotted a student who'd been in her lab group for microbiology in second year and went to sit alongside her.

"Hi, Lorraine." Lorraine quickly finished chewing on a mouthful of bacon roll and swallowed it.

"Hello Alison, haven't seen you in a while. What brings you to Bangour?"

"Surgery. And you?"

"Obstetrics."

"I've just finished mine, at Elsie's. It can be tough getting all the deliveries in."

"Yeah, I've heard that. Sorry I better go now; the ward round starts in five minutes. But hopefully we can catch up for a chat sometime if you're staying over?"

"Yeah, see you around." Alison finished her meal then set off for the surgical unit where she had a tutorial scheduled at nine o'clock. Alison had enjoyed her surgical attachment in third year and was looking forward to the next months. Although she knew she didn't have the psyche required to actually be the person with the scalpel she enjoyed the atmosphere in theatre and was interested in the process of the operations. She wondered if on learning more about anaesthetics that might be something she could envisage working at longer term. It was one of the things on her 'possible' list, along with general practice and hospital medicine of some description.

The week went in very quickly and she was lucky to be offered a lift back to Edinburgh with one of the surgical SHOs after their list was completed on Friday afternoon. She had been the second assistant to his first in theatre. So, while he'd been delicately holding forceps and cutting sutures Alison had been keeping the liver out of harm's way using the liver retractor. This job was often given to medical students, they could get a good view of the proceedings but it was tiring and required a fair amount of stamina to keep the retractor steady.

"How's your arm? Tired?" he asked her as they swung past the farm buildings down towards the main road.

"OK now, but I felt it was getting a bit shaky after a while."

"Any plans for the weekend?"

"Just catching up with friends, maybe going to the cinema."

"Anything good on?"

"This one would be at the Filmhouse, I think it's French. My boyfriend's into arty-type cinema, foreign with subtitles. Sometimes they're OK."

"Right. I'll probably just stick to a football match and the pub then. Hearts are playing at home."

"Are you a big fan?" she asked. He then proceeded to give her his views on the team's recent form for the rest of the journey into Edinburgh, dropping her off at the end of the Western Approach Road with a wave. She set off towards home, walking briskly up Lothian Road. Getting a lift had saved her a lot of time compared with the bus journey. She could fit in a run and have a leisurely bath before meeting James.

Later she retraced her steps to the corner of Lothian Road and Morrison Street where James was waiting for her.

"So, do you feel up to the cinema?" he asked her after a hug and kiss of greeting.

"As long as it's lively enough to keep me awake and not one of those with lots of atmosphere but not much happening."

"I think you'll be OK." The Filmhouse was still undergoing development in what had previously been a church. So, at present the entrance was through a small close which led to the back of the building. Alison found that she was drawn into the drama of 'Le Retour de Martin Guerre' so, despite the subtitles; there was no danger of her falling asleep. When it was over, they retreated to the Golf Tavern.

During their walk and in the pub, they exchanged their views on the film and proceeded to catch up on their respective activities of the past week. James was excited as he'd been asked to go to Cambridge for an interview for a senior registrar post.

"Addenbrookes would be my second choice after London, so I'm really pleased."

"Well done, that's brilliant. And you've got a couple of weeks to prepare for it so that's good."

"The job would be for two or three years and I reckon I should have a good shot at consultants' posts after that."

"D'you still think you'd keep your flat on here?"

"I'm planning to, at least to begin with. Why?"

"Well I might have someone who'd want my room at Spottiswoode Street, in which case I'd take you up on your offer and move my stuff in before I go to Australia. I met a girl from my year, Lorraine, at Bangour. She's friendly with this girl Meg who's currently on her elective. Lorraine knows that Meg will be looking for a new flat when she gets back, as she used to live with her boyfriend and they've since broken up. So, she'd want somewhere just as I'm going away."

"How about Linda and Suzy? Do you think they'd be happy with this Meg?"

"Nothing's definitely settled yet. Lorraine's going to get in touch with Meg and obviously I'll need to talk to Linda and Suzy. But actually, Linda will know Meg from first year, they were on the same body for anatomy before

310

Linda left. I think they got on alright. And Suzy should be OK with it. Actually, she's not been the easiest to live with."

"Oh? You didn't say anything before."

"We thought she might settle down once term was farther on. She's nice enough most of the time, but she comes home reeling drunk at least twice a week. I don't know how she turns up for classes the next day, or plays hockey. I know we've all had times when we've been drunk, but two or three times a week seems a bit excessive, especially when she's thrown up a few times. I'm wondering if that's why her other flat didn't work out."

"Maybe it goes with the rock music. D'you think it's just alcohol, no drugs?"

"I've not seen any sign of that. She just seems so different from the picture her mum painted of the sporty, sweet-voiced, musical girl that night we came here after we moved her stuff in."

"Probably she's kicking out against that image."

"Maybe, but it is her third year, you'd think she might have got it out of her system by now. Anyway, Linda will have to put up with her till the summer. When I'm in Australia I think she'd rather have someone else around, not just my empty room. Though she does spend quite a bit of time at Fred's place."

"Fred's still on the scene?"

"Yeah, he seems smitten and I think Linda seems really happy."

"That's great. Well the thing with Meg certainly seems like a neat solution. I hope it'll work out. Another drink?"

"Yeah I'll have another one before home. Don't think that'll be over-doing it, I wouldn't want to be a hypocrite."

***

The two-week Christmas break arrived and Alison went up to Oban on the 23rd joining Helen and Neil there for the first part of her holiday. Helen announced her pregnancy as planned and even accepted a small glass from the champagne bottle that Mr Scott opened in celebration. Her Mum was delighted by the news of a grandchild in the offing and fussed around Helen. She was less pleased by Alison's plan to move into James's flat.

"I just don't approve of you moving in with him if you're not married," she stated.

"Mum, he won't even be there. He's going to be in Cambridge. He might come up to Edinburgh some weekends. I thought you'd be pleased that I'm saving you some rent money while I'm in Australia."

"Well, thank you, but that's not the point. Living in the city may have given you modern ideas, but it's not how you were brought up."

"But you like James. Why don't you just look on it as me helping him out by house-sitting?"

"She'll get used to it," Helen reassured Alison later. "Just give her some time to come round."

"But there isn't much time. Unless they come down to Edinburgh before the end of February I won't see Mum and Dad before I go away. Probably not till my graduation. I'd hate to go half-way round the world feeling that we'd fallen out."

"I'll have a word with her. Try talking to Dad too, he might be able to get her to back down."

Before Alison left a shaky truce was agreed, perhaps helped by interventions from Helen and Mr Scott. There was still definite frostiness in Mrs Scott's farewells, possibly not helped by Alison's next destination. Because James had been working at Christmas he wanted to spend New Year on the farm with his family and Alison was going to join him there. Helen and Neil were driving her to Perth, where they'd all arranged to meet up with James for lunch.

"Bye Mum. I'll write soon," Alison called through the open car window and waved. She sighed and wound the window back up as the car pulled away.

"Don't worry about Mum. She just finds it hard to let you grow up. The new arrival should help; take over your place as the baby of the family," her Dad had whispered to her as he'd hugged her goodbye.

Twenty-nine

Beeb-beeb-beeb…Beep-beep-beep…Beep-beep-beep…

The crash-call bleeper went off. The anaesthetist that Alison was shadowing grabbed it out of her pocket, checked the screen and began to run.

"DSN2, arrest." she shouted. "Come on."

Alison had never attended a cardiac arrest before. She followed the anaesthetist, running along the hospital corridors, dodging people and trolleys, then up two flights of stairs. When they arrived, panting, on the ward a junior nurse pointed to a single room half-way up the corridor on the left. A female doctor was performing chest compressions on a middle-aged man who had extensive bandaging to his head. There was already an IV line in place attached to a saline drip. A porter arrived with the arrest trolley quickly followed by the medical registrar and a senior nurse. They inserted a board underneath the patient's back to make the cardiac massage more effective. The anaesthetist began to give oxygen by mask and bag while the registrar and nurse applied ECG pads to the man's chest.

"You want to shock him before I put a tube down?" the anaesthetist asked.

"Yeah, just charging up the defibrillator." The registrar put the paddles in place.

"All stand clear." The current from the defibrillator made the patient jerk. As soon as that was done the anaesthetist pulled the man's head back, inserted a laryngoscope and then an endotracheal tube.

"This allows us to give more continuous oxygen, makes a big difference if the resus procedure is lengthy. It's very important in protecting the brain, especially in this chap who's obviously just had neurosurgery," she explained to Alison.

The nurse took over the heart massage now as the houseman looked as if she was tiring. Meanwhile the registrar wasn't happy that the ECG tracing had improved.

"Still in VF, let's shock again. Stand clear." He repeated the shock. "Can someone change that saline for bicarb? What's the history?"

"Age forty-four. Day two after craniotomy for a frontal meningioma. Previously fit, no history of heart disease, surgery was uncomplicated," the surgical houseman reported.

"So, a healthy heart, we should be able to get him back. Aah, looking better," he commented while peering at the ECG tracing. "Can someone check that we have a space ready in ITU once he's stabilised? Is the consultant surgeon coming in?"

"Yes, he's on his way," the houseman confirmed while changing the fluid in the drip. The other junior doctor went to make the phone-call to ITU. Alison was impressed by the coordinated efforts of the team and felt a bit anxious that she'd be one of the team members in just over six months' time.

That evening she confided as much to James.

"Don't worry, as a junior you just do what you're told. If no-one in his family is close enough, there's a register of donors in London. After that you just follow instructions from the reg. They'll be running things."

"It was really satisfying that we got him back."

"Yeah, a good first experience. D'you want me to look at those job lists now?"

Alison had received the information she needed to apply for house-jobs and wanted to ask James's advice.

"I'll get them. Would you like a coffee?"

"Sure."

She put the kettle on to boil before going through to her bedroom to collect the sheaf of papers. Soon she reappeared with two mugs of coffee, a packet of biscuits and the information sheets.

"OK, so I can apply for three units each for medicine and surgery and rank them in order of preference, yeah?"

"Yeah. You're most likely to get in where they know you, so best to apply for units where you've been attached as a student, unless you didn't like the bosses or the rota is too killing."

"What does UMT mean here?" she pointed to the sheet.

"All of the time you work on a rota out-with the normal working day is added up. That figure is divided by four and every four-hour block represents one 'unit of medical time' or UMT."

"So, it's the overtime rate?"

"Yeah, but the rate of pay for a UMT varies. For house-jobs where you have to live on the premises when you're on call it's currently a third of normal hourly rates. In other words, each hour is one twelfth of the usual hourly rate. Some SHO and reg. jobs you can be on-call from home and then the rate is less."

"That's outrageous. I remember Helen telling me she gets paid double time or time and a half for overtime or anti-social hours."

"Yeah, I know, but I think the NHS would be bankrupt if it had to pay doctors proper overtime. For a one in two rota you'd be on call for about two hundred and fifty extra hours a month. They get away with it by saying that you're only on standby and might not actually be working the whole time. If you're on a quiet unit, you might get to sleep all night."

"But think of all the nights you've been up continuously. They don't tell you about this before you start medical school."

"No, but there isn't really a choice. You have to do the house jobs in order to be fully registered. Some people go abroad to work after that if they don't like the system, but most doctors want to stay here so they just have to get on with it. It's actually not so much the money that bothers me, but the worry that if I'm working such long hours and get really tired then I might make a mistake."

"Mmm. I think I need another biscuit to keep my strength up just thinking about it. Want one?" she proffered the packet of Jaffa cakes. "So, for medicine I'll probably put the G-I and chest units at the Royal and the Western medical unit. Maybe I should put the Western first, the rota looks better. It's a two in five rather than a one in two. And for surgery there's Bangour and 9 and 10 at the Royal, but I've not really been anywhere else."

"I'd put Bangour first, the keen surgical types will apply for the Royal. Then just put another quieter unit as number three, but I'm sure you're likely to get in at Bangour. It'd be worth going to have a chat with one of the consultants at each of your first choices since you're going to be out of the country."

"OK, thanks. I'll mull it over for a bit, but I think that's a reasonable plan. I think I'd need to buy a car, though, if I end up working out at Bangour for six months."

"Well, that shouldn't be a problem once you're working. It took me a wee while to get used to having money and then I was working such long hours I didn't have any time to spend it. So, anyway, how's the rest of anaesthetics going so far? Still on your possible list?"

"Yeah, it's been really interesting. I like being in theatre doing the G.A.s, but I've also seen a spinal and a Bier's block today."

"That's good…sounds like company arriving," as the front door was closed and voices approached from the hall. Linda and Fred appeared in the lounge doorway.

"Hi, you guys," Linda greeted them.

"Excellent, we'd planned to play cards, but it's much more interesting with four," Fred announced, roping them in.

"OK, what do you suggest?" Alison asked.

"I could teach you all to play Euchre. I learned it on my elective in Canada and its good fun. Best to separate couples though, Alison with me and Linda with James. I'll set it up at the table." They followed Fred through to the kitchen and let him organise the rest of their evening.

***

Smoothing the wet plaster-of-Paris to make a cast for her patient's broken wrist reminded Alison of pottery classes at school. Was it just the feel of it? The smell

319

seemed familiar too. The plaster technician was keeping watch over her progress, talking her through each stage. She enjoyed the opportunity to practise a hands-on skill and the plaster room was a small oasis of calm in the hinterland of the busy A and E department at the Royal Infirmary.

"There you go. Maybe not as smooth as one of mine, but it'll do the job," the technician commented.

"Does it feel OK?" Alison asked the elderly woman who'd slipped and fallen on an icy patch of pavement that morning.

"Yes, dear, it's much more comfortable now. But I wish it was my left arm, I'm going to be useless at everything."

"Who else is at home with you?" Alison asked.

"Oh, my husband, but he's not much use at cooking and such-like."

"You'll just have to tell him what to do," Alison suggested.

"Aye, most women are good at that," the male technician joked.

After she'd washed the hardening clay off her hands, scrubbing around her finger-nails Alison escorted her patient to reception. There the woman was given a date for a review appointment at the fracture clinic and then allowed to go home. When Alison returned to the main department another patient's X-rays were back, ready to be studied. She thought that she could see a fracture of the nasal bone and checked with one of the SHOs.

"Yip, you'll need to get him an ENT appointment. Any other injuries?"

"No just a few abrasions, they've been cleaned. Nothing to be sutured," Alison reported.

"OK, I'll come along with you to sign things off and then you can arrange the follow-up," he said.

Alison enjoyed being allowed to see a variety of patients semi-independently with supervision by the regular A and E doctors. She was encouraged to carry out any treatments that were needed, like today's arm cast. Last week she'd been taught how to do basic suturing and felt satisfied with her first results, although she was quite glad that it had been a scalp laceration so the scar wouldn't be on view once the patient's hair grew back in. She gave an appointment card to the man with the broken nose then, looking at her watch, decided to sign off for the day as it was ten past five.

Tonight, she planned to start packing up her belongings ready to move out of Spottiswoode Street. Tomorrow James was coming with his car to take everything to Harrison Gardens. It was his last day at the Western on Friday and then he'd be setting off for Cambridge at the weekend. So, because of his last on-call slot and his farewell night out, tomorrow was the only night that he had left to help with her flitting. After three and a half years in the flat she'd amassed a sizeable amount of possessions so she'd gone to the Co-op supermarket round on Marchmont Road last weekend and asked for some cardboard boxes. She felt daunted at the thought of sorting through everything. "Oh well, it's got to be done," she thought as she set off along Jawbone Walk.

After a bowl of soup and a sandwich for sustenance she decided to start with her chest of drawers. She put David Bowie on her music system and opened the bottom drawer. Attracted by the music Linda appeared, she leant on the doorframe, watching.

"Funny, us growing up and moving on."

Alison looked up.

"Yeah, it's a bit sad moving out, but I'm excited too. You sure you're alright about Meg?"

"Yeah, it's only for a few months and anyway I'm going to be working like a slave to get my dissertation in and then for my finals. Just think you'll have all of that behind you in a few weeks."

"As long as I pass."

"You will. I need to get decent grades to get that training placement at the London clinic. Speaking of which, I'd better go and do some work."

Alison started on the next drawer up, she was taking this opportunity to sort through her clothes and discard things that she'd stopped wearing. The cassette came to an end and she stood up to change the music. She realised that her left foot had been folded underneath her while she was kneeling and it had gone to sleep. She hobbled as the blood flowed back in giving her pins and needles. This caused her to stagger slightly into the furniture and knock over a shallow glass dish containing Kirby grips and safety pins.

"Oh drat," she muttered and got down on hands and knees to gather up the pins. Some had scattered under her desk drawers and she scrabbled around trying to get at them. Eventually she pulled the desk out from the wall, thinking that she should probably hoover up the collection of dust that she could see behind them. There was also a sheet of paper which must have fallen down the back of the desk. She picked it up, glanced at it, and then froze. The handwriting and purple ink couldn't belong to anyone but Karen. She sat on the edge of her bed and began to read.

Why can't I get better? It's been three months now, I should be picking up. The iron hasn't really helped. Is it something serious? The doctor seemed concerned.

What is the lump? An infection? Is it serious? Is it cancer? What would cancer mean? Will it be painful? Will I lose my hair? Am I going to die? Oh, stop thinking the worst!!!

I'm frightened.

Mum will fuss and worry and Dad will go quiet and worry.

I'll have to cancel the chambermaid job. I don't think I have the energy to do it, or am I being pathetic?

What will I do about money if I don't have a job? I don't want to be dependent on Mum and Dad. Can I sign on the dole? Or if I'm ill maybe I qualify for sickness benefit. I'll need to ask the doctor.

How long will it take to get better? Will I ever get better?

I might need hospital treatment. I've never been in hospital. It'll be scary, and lonely

They can cure cancer now, though, can't they?

Will I have to cancel France? What about my degree? I'll need to see my director of studies.

Maybe it'll be OK. Maybe it's just an infection.'

Alison was weeping by the time she got to the end of the page. Karen must have written this before she moved out of the flat at the beginning of that first summer. She wondered if she was still in Edinburgh herself when it was written, or back up in Oban. How worried her friend had been, trying to sort out her thoughts by writing them down. Her beautiful friend, they'd thought she had been cured. This weekend would be the first anniversary of her death.

Linda found Alison lying on her bed staring at the wall when she peeped in two hours later to see how the packing was progressing.

"Are you OK?" she asked, surprised to see so little progress. Alison held out the piece of paper, wordlessly. Linda sat at the foot of the bed to read it through.

"Karen. Poor girl," she said, returning the paper to Alison. "I was going to ask you if you'd like to do something together on Sunday. I know James will have left to be in time for starting his new job."

"Yes, thanks, that would be nice. I don't want to be on my own, maybe we could go for a walk or something, I don't know. What should I do with this?" Alison asked.

"I suppose you should give it to her parents."

"I can hear her voice in it."

"Well you don't need to decide on anything right now. Why don't you sleep on things? Maybe you should just stay home tomorrow and do the rest of your packing then, they won't miss you at A and E for one day. Come on, I'll make you a hot chocolate." Alison let Linda steer her towards the kitchen and gave in to being looked after.

Thirty

"Excuse me Miss, would you like breakfast?"

Alison opened her eyes to see a petite Asian airhostess offering a plastic tray. She unclipped the fold-down table in front of her and her breakfast was deposited with a smile. She was amazed that so much time must have passed already, not having expected to sleep so well. When she checked her watch, it confirmed that they should be landing in Singapore in about an hour.

The past few weeks had been hectic, no wonder she was tired. Living on her own in James's flat had felt strange at first, however since she had her surgical exams on the horizon she had plenty to keep herself occupied and it was helpful to have few distractions. She'd worked out a new running route along the canal and got used to catching different buses. Her new location was less central but her last attachment had been in orthopaedic surgery at Princess Margaret Rose hospital. This was out on the southern edge of the city near Hillend ski-slope, so she'd have had to travel by bus from the old flat too.

She'd taken James's advice and arranged to go to speak with one of the consultants at the surgical unit at Bangour and also at the medical unit at the Western about house jobs. Then she'd filled in the application form and sent it off.

James seemed to be enjoying his new job in Cambridge and currently was staying in a guesthouse while he looked for a place to rent. It was great having a phone in her flat, she could contact James really easily and had also spoken to her parents and Helen more regularly too. Her mum and dad had come down to Edinburgh before she left. They'd even come to visit at the flat, picking her up there before going out for dinner. Her mum hadn't made any comment but the atmosphere between them had seemed relaxed again. Alison had been relieved.

She opened a container of fruit salad, and had difficulty spearing a piece of melon with the plastic fork provided. She got it eventually and chewed. The final surgical exams had been scarier than she'd expected. It wasn't so much the difficulty of the subject, but worry that she'd make some dreadful mistake causing her to fail and upset all her plans. After her initial anxiety, she'd managed to settle down into the now familiar routine and had tackled the papers methodically. She'd been assigned an extremely chatty patient for the clinical part of the exam and had trouble keeping the dialogue on track in order to collect all the relevant information in the allotted time. On reporting back to the examiner, she was questioned on a subject that had a famous mnemonic that students used. It was quite rude, as these things often

327

were. She'd struggled, trying to format the answer so that it wasn't obvious where her mind was going. She was sure that the surgeon who had asked the question had a twinkle in his eye, so she reckoned that he knew the rhyme perfectly well himself. Anyway, she'd passed. It was a great relief and there was a long celebratory night in the pub with other members of her group who were now all also on their elective period.

Having finished the fruit salad, she spread a roll with butter and jam and opened a carton of orange juice. The last time she'd been on a plane was that trip to Paris to visit Karen. That had been fun.

She'd eventually sent the sheet with Karen's writing to Mr and Mrs Douglas with a short covering note explaining the circumstances of its discovery. She'd considered making a photocopy to keep for herself, but had decided that it was best to let it go. On Sunday 30th January, the first anniversary of Karen's death, she and Linda had climbed Arthur's Seat. They'd been lucky with the weather, it was a crisp bright day and the views from the hilltop sparkled with frost. It was a positive experience which they'd both agreed that Karen would have appreciated. Then they'd changed into smarter clothes and gone to the North British Hotel for a stylish afternoon tea as Karen had enjoyed this as a treat in the past. There wasn't quite the same ambience, as the live music was now provided by a pianist at a baby grand rather than Chris's string quartet, but the sandwiches, scones and cakes were just as good.

The cabin crew was collecting up the debris from breakfast and a notice was given over the tannoy asking passengers to ready themselves for landing. Alison replaced her table and fastened her seat belt. Her stop-over at Singapore airport was only three hours. Enough time to stretch her legs and look around before catching her connecting flight to Perth.

***

As Alison emerged from the baggage reclaims area into the arrivals hall at Perth airport, she scanned the crowd wondering how she'd recognise her Dad's old friend. She needn't have worried. A couple stood, slightly to her left holding a large banner which read, 'Welcome Alison' between them, it seemed to be decorated with pictures of kangaroos and koalas. The man was tall and had close cropped hair. Alison thought he looked younger than her dad, but that was maybe the effect of a suntan and his casual clothes, a loose bright Hawaiian style shirt, baggy shorts and sandals without socks. The woman was also tall with blonde hair caught back in a low ponytail. She wore a bright sundress and sandals. Seeing her reaction to their banner they approached her and the man shook her hand energetically, the woman kissed her cheek.

"Well, I'm Harry and this is my wife Pat. Give me that case and we'll get moving."

"You must be tired after the journey. You can relax with us for the next few days," folding the banner Pat fell in beside Alison and they both followed Harry towards the exit.

"The banner is courtesy of Kim, our youngest. She loves a project," Pat explained.

"It was a good idea," Alison responded.

"Well I think she intends for you to keep it now. Here," and she handed over the folded banner.

They reached the automatic doors and stepped outside. Immediately Alison was hit by what seemed to be a wall of heat.

"Wow, it's hot," she couldn't help exclaiming.

"Been quite a warm day," Pat agreed. "You'll feel it hot, just the contrast with Scotland, but it's cooling down a bit now towards evening. It's always a bit airier where we stay by the beach."

Harry and Pat had kindly invited Alison to stay with them for the rest of this week and the weekend, in their house at Cottesloe. She would go to the hospital with Harry on Monday and move into her accommodation then.

"So, how's George?" Harry asked her once they were installed in his car and he'd negotiated a route out of the car park.

"He's well. Still working at the bank and golfing," Alison replied.

"And you've got one sister, is that right?"

Alison confirmed this and told him about the baby that was expected.

"Wow, George to be a grandpa, hard to believe it," Harry laughed. "We've got three kids," he told her. "Darren, who'll be a bit younger than you, is studying medicine in Sydney, then there's Sandra who's in her final year at school and our wee afterthought, Kim, she's twelve."

"Sandra and Kim are dying to show you around," Pat told her. "And if you feel lonely or homesick once you move up to Perth you just come right back to us."

Given the friendliness of their welcome and their enthusiasm to be helpful Alison didn't think that she'd be in danger of feeling lonely. When they reached Cottesloe, they drove through a gateway up to a spreading bungalow set in extensive grounds. Alison could see a tennis court and discovered that there was also a swimming pool when they went through the house and out onto the patio at the rear to greet the two MacDougall daughters.

"Do you play tennis?" Sandra asked her.

Alison explained that she could get by in tennis but that badminton was really her game.

"A good choice to play an indoor game in Scotland where it rains all the time," Harry explained to his daughter. "But I'd say you'd better watch out, she'll probably beat you. If she played any racquet sport at Uni level, she'll be good." Alison felt embarrassed but happily agreed to play tennis with Sandra after school tomorrow.

"And thank you for the lovely banner," she said to Kim. "It was really welcoming, I'll use it to decorate my room at the hospital."

The next days allowed Alison to acclimatise to her new surroundings, a different time zone and the hot weather. She covered herself in sun cream and went to the beach, played tennis against Sandra, and won, and enjoyed lounging around the MacDougall's beautiful garden. While reading her book on the patio she was distracted by glimpses of grey and pink parrots called galah, bright green parrots and, once, a kookaburra. On Saturday Sandra borrowed her Mum's car and drove Alison to Caversham Wildlife Park which was just to the north of the city. Kim and one of Sandra's school friends came along for the ride. The girls enjoyed Alison's reaction to the unique Australian animals, and shot her photograph with koalas, kangaroos and a very portly wombat. On Sunday, they spent most of the day on the beach returning to a Bar-B-Q feast cooked by Harry in the garden.

Once she was established at the Royal Perth Hospital Alison discovered that the friendliness shown to her by the MacDougall family seemed to be universal. The other medical students attached with her in the A and E department, the nurses and junior doctors all made her feel welcome. In the end she'd elected to spend eight weeks in the A and E department, and for the second eight she'd chosen an anaesthetics attachment. She was invited out for drinks, to the beach, to bar-B-Qs, for more tennis and to parties. The hospital was situated in the centre of downtown Perth, so she felt right in the thick of things. She loved the nearby Kings Park and had managed to run there a few times in the early morning before it got too hot. Three weeks had flown past with busy days in the department and a hectic social life when she realised that she hadn't been in contact with Gordon yet. She was conscious that she'd probably been putting it off. She dug out the letter that she'd brought with her which contained the details of his address and sent a post card with a picture of the famous Bell Tower suggesting that they meet up, perhaps at the weekend. She wasn't sure what hours he'd be working. Later that week she had a reply from him explaining that weekends were busy so proposing an evening drink next Monday.

'How about meeting at the Bell Tower, re your PC, at 6.30?

Sincerely yours, Gordon'.

It was only two blocks to walk and then a stroll through the Supreme Court Gardens to reach the Bell Tower from the hospital. Alison left in plenty of time so that she didn't need to hurry and risk getting sweaty. She'd noticed that since her arrival the temperature was cooler, but still autumn weather here didn't bear any resemblance to a Scottish autumn. She could see Gordon waiting for her at the tower from across the road and waved to him. He looked so familiar and when the pedestrian light turned green he crossed over to meet her.

"Hi, you're looking good, Alison." He kissed her on her cheek and she didn't feel awkward, but neither was there the old quickening of her heartbeat.

"Thanks, you too."

"How are you enjoying Perth?"

"Oh, it's been great and everyone's so friendly." Alison chatted to him about her experiences of the past weeks while they walked along, amazed to feel so relaxed.

"There's a nice bar along here that has some tables out on the square," he suggested.

"So, what exactly brought you here?" Alison asked after they had ordered their drinks, a beer for Gordon and a Gin and tonic for Alison.

"I'm attached to the Yacht Club. I answered an advert, it seemed a great chance to sail in a different environment. So, I do sailing instruction and I also skipper for some charters. That's why I'm mainly busy at weekends. There's a lot of excitement about sailing here at the moment. You probably don't know, but there's a team from the yacht club here preparing for the America's Cup challenge later in the year."

"I feel ignorant, but don't think I've heard of it."

"Well basically the USA has held the cup since 1851 unbeaten and seven teams have challenged them to defend it later this year, including ours. So, it's a big event in sailing circles, but possibly not elsewhere."

"I'll need to look out for it on the news. Will it be here?"

"No, it'll be in the States at Rhode Island. The defending team gets to host it in their country."

"Pity, it would have been fun for you to be able to watch. How long do you plan to stay on here?"

"I haven't really planned, probably for at least another year. I'm enjoying it, as you've said people are very welcoming and the warm weather is a bonus. What about you? What happens after graduation?"

Alison explained about house jobs and the application process.

"I'm expecting James to contact me once the posts are finalised. He'll probably be up at the flat sometime in April and will check my mail."

"That's the chap I met at Windermere?"

"Yes, we're still together, although obviously not geographically."

"Well I hope the separation doesn't have drastic results."

"Have you been dating anyone?" Alison asked, ignoring the barb.

"A few social dates, but nothing serious. Want another drink?"

Alison gazed around the square at the other bar patrons and took an internal inventory as Gordon fetched their refills. She was still feeling perfectly poised and at ease, there had been no blushes or butterflies in her stomach. Could it really be true that she was eventually over Gordon?

"I was so sad to hear about Karen," he said as he sat down across from her. "It must have been an awful time."

"Yes, it's been pretty grim. Things still sometimes crop up that bring everything back." She told him about finding the writing and the anniversary.

"Hard for her parents. Did they write back to you?"

"I sent it just before I left so there might be a reply at the flat. I had considered going down to see them, thought about it a lot. But in the end, I couldn't face it, so that's why it took me so long to get around to posting it. A bit chicken of me really, I hope everyone doesn't avoid them like me."

"It was hardly avoiding them; it would have been a long way to go. You don't have a car yet do you?"

"No, I might need to get one for work, but I'd have had to get the bus. Still I don't feel good about it. I really liked Mr Douglas, Mrs Douglas could be hard work, though."

Gordon decided to try and change the mood.

"Do you have plans for Easter weekend? It's going to be amazingly busy at work."

"I'm quite spoiled at the moment, no studying so all my evenings and weekends are free. The MacDougalls,

Harry's my dad's friend from school, have invited me to go with them to Busselton for Easter weekend, apparently, they go there every year and stay in a nice villa by the beach. Their house in Perth is amazing and not that far from the beach, so it sounds like a home from home. And on Anzac weekend I'm going camping on Rottnest Island with a group of students from the A and E department."

"I'll be able to wave to you if I sail past."

"Yes. It's been nice to meet up."

"Maybe we can do this again some time. Just as friends?"

"I'd like that."

Thirty-one

Alison arrived back in Edinburgh ten days before her graduation ceremony. She had a lot to organise and was busy catching up with everyone. Today she was meeting Linda for a picnic in Princes Street Gardens. They'd arranged to meet by the floral clock at five to twelve, as Linda wanted to see the cuckoo at midday. Alison arrived first and spotted Linda striding down the Mound, blonde ponytail swinging. The friends exchanged a hug.

"I can't believe it's been over four months since I saw you. Look at how tanned you are, disgusting," Linda proclaimed.

"Better get into a good position to see your bird," Alison advised.

"Yeah, I'm feeling nostalgic about lots of Edinburgh things already, including the wee cuckoo."

"Don't worry, you'll be back to visit."

"I will, I'll have to keep an eye on you," Linda agreed.

They witnessed the sounding of the hour and then made their way to a sunny spot where Alison spread out a tartan rug. She'd brought egg mayonnaise sandwiches, mini sausage rolls and salt and vinegar crisps. Linda provided cheese salad sandwiches, grapes, two chocolate cream éclairs and a large bottle of coca cola.

"So, well done for getting a first." Alison touched her paper cup against Linda's. "We should have had proper fizz to toast you, coke will have to do. All set for tomorrow?" Alison asked, referring to Linda's graduation ceremony which was on the next day. The girls chatted as they tucked in to the food.

"Yes, my parents should be arriving at about five this evening. They're staying at the Bruntsfield Hotel, so handy for the flat. I'm going to pop over to see them this evening. I've started packing up as they'll take me and all my stuff back with them. It made me think of you earlier in the year."

"What'll you do about a place to stay in London?"

"Once I get home I'll contact some London letting agents, but I've got a bit of time before I start."

"And how long's the trainee attachment at the clinic?"

"Two years to begin with, and a possible option to extend. I'm not sure how I'll feel by then, some people have advised me it'd be better to move and get wider experience at that stage. Anyway, I don't need to decide about that for ages."

"And how about Fred? You guys have been together for more than a year now, what's going to happen when you go down south?"

"He's fine and we're still good but he's got another year of his SHO rotation here. Maybe after that he'll move, he's suggested it. He thinks he could get a GP trainee post in London."

"Yeah, I hope it all works out. So you'll be up here to see Fred, not just me. Hey, did I tell you I'm an auntie?"

"Only a million times. How's Helen?"

"She sounds great on the phone. But she won't be able to come through for my graduation, Kenneth's too wee to leave, breast-feeding every three hours apparently. I'm going through to Glasgow tomorrow to meet him. Brought him a fluffy koala from Oz."

"And have you seen James yet?"

"No. He's arriving at the weekend. He's got two weeks' holiday, so he's staying for my graduation and the ball and then going up to see his folks."

"Whoa, I'm stuffed."

Linda lay back on the rug and closed her eyes against the sun and the friends continued their catching up over the next three hours. They were interrupted by the one o' clock gun which startled them, making them jump and giggle and sending a flurry of pigeons flapping and whirling round the park. Later they had an urge for ice-cream so Alison queued at the nearby Mr Whippy van and brought back two '99s'. At three thirty Linda stretched and stood up regretfully.

"I'm afraid my packing is calling."

The girls collected up their picnic debris and folded the rug. They hugged goodbye and promised to keep in touch by phone and writing. Linda expected to be back visiting before long, so it wasn't too sad a parting.

***

As she descended the steps from the McEwan Hall, Alison clutched her degree certificate in its red tube like a baton. Her academic gown swirled around her knees as she stepped down into the concourse, searching through the crowd for her parents and James. She was greeted and hugged by fellow graduates all looking smart in black and white, the red hoods of their robes trimmed with white fur. There was an occasional kilt adding a different splash of colour. She'd walked past the McEwan Hall on graduation days many times; it felt strange that this time she was on stage. She was Dr Scott and would be starting work at the Western General Hospital on the first of August, which happened to fall on a Monday this year. She bumped into Robert who was flanked by his parents, his dad looked just like him except that his red hair had thinned and faded slightly. He and Robert even wore matching kilts, predominantly blue and green with a dash of yellow, which she presumed was the Johnstone tartan.

"Well we made it," Robert exclaimed, giving her a hug.

"There was never any doubt that you would make it, Dr Johnstone, with distinction." Alison hugged him back. Only two individuals out of their year of one hundred and fifty students had attained a distinction, so it was a big achievement. She shook hands with Robert's parents and then spotted her dad at the top of the steps scanning the crowd. She waved and managed to attract his attention.

"So how does it feel? Were you all emotional?" Mr Scott asked after they'd all been introduced and exchanged greetings.

"It all feels a bit unreal. It's great to see everyone together again. We've not all been in the same place as a year group since third year lectures." Robert replied

"I was scared I'd trip up and fall walking up to the dais so I was relieved once that bit was over," Alison admitted.

"I remember being quite choked up when we were taking the Hippocratic Oath," James admitted.

"Yes, it's quite heavy," Robert agreed.

"Where are you lunching?" Mrs Scott asked the Johnstones.

"At the North British Hotel," Mrs Johnstone replied.

"We're going back to Denzlers," Alison said. "We went there for my twenty-first and really liked it."

"I suppose we should be giving our gowns back and then making a move," Robert suggested.

"Oh, let me take some photos first," Mrs Scott rummaged in her handbag for her camera. This was a cue for other cameras to appear. Alison and Robert posed patiently in various groupings and settings until the photographers were content. Then they went around the side of the hall to the cloakroom where they could return their gowns, continuing to greet fellow year members on their way.

"I'm really looking forward to the ball," Alison said. "Today has made me realise how many people I need to catch up with."

"It'll be easier at the ball without all the parents there too," Robert commented.

"Yes, but it's kind of nice to see everyone with their family groups, gives you a different insight to people. For instance, I now know what you'll look like in thirty years' time."

"And no doubt you'll still be a cheeky wee buggar," Robert rejoined.

***

Alison and James walked hand in hand through patches of sunlight and shade on the riverside path. It was warm when they left the shadow of a tree and there was a scent of freshly mown grass from the playing fields across the river.

"Quite a contrast to the last day we were here," James commented.

"Yes. Thank you for coming with me, I'm glad we came."

James squeezed her hand in reply and they carried on in companionable silence.

Alison had found a lot of mail waiting for her when she returned from her elective, including a letter from Karen's Dad. It thanked her for sending Karen's writing and mentioned that they had come across a few other similar sheets when tidying away her effects. Alison could have let things lie at that but she still had an uncomfortable niggle that there was unfinished business and that she should go to see the Douglases. She kept pushing it away, knowing that a visit would be hard and possibly awkward but the idea continued to bubble up into her thoughts. Eventually she mentioned it to James after graduation was over.

"If it's been bothering you for all these months, then you should go and see them," he advised. "I could give you a lift, easier to do it now before you start work."

"Should I phone them first?" She asked his advice, unsure.

"Well it might be sensible. It is the summer holidays and they could be away somewhere. Isn't Mr Douglas a teacher?"

When she called to check, it turned out that Heather had just had four pups, so Mr and Mrs Douglas were at home and would be delighted to see Alison and James. They were invited for afternoon tea, the reason for their trip to Peebles today.

The pups were a lively diversion, a source of comment and conversation when the flow threatened to run dry.

"Heather's whelping wasn't the best of timing, but hopefully we'll have all of the puppies homed by the October holiday week, so can arrange to go away for a break then," Mrs Douglas explained. She was looking so much better. Her hair had been recently coloured and styled, she had regained weight and was wearing neat casual clothes in bright colours.

"I wish I could take one," Alison confided, cuddling a puppy and nuzzling the soft top of its head with her nose.

"I don't think you'd manage to cope with a dog, you'll be working such long hours," Mrs Douglas was practical.

"I know. But they're so cute." Alison turned to Mr Douglas. She thought that he had aged since she'd last seen him. His hair was greyer, he seemed to have developed deep wrinkles on his forehead and his moustache had been trimmed to a less flamboyant style. "You mentioned in your letter about other writing of Karen's."

"Yes. We think it was something she did to try and sort out her thoughts or to help make a decision. We found some writing in a notebook, like a diary but not kept on a daily basis and also some loose sheets like the one you sent, sometimes she's written out lists of pros and cons. We've kept everything together in a folder. Do you want to see it?" Mr Douglas asked.

Alison wasn't sure. She knew how it might upset her, but to say 'no' would make her appear disinterested to Karen's parents. In the end she agreed, after all they'd had to cope with the same grief as she had, only worse. They wouldn't mind if she got upset. However, when presented with the folder she found it hard to concentrate on the words in front of her. She could see Karen's script, distinctive in purple pen, but found herself staring blankly at a page before flipping to the next.

"That's one she wrote just after finishing her chemo," Mr Douglas was keeping track of her progress. The sheet looked similar to the one from the flat. Alison tried harder to focus.

'I hope I don't need any more treatment. I hope it's worked. Please, please, please, please make it have worked.

If I was religious, I could pray.

I never want to have to go back to the day hospital. I always managed to keep it together but every time I could imagine a dark force like a chill spreading through my whole body from the drip.

I want to feel well again, to be hungry, for my mouth not to be sore and for things to taste nice again.

When will my hair grow?? No more wigs and scarves would be good.

I look like someone out of Belsen. I want to feel attractive and confident again.

I hate to think of all the things I've fallen behind with or let slip completely.

I need to take control again.

What will happen if it hasn't worked? What would they do next?

It has to have worked. I don't think I could go through that again. Please.'

"She did take charge again and had that great year in Paris," Mr Douglas commented.

"Yes, she was so well and enjoying life so much. That's what I try to remember," Alison replied. She handed the folder back to Mr Douglas and she and James talked politely for another five minutes before taking their leave.

"Thank you for coming, I know it couldn't have been easy but we've appreciated it," Karen's Mum said as they shook hands on the doorstep. They waved from the pavement then turned down the hill towards the riverside car park.

"Do you want to go to the cemetery?" James asked.

"No, I don't like to think of Karen there. Let's go for a walk along the riverside. I did that with Karen once when I came to see her here."

So, they carried on down the hill, crossed the road before the bridge and set off along the south bank of the Tweed. As they drew level with the park on the opposite bank, Alison could see the old tower standing out beyond it, marking the site of the cemetery. But she refrained from remarking on it and concentrated on the water sparkling by her side, the ducks powering their feet madly to swim against the current, blue-tits acrobatic in the bushes next to her. She swung James's arm and pointed out a cloud that looked a bit like a dinosaur.

"Look it's a diplodocus, there's its long neck, its blobby body and its pointy tail."

"No legs though," James commented.

***

On the first of August Alison's alarm was set for six o' clock, but she was already awake and feeling nervous. She'd been to the hospital on Friday to organise paperwork, arrange a supply of white coats and collect a key for her assigned room in the residency. She'd also been given her rota and was relieved to find that she wasn't on call on the first day. So at least she'd have time to find her feet and get to know her current patients before a deluge of new acute cases came in. She arrived at the hospital at eight o'clock and collected her coats from the laundry and her bleep from switchboard. The operator explained how to use the pager.

"If it's an internal call, the number will come up on the display and you just find the nearest phone and call that number. You'll find you get to know the common numbers, like your ward or the X-ray department. Outside calls will come up as a zero on the display, then you need to call us here at switchboard and we'll put the call through to you. OK?"

Alison nodded and took the pager with her. She went to the residency which was situated in a stone house across the driveway from the main hospital buildings. She wanted to find her room and drop off her belongings there. She'd been allocated a small room under the eaves and above the front door. The first thing that she saw when she opened the bedroom door was a bouquet of pink roses lying on the bed. There was a note attached:

'Good Luck Dr Scott, With Love from James.'

Alison smiled. He knew the housekeeper well from his own time at the Western, so had probably roped her in to have the flowers put in position. She donned one of her white coats and put the things that she would need in the pockets, pen, bleep, stethoscope and torch. She had some text books which she planned to keep in her desk on the ward so she tucked those under her arm. As she came downstairs, she met one of her classmates, Neil, going up.

"Hi, you OK?" he asked.

"Yeah, a bit nervous but I'm on my way up to the ward now to get settled in."

"I think there's an orientation meeting at ten in the education suite," he informed her.

"OK, see you there then." She was almost out of the front door when her pager sounded. She went back into the house to the sitting room where she'd spotted a phone when she looked around earlier. She dialled the number on the display.

"Dr Scott?" a female voice asked.

"Yes."

"Staff nurse Thomson, C 8. Could you come and look at Mr Wilson's drip? I've tried flushing it through, but I think it's tissued. He's still got a few units of blood to get so it'll need to be re-sited."

"OK, I was just coming up anyway, be there in five minutes," Alison replied. She was grateful that she'd had lots of practice at inserting drips during the anaesthetics part of her elective as previously it had been something that worried her. But now she felt fairly confident that this was something that she could cope with. She exited the house, turned left up the driveway and approached the hospital entrance. She walked between the two rusty lions lying on their plinths, climbed the steps and pushed through the double doors striding out towards her ward.